Fiscal Federalism

A National Bureau
of Economic Research
Project Report

Fiscal Federalism: Quantitative Studies

Edited by   Harvey S. Rosen

The University of Chicago Press

Chicago and London

Harvey S. Rosen is professor of economics at Princeton University. He is the editor of *Studies in State and Local Public Finance* (1986), also published by the University of Chicago Press in association with the National Bureau of Economic Research.

The University of Chicago Press, Chicago 60637
The University of Chicago Press, Ltd., London
© 1988 by The National Bureau of Economic Research
All rights reserved. Published 1988
Printed in the United States of America
97 96 95 94 93 92 91 90 89 88   5 4 3 2 1

Library of Congress Cataloging-in-Publication Data

Fiscal federalism : quantitative studies / edited by Harvey S. Rosen.
     p.   cm. — (A National Bureau of Economic Research project report)
    "Papers presented at a conference held at Halloran House in New York City, 10–11 April 1987"—P.
    Bibliography: p.
    Includes index.
    ISBN 0-226-72619-3
    1. Intergovernmental fiscal relations—United States—Congresses.
I. Rosen, Harvey S. II. National Bureau of Economic Research.
III. Series.
HJ275.F558 1988   87-28726
336.1'85—dc19   2 - 6 - 90   CIP

Relation of the Directors to the
Work and Publications of the
National Bureau of Economic Research

1. The object of the National Bureau of Economic Research is to ascertain and to present to the public important economic facts and their interpretation in a scientific and impartial manner. The Board of Directors is charged with the responsibility of ensuring that the work of the National Bureau is carried on in strict conformity with this object.

2. The President of the National Bureau shall submit to the Board of Directors, or to its Executive Committee, for their formal adoption all specific proposals for research to be instituted.

3. No research report shall be published by the National Bureau until the President has sent each member of the Board a notice that a manuscript is recommended for publication and that in the President's opinion it is suitable for publication in accordance with the principles of the National Bureau. Such notification will include an abstract or summary of the manuscript's content and a response form for use by those Directors who desire a copy of the manuscript for review. Each manuscript shall contain a summary drawing attention to the nature and treatment of the problem studied, the character of the data and their utilization in the report, and the main conclusions reached.

4. For each manuscript so submitted, a special committee of the Directors (including Directors Emeriti) shall be appointed by majority agreement of the President and Vice Presidents (or by the Executive Committee in case of inability to decide on the part of the President and Vice Presidents), consisting of three Directors selected as nearly as may be one from each general division of the Board. The names of the special manuscript committee shall be stated to each Director when notice of the proposed publication is submitted to him. It shall be the duty of each member of the special manuscript committee to read the manuscript. If each member of the manuscript committee signifies his approval within thirty days of the transmittal of the manuscript, the report may be published. If at the end of that period any member of the manuscript committee withholds his approval, the President shall then notify each member of the Board, requesting approval or disapproval of publication, and thirty days additional shall be granted for this purpose. The manuscript shall then not be published unless at least a majority of the entire Board who shall have voted on the proposal within the time fixed for the receipt of votes shall have approved.

5. No manuscript may be published, though approved by each member of the special manuscript committee, until forty-five days have elapsed from the transmittal of the report in manuscript form. The interval is allowed for the receipt of any memorandum of dissent or reservation, together with a brief statement of his reasons, that any member may wish to express; and such memorandum of dissent or reservation shall be published with the manuscript if he so desires. Publication does not, however, imply that each member of the Board has read the manuscript, or that either members of the Board in general or the special committee have passed on its validity in every detail.

6. Publications of the National Bureau issued for informational purposes concerning the work of the Bureau and its staff, or issued to inform the public of activities of Bureau staff, and volumes issued as a result of various conferences involving the National Bureau shall contain a specific disclaimer noting that such publication has not passed through the normal review procedures required in this resolution. The Executive Committee of the Board is charged with review of all such publications from time to time to ensure that they do not take on the character of formal research reports of the National Bureau, requiring formal Board approval.

7. Unless otherwise determined by the Board or exempted by the terms of paragraph 6, a copy of this resolution shall be printed in each National Bureau publication.

(Resolution adopted October 25, 1926, as revised through September 30, 1974)

Contents

Acknowledgments

This volume, consisting of papers presented at a conference held at Halloran House in New York City, 10–11 April 1987, presents research carried out as part of the NBER's project on state and local government finance. The National Bureau has undertaken this project with the support of the Ford Foundation and the John M. Olin Foundation, Inc.

The many people whose advice and assistance have helped to make this volume possible include National Bureau directors Robert S. Hamada, Robert C. Holland, and Burton A. Weisbrod; National Bureau research associate Daniel Feenberg; and Charles L. Ballard.

The opinions expressed in this volume are those of the respective authors. They do not necessarily reflect the views of the National Bureau of Economic Research, or any other organization.

Introduction

Harvey S. Rosen

Discussions of public finance in the United States often refer to the role of "the" government. While for many purposes it is useful to think of fiscal decisions as being made by a single government, the reality is that in the United States, an astounding number of entities have the power to tax and spend. Including states, countries, municipalities, townships, school districts, and special districts, there are over 82,000 governmental jurisdictions. The interaction of state, local, and federal governments plays a crucial role in the U.S. fiscal system. In recognition of this fact, the National Bureau of Economic Research sponsored a conference on Fiscal Federalism in April of 1987. The seven papers presented at that conference, and the comments of the discussants, are contained in this volume. Although the papers cover a diverse array of subjects, they share a quantitative orientation and a concern with policy issues.

The first three papers, by John Joseph Wallis and Wallace E. Oates, Robert P. Inman, and Jeffrey S. Zax, examine the distribution of power and responsibilities among the various levels of government. The Wallis-Oates paper provides a broad historical perspective on the extent and evolution of fiscal decentralization in the state and local sector. They begin by noting that in 1902 local governments accounted for 82 percent of the tax revenues of the state and local sector; by 1981 this had fallen to 42 percent. The major part of this centralizing trend occurred in the first half of the century. Similarly, at any given point in time, there are wide variations in the extent of fiscal decentralization among states. Wallis and Oates discuss several theories that might help explain differences in fiscal

Harvey S. Rosen is professor of economics at Princeton University and a research associate at the National Bureau of Economic Research.

decentralization, and then test these theories econometrically. They find that a state's share in state and local spending is inversely related to both population size and urbanization, and in some specifications of the model, it is directly related to the level of per capita income. While noting that it is very difficult to make predictions about the future course of centralization, on the basis of their results Wallis and Oates conjecture that in the future the tendency toward centralization (which has already slowed in recent decades) is likely to stop altogether.

While the Wallis-Oates paper focuses on economic explanations for the development of the federal structure, Inman concentrates on political issues. He observes that the federal fiscal structure has been evolving steadily toward the centralization of the financing of government spending. Revenues are raised centrally and then transferred, via grants-in-aid, to state and local governments. Inman explores two different hypotheses to explain this trend. In the first, federal aid is allocated to correct for the presence of market failures such as externalities. In the second, aid is allocated only when it is in the political interests of congressional representatives. Inman's examination of the relationship between the level and composition of federal grants and the structure of congressional decision-making suggests that the political theory provides a better explanation of the facts.

The paper by Zax investigates the effects of the number and types of government jurisdictions on aggregate local public debt and expenditures. From a theoretical point of view, it is unclear whether more jurisdictions will lead to greater or less spending. On the one hand, when there are fewer governments they may be able to capture economies of scale in the production and distribution of local public services. On the other hand, political and bureaucratic tendencies toward excess public spending may be reduced by competition among a large number of jurisdictions. Zax examines county-wide data and finds that aggregate debt and expenditures are positive functions of jurisdictions per capita, suggesting that small jurisdictions are inefficient. However, the data also suggest that when jurisdictions have large average "market shares," they use their market power to expand the size of the local public sector.

The next three papers, by Douglas Holtz-Eakin and Harvey S. Rosen, Lawrence B. Lindsey, and George R. Zodrow examine the relationship between the deductibility of state and local taxes on federal tax returns and the structure of subfederal public finance. This question has assumed great importance in light of the recent public debate about the merits of partially or totally eliminating deductibility. Holtz-Eakin and Rosen focus on how changes in the tax price of local spending induced by deductibility affect the mix between deductible and non-deductible revenue sources, and the level of expenditures. Their econometric analysis is based on a panel data set that tracks the fiscal behavior of 172 local governments from 1978 to 1980. They estimate that the elasticity of deductible taxes with respect to the tax price is in the range -1.2 to -1.6; the tax price has no statistically significant effect on the use of nondeductible revenue sources; and the elasticity of local expenditures with respect to the tax price is about -1.8. Hence, their estimates imply that if deductibility were eliminated, there would be a substantial decline in local government spending.

Like Inman's paper on the growth of grants, Lindsey's paper on deductibility emphasizes political issues. He emphasizes that unlike conventional price changes, changes in the price of local taxation do not translate directly through consumer optimization into changes in the equilibrium quantity of services demanded. The response depends on how the political mechanism translates the price change into a public decision. Lindsey examines the implications of several different theories for the appropriate measure of the tax price of state and local spending. Like Holtz-Eakin and Rosen, Lindsey finds that the level of state and local spending is significantly affected by deductibility. He also finds that voter-based measures (e.g., the median tax price among voters) does better at predicting state and local spending than aggregate measures of cost such as the average tax price measured over all individuals.

Both the Holtz-Eakin/Rosen and Lindsey papers examine deductibility in a partial equilibrium context. A potential problem with this approach is that the state and local sector is "large" relative to the economy as a whole. Thus, predictions regarding (say) the revenue effects of deductibility may be affected by feedbacks from other sectors of the economy. Zodrow constructs a two-sector general equilibrium model to investigate such effects. The model permits the allocation of capital to respond to changes in state and local capital taxes and the associated changes in the net return to capital, wages, and income. These in turn permit an explicit calculation of the impact of eliminating deductibility on both personal and corporate federal tax revenues. Zodrow's results indicate that the increase in federal revenue from eliminating deductibility is likely to be less than that predicted by partial equilibrium techniques. The amounts involved are substantial; the revenue shortfall is 25 to 58 percent of the partial equilibrium estimate.

The final paper, by Charles R. Hulten and Robert M. Schwab, tackles the problem of developing a set of income and product accounts for the state and local sector. Hulten and Schwab note that conventional estimates of the production of the state and local sector assume that its capital income is zero, despite the fact that the state and local sector is one of the most capital intensive in the U.S. economy. In addition to leading to a downward bias in the income of the state and local sector, this assumption obscures the existence of an important implicit subsidy in the federal fiscal system—under the federal tax code, state and local capital is treated like owner-occupied housing in the sense that the noninterest portion of income accruing to capital is excluded from the tax base. Hulten and Schwab's empirical results indicate that conventional accounting procedures underestimate the amount of income generated by the state and local sector by about $100 billion.

1 Decentralization in the Public Sector: An Empirical Study of State and Local Government

John Joseph Wallis and Wallace E. Oates

1.1 Introduction

Decentralized choice in the public sector (as in the private sector) provides an opportunity to increase economic welfare by tailoring levels of consumption to the preferences of smaller, more homogeneous groups. More centralized decisions typically involve relatively uniform levels of consumption that circumscribe the diversity of outputs needed to accommodate differences in tastes. The existing literature in local public finance has explored the normative theory of decentralization in substantial depth. The important Tiebout model, for example, describes the way in which mobile consumers through their location decisions can make use of decentralized choice in the public sector to enhance the efficiency of resource allocation.

The purpose of this paper is to explore empirically the extent and variation in fiscal decentralization in the state and local sector in the United States. The state-local sector exhibits wide variation in the relative roles of state and local government both over time and across states. In 1902, local governments accounted for 82 percent of the tax revenues in the state-local sector; by 1982, this had fallen to 43 percent.

John Joseph Wallis is assistant professor of economics at the University of Maryland and a faculty research fellow of the National Bureau of Economic Research. Wallace E. Oates is professor of economics at the University of Maryland, where he is also a member of the Bureau of Business and Economic Research.

We are grateful to our discussant, James Hines, and to the other participants of the NBER Conference on Fiscal Federalism for some very helpful comments on an earlier draft of this paper. We also thank our colleague Harry Kelejian for his counsel on some econometric issues. For their assistance in the assembling of our large data set, we are deeply indebted to Mark Eiswerth, Christopher Graves, Deborah Shiley, and Calvin Timmerman. Finally, we express our appreciation to the NBER for the support of this research.

Likewise, wide variations in the extent of fiscal decentralization are evident among states. In 1981, for example, state government spending in New York accounted for only 28 percent of total state-local expenditures in contrast to Vermont, where the state government share of spending was 60 percent.

In this paper, we shall investigate the extent to which the existing theory of decentralized fiscal choice can explain the observed patterns in the structure of the state-local sector both over time and across states. Our approach is to set forth the conditions that would enhance the potential welfare gains from a more decentralized public sector and then to see if the presence of these conditions is, in fact, associated with greater fiscal decentralization. Using a large panel data set of the U.S. state-local sector reaching back to 1902, we explore econometrically the variation both over time and across states in various measures of fiscal centralization.

In the first part of the paper we provide a historical overview of the trends in fiscal centralization during the twentieth century. A pervasive tendency toward centralization in the state-local "fisc" is evident; there are also some interesting regional differences with historical roots. In the second section, we discuss the circumstances that enhance the potential welfare gains from fiscal decentralization and formulate some specific testable hypotheses concerning the determinants of the optimal degree of decentralization. The third section then presents the findings from our econometric analysis, where we make use of the error-components approach to our panel data set to test the hypotheses. The final section of the paper offers some reflections on likely future tendencies in the centralization of the state-local sector. In addition, we include an appendix that describes our data base.

1.2   Trends in Fiscal Centralization in the State and Local Sector during the Twentieth Century

We begin our investigation of fiscal centralization with an overview of the trends in the vertical structure of the state and local sector during the present century. At the outset, we acknowledge the difficulty of developing a fully satisfactory measure of the extent of decentralization (see Oates 1972, 196–98). Available data essentially limit us to fiscal measures, and, following earlier work, we will use the fiscal share of the state government in the state-local sector as our measure of fiscal centralization.

Even this does not resolve all the ambiguities, since we can construct fiscal "centralization ratios" (i.e., the state share in the state-local fisc) on either an expenditure or revenue basis. Should we measure the relative importance of a level of government by the share of public revenues that it raises or by its share of public expenditures? The basic issue here is how to treat intergovernmental transfers of revenues. If we use a revenue measure, we attribute such funds to the grantor. This seems sensible if the grantor prescribes to a significant extent the use of the funds. However, where such funds are transferred unconditionally (say, under a revenue-sharing program) so that the grantor is simply a revenue-collection agent for the recipient, it may make more sense to attribute the funds to the transfer recipient. Since grants of both kinds are widely used in the public sector, we shall not opt for one measure over the other; instead we shall present fiscal centralization ratios in both revenue and expenditure terms and note where the two measures generate divergent results.

Table 1.1 presents the state and local government shares in public expenditure for selected years.[1] These are the respective shares in "direct expenditure" (that is, in disbursements to final recipients of government payments) so that intergovernmental transfers of funds are attributed to the recipient level of government. The most striking feature of table 1.1 is the dramatic increase in fiscal centralization that it reveals over the current century. The state share of state and local spending was only 12.4 percent in 1902; by 1982, this figure had risen to 40.5 percent. On closer inspection, however, the table reveals an interesting feature of the process of centralization: nearly all of this process seems to have taken place in the first half of the century. By 1952, the state share had risen to 35 percent (in fact, in 1950 this share was 39 percent). Since 1950 the state share in state and local sector expenditure has grown only very slightly.

What accounts for this trend toward centralization? There are logically three ways in which changes in these shares can occur: the services that states perform may have grown in fiscal terms relative to

Table 1.1   **State and Local Government Shares in State-Local Expenditures for Selected Years (in percentages)**

Year	State Share	Local Share
1902	12.4	87.6
1913	13.2	86.8
1922	19.2	80.8
1932	24.1	75.9
1942	32.6	67.4
1952	35.0	65.0
1962	36.1	63.9
1972	38.1	61.9
1982	40.5	59.5

Source: The figures from which these percentages were computed come from Tax Foundation, Inc., *Facts and Figures on Government Finance*, 23d biennial ed., (New York: Tax Foundation, Inc., 1986), Table D1, p. d3.

those of local governments; there may have been a shifting of services from local to state governments; or certain new services may have been introduced with a disproportionate assignment of these new services to the state government level. A closer investigation indicates that the explanation is largely a matter of the last of these alternatives: the state-local sector was called upon to provide a number of new services in the first half of the century with state governments playing the more important role. In particular, state governments over this period entered into the provision of highways, higher education, public welfare, and various retirement and unemployment compensation programs that account for the bulk of the expansion in the state share. For highways, for example, state governments in the aggregate spent only $4 million in 1902; with the advent of the automobile, state level expenditures rose to $2.56 billion by 1952. This represents an increase in the state share of total state and local spending on highways from 2.0 percent in 1902 to 55 percent in 1952. The relative role of state government in education likewise exhibits a striking expansion. In 1902 we find state governments in the aggregate spending only $17 million on education; by 1952 this figure has become $1.49 billion. This represents an increase in the state share of educational spending from 7 percent in 1902 to 18 percent in 1952. The major portion of this spending is for public higher education in which state governments have taken the lead.

Similarly, state governments in the first half of the century greatly expanded their efforts in the provision of public welfare support. Aggregate spending by state governments on public welfare grew from $10 million in 1902 to $1.4 billion by 1952, representing an increase in the state share of public welfare expenditures from 27 percent in 1902 to 51 percent in 1952. Much of this growth, incidentally, took place during the New Deal years when the federal government relied heavily on state governments for the operation of relief programs (see Wallis 1984, 1987). Finally, there was a rapid expansion of state insurance trust fund expenditures, including unemployment compensation and retirement benefits (again associated with the New Deal), from virtually zero in 1902 to $1.4 billion in 1952.

We thus find that the centralizing trend in state and local expenditures is largely a phenomenon of the first half of the century and represents an expansion of state governments into the provision of several major new public services. State governments, in fact, played a very minor fiscal role at the turn of the century, but in the ensuing 50 years they became an equal fiscal partner in the state and local sector. This expansion of the relative role of the states would seem not to be purely politically motivated; there is a sound economic case for state provision of the services that expanded so rapidly in this period. The need for a highway system to link localities within a state clearly calls for a level of government transcending that with a purely local orientation. Likewise, the development of a viable system of higher education reaching out beyond major urban centers requires a supra-local presence. And, finally, as has been argued in the pubic finance literature (e.g., Oates 1972), there are serious constraints on the ability of local governments to provide assistance to the poor; the need for programs at higher levels of government for poor relief is widely recognized.

If we examine the trends in fiscal centralization from the perspective of revenues rather than expenditures, we find roughly the same picture except that levels of centralization are generally a bit higher for revenues than for expenditures. Table 1.2 reports state and local shares in revenues from own sources. The major difference between tables 1.1 and 1.2 is that the latter attributes intergovernmental revenues to the level of government that is the source (not the recipient) of the funds. Using a revenue measure of fiscal centralization, we find again a quite dramatic trend toward fiscal centralization. The state share of state-local revenues from own sources was only 17.6 percent in 1902; by 1982 this had risen to 56.8 percent. Thus, state governments shifted from being a relatively minor partner in the fund-raising function of the state and local sector at the beginning of the century to becoming the major partner by 1982. Once again, we find that the bulk of this centralizing process took place in the first half of the century; by 1952, the state's share in state and local revenues was already over 50 percent. Since midcentury, there has been some further centralization of revenues, but the trend has slowed significantly. This has been accompanied by a continuing increase in the reliance on state intergovernmental grants to local governments. Table 1.3 documents this trend with figures indicating the fraction of local revenues coming from intergovernmental transfers; the rise in this figure over the first half of the century has continued since 1950.

Table 1.2   **State and Local Government Shares in State-Local Revenues from Own Sources for Selected Years (in percentages)**

Year	State Share	Local Share
1902	17.6	82.4
1913	17.8	82.2
1922	24.4	75.6
1932	29.7	70.3
1942	48.9	51.1
1952	50.4	49.6
1962	48.9	51.1
1972	52.9	47.1
1982	56.8	43.2

Source: Same as Table 1.1.

Table 1.3   **Intergovernmental Transfers as a Percentage of Local Government Revenues for Selected Years**

1902	6.6
1913	6.0
1922	8.3
1932	14.3
1942	27.8
1952	31.6
1962	30.6
1972	37.7
1982	41.5

Source: Tax Foundation, *Facts and Figures*, Table F14, p. f19.

The fiscal evolution of the state and local sector thus reveals a very striking tendency toward centralization in both spending and revenues over the first half of the century. This trend has moderated since 1950, however, with only a very slight increase in the state share of fiscal activity since then.

In addition to a strong secular trend toward a more centralized state and local sector, there is also a persistent and interesting historical pattern of centralization across regions. The southern regions of the country in 1902 had much more concentrated public sectors than did the other regions of the nation. Table 1.4 presents our fiscal centrali-

Table 1.4   **Fiscal Concentration Measures by Region, by Year — 1902 to 1982**

Region	Revenues/Expenditures				
	1902	1922	1942	1962	1982
New England	0.195	0.259	0.494	0.468	0.591
	0.191	0.237	0.450	0.454	0.523
Mid-Atlantic	0.159	0.194	0.455	0.405	0.526
	0.131	0.198	0.338	0.282	0.358
East North Central	0.155	0.187	0.517	0.441	0.539
	0.139	0.194	0.333	0.298	0.384
West North Central	0.172	0.209	0.448	0.432	0.546
	0.165	0.221	0.357	0.386	0.425
South Atlantic	0.284	0.311	0.620	0.604	0.612
	0.268	0.305	0.487	0.421	0.452
East South Central	0.281	0.284	0.597	0.584	0.619
	0.273	0.281	0.429	0.473	0.481
West South Central	0.248	0.272	0.629	0.612	0.605
	0.241	0.255	0.466	0.472	0.446
Mountain	0.246	0.335	0.529	0.534	0.583
	0.238	0.307	0.441	0.430	0.411
Pacific	0.179	0.241	0.571	0.515	0.570
	0.186	0.260	0.430	0.379	0.396

Note: First row for each region is revenue measure; second row for each region is expenditure measure.

zation measures for both expenditures and revenues for twenty year intervals from 1902 to 1982. In 1902 state governments in the South Atlantic and East South Central regions accounted for roughly twice as much of the state-local fisc as did state governments in the Mid-Atlantic or East North Central regions; other regions fell between these two extremes. While regional differences have narrowed with time, the southern regions still remained slightly more centralized in 1982.

These regional differences may reflect to some extent the variation in the underlying economic, social, and demographic factors that we discuss in the next section. There are, however, strong historical differences in the structure of the state-local sector that must be kept in mind. Colonial land laws were particularly important. Although both the southern and northern colonies began under the same Virginia Company charter, the two regions developed distinctly different ways of establishing private property rights in land. In Virginia and surrounding colonies, an individual was allowed to decide which specific parcel of land he would take title to. People took their 50-acre head rights, for example, in the best bottomland available, leaving hilltops and scrub land to the colonial government.

In the New England colonies, under the joint influence of the Virginia Company charter and the Massachusetts Bay Colony charter, the colonial government generally made large grants of land to towns. These grants were typically ten miles square and were made to an already existing group of prospective townsmen. The colonial land grant was to the town, not to individuals, and the town council then distributed lands to the members of the community (occasionally selling land directly). This method of land distribution accounts for (perhaps it would be better to say "was endogenous with") the importance of community leaders and institutions like the local minister and the church, as well as for the vigor of the typical New England town meeting.

The New England method of distributing land led naturally to a very active local political life, and it created local governments which had, from the very beginning, considerable real assets at their disposal. In contrast, the process of distributing land in the South did very little to encourage local governments. In many areas large land owners were the effective government, and local agreement to levy taxes on themselves would only occur on issues on which there was considerable agreement. Indeed, the effects of land policy are still visible on the maps of southern states today. The numerous small counties and tortured boundary lines follow the borders of the existing private property distribution at the time the counties were formed. This contrasts sharply with the geometric precision of New England townships.

The compromise between northern, southern, and other interests that led to the Northwest Ordinances of 1785 and 1789 created a method for establishing private property rights over federal lands in the Old

Northwest and eventually the trans-Mississippi West that followed the New England model in geometry and the southern model in individuality: land was sold in rectangular plots, but sold directly to individuals. And, importantly, the ordinances retained the New England principle of providing for the support of local government by allotting fixed amounts of land for the support of schools and other public functions.

The result of this historical development was relatively strong local governments in the northern and western regions of the country and relatively weak local governments in the southern regions. These regional differences persisted well into the twentieth century. Unlike the trend toward centralization (most of which had taken place by mid-century), the near equalization of fiscal centralization ratios across regions appears to be a phenomenon of the latter half of the century. Centralization ratios take a sharp jump upwards between 1922 and 1942, but they retain their pattern of regional differences into the 1960s.

1.3   The Economics of Decentralization in the Public Sector: Toward Some Testable Hypotheses

The decentralized provision of public services provides a means to increase the level of economic welfare by differentiating levels of public outputs according to the demands of local constituencies. The magnitude of the potential gains from such decentralization depends upon the variation in the optimal levels of public outputs across jurisdictions. If the optimal level of output varies little from one jurisdiction to another, then the welfare losses from providing a uniform level of output of public services across all jurisdictions will tend to be relatively small. The case for decentralized provision will, in such instances, be less compelling than where desired outputs vary widely from one area to another.[2]

The general approach in this study will be to identify the conditions that enhance the welfare gains from decentralization and then to see (in the next section) if these conditions can "explain" in econometric terms the observed variation in fiscal decentralization in the state and local sector both over time and across states. The primary determinants of the optimal degree of fiscal decentralization encompass three classes of variables:

1. Conditions relating to the land area of the state, the size of its population, and the geographical distribution of the population
2. The level of income and wealth in the state
3. The extent of diversity of tastes for public outputs and their geographical distribution among the population

We shall consider each of these classes of determinants in turn and see what they imply in terms of testable hypotheses.

The size of the state both in terms of population and land area has potentially important implications for the optimal degree of decentralization. That is, in certain ways, a fairly obvious point. A large jurisdiction with a sizeable population offers more opportunities for welfare-enhancing decentralization. As John Stuart Mill observed over a century ago in his tract on *Representative Government,* "There is a limit to the extent of country which can advantageously be governed, or even whose government can be conveniently superintended, from a single centre." This immediately suggests

Hypothesis 1: The larger the size of a state in terms of land area, the less centralized, other things equal, should be its public sector.

However, there is a bit more to the economics of size and geography. Many public services have important economies of scale with respect to population size. For services with important dimensions of "publicness" (i.e., where units of output can be consumed by additional persons without reducing the level of consumption of anyone else), cost per unit of services *per person* varies inversely with the size of the population. In relatively small states, population size at decentralized levels may simply be insufficiently large to exhaust the available economies of scale. In such instances, it may be more economical to provide these services at the state rather than the local level. This suggests

Hypothesis 2: The larger the population of the state, other things equal, the less centralized should be its public sector.

More than simply aggregate population size is at issue here. The way the population of a state is distributed among its local jurisdictions is of central importance for the optimal degree of decentralization. The point is that to take advantage of existing economies of scale with respect to population at the local level requires a certain concentration of economic units. Certain public outputs (including things like zoos, museums, and various specialized services) involve significant indivisibilities; the first "unit" of output of such goods may require a substantial expenditure. Even if all persons have similar demand functions for such a good, it does not become efficient for a locality to provide the good until the sum of the individual demands exceeds its cost. In short, the range of services provided at the local level will depend on the extent of the concentration of the population in urban areas.

In an intriguing study of one metropolitan area, Schmandt and Stephens (1960) found that the number of distinct "subfunctions" (or particular services) that were provided in a municipality was strongly and positively associated with population size. The larger a local jurisdiction, the greater the range of services it provides. This suggests that if the population of a state is thinly spread throughout its land area, there will be a relatively small role for local government. In contrast, the concentration of population in urban areas will make it economically desirable for the local sector to provide a wider range of services.

Hypothesis 3: The larger the fraction of a state's population residing in urban areas, the less centralized, other things equal, should be the state and local sector.

The second set of considerations influencing fiscal decentralization involves the level of income and wealth in the state. Higher levels of income seem to have two effects on the extent of decentralization—effects that work in opposite directions. First, it has been observed in a number of empirical studies (Martin and Lewis 1956; Oates 1972; Kee 1977; Oates 1985; Bahl and Nath 1986) that the higher-income, developed countries have much more decentralized public sectors than do the poorer, developing countries. In one of these studies using data for the mid-1970s, Oates (1985) finds that for a sample of 18 industrialized nations, the mean central government share of total public expenditure is .65; for the corresponding sample of 25 developing countries, the central share is .89. Higher-income countries seem to have a much stronger tendency toward (or history of) decentralization in the public sector. Several explanations have been suggested for this pervasive finding. Wheare (1964), for example, contends that decentralization is expensive and that a country must be relatively affluent to adopt a relatively decentralized form of government. Alternatively, Martin and Lewis (1956) suggest that centralization is necessary in the early stages of development to economize on scarce administrative talent.

This particular line of argument, however, does not seem relevant to a study of the state and local sector in the United States, for the finding of a significant negative relationship between per capita income and fiscal decentralization is limited to comparisons of developed and developing countries. Where the sample is limited to higher-income, developed countries, the relationship between income and decentralization disappears (see Kee 1977; Oates 1985). This suggests that among the states within the U.S., which all fall within the "developed" classification on a world scale, this "income effect" on decentralization is unlikely to be of importance.

There is, however, a second way in which the level of income can influence the extent of fiscal decentralization. It has been observed that the propensity to engage in income redistribution has a relatively high income elasticity. Wealthier polities tend to provide much more in the way of transfers (as a fraction of total income) to lower-income (and other) groups. Local governments tend to be notably circumscribed in their capacity to redistribute income to poor economic units because of the mobility of potential recipients (and sources) across local jurisdictions (see, e.g., Brown and Oates, 1987). For this and other reasons, programs aimed at assisting the poor tend to be more centralized than those involving direct services. On these grounds we might expect higher-income states, other things equal, to have more centralized state and local sectors.

Hypothesis 4: The higher the level of per capita income in a state, the more centralized, other things equal, should be its public sector, as a result of a higher level of involvement in redistributive programs.

The third set of considerations relating to fiscal decentralization encompasses the effects of variations in tastes and demands for public services. The general idea here is a straightforward and seemingly unambiguous one: the greater the diversity of tastes and demands among economic units, the more likely, other things being equal, will be significant differences in the optimal levels of outputs across local jurisdictions. This suggests that we seek some proxy variables for taste and demand differences for public services.

We expect the demand for public (like private) goods typically to vary positively with income; thus, one determinant of the variation in demand should be the degree of inequality in the distribution of income. This suggests that the value of the Gini coefficient will be positively associated with the variation in the demand for public services.

Hypothesis 5: The more unequal the distribution of income. the less centralized, other things equal, should be the state and local sector.

Other proxy measures for the variation in demand for public services are less clear. We expect various socioeconomic differences in the population to manifest themselves in varying demands for public services. Variation in such things as the age distribution of the population, racial composition, and religious affiliations may well contribute to an increased diversity in demands for publically provided services. There may exist, for example, a certain life-cycle pattern to demand for public services with younger households with children present exhibiting a higher demand for things like public education than older households. Or, to take another possible case, states with a substantial mixture of religious groups, some of which provide their own schools, may tend to have widely varying demands for public education. While all this admittedly requires closer examination, we take as a "working hypothesis"

Hypothesis 6: States exhibiting more in the way of diversity as indicated by socioeconomic indicators should tend to have, other things equal, more decentralized public sectors.

This last set of considerations relating to the extent of differences in demands for public services is subject to one important qualification. In order for the variation in demand for local services among the population of a state to manifest itself in the form of welfare gains from increased decentralization, there must be some tendency for people with similar demands to be grouped together in local jurisdictions. If the intrastate diversity in individual demands is mirrored in each local jurisdiction, then there will be little in the way of differences in demands aggregated at the local level. It is where individuals separate themselves into groups with relatively homogeneous demands for public services (as in the Tiebout model) that the welfare gains from fiscal decentralization reflect the diversity of household demands. This suggests a further reason for expecting the optimal degree of decentralization to vary directly with the extent of urbanization within a state. It is within metropolitan areas where individuals can conveniently work in one jurisdiction (the central city) and live in another (a suburban community) that the opportunity for sorting of households in residential communities according to demands for local services has its greatest potential.

As will be discussed in the following section, our measures of socioeconomic diversity are rather naive. The two measures available over the entire sample period are the population living on farms and the ethnic composition of the population.[3] Our "homogeneity" measure is simply $(PC - .5)^2$, where PC is the percentage of the population that is white or (under the alternative definition) living on farms. This variable takes on its maximum possible value of $\frac{1}{4}$ for a completely homogenous population and declines to a minimum possible value of zero for a population that is evenly divided between the two groups. This measure is admittedly crude, but we hope that it captures the essential point of the hypothesis.

Historically, however, simply the proportion of farmers and that of whites in the population have also been important determinants of public policy. Farmers are a diverse lot, but their late nineteenth-and early twentieth-century political goals can be subsumed under the common label of "populism." While supporting a fairly wide range of social and economic reforms, the populists stood firmly behind the notions that a small government was better than a large one and that local governments were better than more centralized governments. Agrarian elements, reformer or otherwise, were also leery of the "city," and states with farm majorities often apportioned state legislative districts to give rural areas disproportionate representation. The net effect of having a large share of the population living on farms is not altogether clear: farmers were against large cities which would tend to promote a more centralized state-local fisc, but they also supported smaller and more decentralized governments as a general principle. As the following section will show, accounting for the share of farmers in the population is important econometrically, even if we do not have a clearcut theoretical prior on the sign of the variable.

The percentage white variable is unavoidably connected with historically centralized southern governments and with a difficulty in interpreting how race relations would affect the structure of government in the South. Since Southern states have historically been more centralized, we expect that

Hypothesis 7: States in the southern region of the country will, other things equal, have more centralized public sectors.

Since the percentage white is considerably lower in most southern states than elsewhere, simply including the percentage white will pick up a "southern" effect. We try to control for this with a dummy variable, but a more complicated problem remains. In many states, especially in the South, a large part of the black population was denied the right to vote until the 1960s. We do not know whether the enforcement of laws (or more informal measures) designed to control and coerce a substantial part of the community requires a more or less centralized government. We also do not know whether the granting of black suffrage would have led to a movement for more or less centralized government; it might have encouraged decentralization as black majorities in local government attempted to use their newly obtained political power in those governments over which they had the most control. As we shall see, it appears as though the level of the black population, as well as our diversity measures, may be an important determinant of the degree of centralization.[4]

1.4   An Econometric Study of Fiscal Decentralization

To test our set of hypotheses on fiscal decentralization, we shall make use of a large panel data set on the state and local sector that we have assembled in the course of a broader historical study of U.S. government finance. Drawing on the U.S. *Census of Governments* and various other sources, we have collected data on state and local governments and on other relevant socioeconomic variables at roughly decade intervals beginning in 1902. We thus have nine sets of cross-sectional observations on the 48 contiguous states that include data on expenditures, revenues, and tax receipts for state government and for local governments in each state. For a description of our data base, we refer the reader to the appendix at the end of this paper.

With this panel data set, we can explore both changes over time and differences among states in the extent of fiscal decentralization. For this purpose, we have adopted the error-components technique for the estimation of our regression equations. Using the error-components estimator, our general approach to the testing of our various hypotheses takes the form:

(1) $$C_{it} = a + bX_{it} + cZ_{it} + s_i + t_t + e_{it},$$

where C_{it} is our measure of fiscal centralization (i.e., the state share of state-local spending or revenues), X_{it} is a vector of control variables, Z_{it} is the vector of variables representing our hypotheses, s_i is a state-specific disturbance term, t_t is a time-specific disturbance term, and e_{it} is the normal disturbance term with zero expected mean. Part of the appeal of the error-components approach is that it allows us to separate out an effect that is specific to each state in our sample and also to each time period. The remaining component of the disturbance term is the usual random error term with zero mean.

We begin the econometric analysis by presenting the simple regression equations involving our measures of fiscal centralization and each of the variables chosen to test one of our hypotheses. We are unable unfortunately to test all the hypotheses we set out in the preceding section because of limitations on our data. We have measures for each state and time period on land area, population size, urbanized population, and per capita income. This allows us to test hypotheses one through four. We do not, however, have data on the distribution of income so that we are unable to test hypothesis five.[5] Next, we have a set of socioeconomic variables from which we will create proxies for variations in tastes for public services so that we can explore hypothesis six. And, finally, the use of a dummy variable for southern states will provide a test of hypothesis seven.

The results of the simple regressions appear in table 1.5. Each row of the table reports the results of the univariate error-components regressions for one of our proposed explanatory variables; the first two columns indicate the results using the state share of total state-local expenditures as the dependent variable, and the second two columns report the estimated equation with the state share of total state and local revenues as the dependent variable. The first set of hypotheses, numbers one through three, relate to the size and urbanization of the state. Here we find that the simple regressions provide support for two of the three hypotheses. The size of the state (measured in terms of population) and the extent of urbanization both have the hypothesized negative coefficients, and these coefficients are statistically significant at the .01 level regardless of whether the expenditure or revenue variable is employed to measure fiscal centralization. Size as measured by land area, although it has the hypothesized sign, is not statistically significant.[6]

Hypothesis four proposes a positive relationship between fiscal centralization and the level of per capita income. In the univariate regression, however, we find an inverse association. [More on this shortly.] To explore hypothesis six concerning variation in tastes, we have used two proxies for the homogeneity of the state's population. As noted earlier, the measures are the squares of the difference between .5 and

Table 1.5   **Simple Univariate Error-Components Regressions, Fiscal Concentration Measure on Selection of Independent Variables (Absolute t-Statistics)**

	Expenditures		Revenues	
	Constant (1)	Coefficient (2)	Constant (3)	Coefficient (4)
LAND AREA	0.3622	−1.94E−07	0.4309	−7.38E−08
	(10.3)***	(.90)	(7.7)***	(.34)
POPULATION	0.3802	−1.01E−05	0.4392	−4.3E−06
	(12.4)***	(5.9)***	(9.0)***	(2.5)***
PERCENTAGE	0.4587	−0.2147	0.4956	−0.1371
URBAN	(15.2)***	(6.7)***	(11.7)***	(4.3)***
PER CAPITA	0.3853	−1.9E−05	0.476	−2.71E−05
INCOME	(11.7)***	(1.54)	(10.5)***	(2.06)**
HOMOGENEITY	0.3816	−0.3009	0.4517	−0.2428
FARM	(13.6)***	(3.3)***	(10.5)***	(2.8)***
HOMOGENEITY	0.3849	−0.2075	0.4865	−0.3602
WHITE	(10.6)***	(2.13)**	(8.6)***	(4.0)***
PERCENTAGE	0.3396	0.0442	0.4265	−0.0008
FARM	(13.8)***	(1.21)	(11.3)***	(.02)
PERCENTAGE	0.4962	−0.1642	0.6003	−0.1958
WHITE	(8.5)***	(2.9)***	(8.5)***	(3.8)***

Notes: Every row represents two univariate regressions. In columns (1) and (2) the constant and coefficent are from a regression of the percentage of total state and local expenditures undertaken at the state level, regressed on the individual independent variables. In columns (3) and (4) the constant and coefficent are from a regression of the percentage of total state and local revenues undertaken at the state level, regressed on the individual independent variables.

N = 432 for all regressions

*** = 1% significance level

** = 5% significance level

* = 10% significance level

the percentage white or the percentage residing on farms. A state with 50 percent of its population living on farms, for example, would be as diverse as possible, and the farm homogeneity variable would, in this instance, equal zero. We find in table 1.5 that the univariate results support neither version of hypothesis six: the estimated coefficient on both the farm and white homogeneity variables is negative and statistically significant in both equations, indicating that more homogeneous populations are associated with more decentralized governments.

The percentage white variable has a significantly negative association with fiscal centralization, which probably reflects the southern effect. The percentage of the population living on farms does not exhibit a significant association with centralization (with opposite signs for the revenue and expenditure equations).

While the univariate equations are of some interest, a multiple-regression model containing a set of control variables is obviously needed to provide a more reliable test of the various hypotheses. We present in table 1.6 the results of our error-components multiple-regression analysis. The first two columns indicate the estimated coefficients for the equation using the expenditure measure of fiscal centralization, while the second two columns report the results using the revenue definition for the fiscal centralization variable. The multivariate tests for the first three hypotheses confirm the univariate findings: the extent of fiscal centralization is significantly and negatively related to the size of the population and the percentage urban, but is not significantly associated with land area. Larger states in terms of population and states whose population is more highly urbanized tend to have more decentralized fiscal systems.

Table 1.6   **Error-Components Regressions, Fiscal Concentration Measure on Selection of Independent Variables (absolute t-statistics)**

	Expenditures		Revenues	
	(1)	(2)	(3)	(4)
LAND AREA	$-2.05\mathrm{E}-07$	$-1.37\mathrm{E}-07$	$-6.13\mathrm{E}-08$	$-1.21\mathrm{E}-08$
	(1.3)	(.87)	(.37)	(.07)
POPULATION	$-9.30\mathrm{E}-06$	$-7.02\mathrm{E}-06$	$-5.48\mathrm{E}-06$	$-3.37\mathrm{E}-06$
	(5.2)***	(3.9)***	(3.1)***	(1.87)*
PERCENTAGE	-0.1966	-0.2917	-0.0783	-0.1933
URBAN	(4.7)***	(6.2)***	(1.9)*	(4.15)***
PER CAPITA	$2.39\mathrm{E}-05$	$3.58\mathrm{E}-05$	$3.01\mathrm{E}-06$	$1.62\mathrm{E}-05$
INCOME	(1.76)*	(2.5)***	(.20)	(1.09)
HOMOGENEITY	-0.045	-0.1707	-0.0092	-0.2134
FARM	(.41)	(1.48)	(.08)	(1.89)*
HOMOGENEITY	-0.1628	0.5812	-0.3573	-0.0331
WHITE	(1.81)*	(2.11)**	(3.8)***	(.12)
PERCENTAGE	—	-0.2284	—	-0.2477
FARM		(4.3)***		(4.7)***
PERCENTAGE	—	-0.4305	—	-0.1748
WHITE		(2.9)***		(1.19)
SOUTHERN	—	0.0377	—	0.0416
DUMMY		(1.67)*		(1.84)*
Constant	0.4686	0.8073	0.5411	0.7343
	(13.3)***	(7.5)***	(11.8)***	(6.7)***

Notes: The dependent variable in columns (1) and (2) is the concentration measure for expenditures and in columns (3) and (4) is the concentration measure for revenues.
N = 432 for all regressions.
*** = 1% significance level.
** = 5% significance level.
* = 10% significance level.

When we come to the income variable, however, the results differ from the univariate cases: for the multivariate equations, the estimated coefficient on per capita income possesses the hypothesized positive sign and is statistically significant in the expenditure equation. Higher income states thus exhibit a tendency toward more centralized state and local sectors (at least in terms of the expenditure measure of centralization).[7]

The estimated coefficients for the southern dummy variable are positive (as hypothesized) and statistically significant. Simply being a southern state seems to explain roughly a third of the difference in fiscal centralization between southern and northeastern states. However, the results for the socioeconomic variables are more difficult to interpret. The estimated coefficients on our homogeneity variables, both percentage white and farm, are extremely sensitive to the specification of the equation, and we hesitate to place much confidence in these estimates. The coefficient on the farm homogeneity variable is negative in all four equations, which runs counter to hypothesis six. There is another intrepretation of this variable in conjunction with the percentage farm variable in equations (2) and (4) in table 1.6. Having more farmers appears to produce a more decentralized government, but at a decreasing rate. Or, what may be the more appropriate way to phrase that statement in the American historical context: having fewer farmers (as has happened over time) leads to a more centralized government, and does so at an increasing rate. This effect is quite interesting in light of the strong negative effect that urbanization exerts on centralization, as it indicates that we cannot simply think of percentage farm and percentage urban as proxies for one another.

The racial homogeneity variable has the predicted positive sign in equation (2) and is statistically significant. But it is negative in the other three equations in Table 1.6. The estimated coefficient for percentage white is negative in both instances, but statistically significant only in equation (2). We find these results difficult to interpret. Taken at face value, the results in equation (2) indicate that a larger white population results in greater decentralization but at a diminishing rate. The white "decentralization effect" is increasingly offset by the "diversity effect" as percentage white rises toward 100 percent.

Finally, we thought it would be of interest to compare our results for the error-components analysis covering the entire period of eighty years with the set of cross-sectional multiple-regression equations for each decade. We present in table 1.7 the estimated cross-sectional equations for each of our observed years (using ordinary least squares). The estimated equations use the expenditure definition of the dependent variable.[8] While the overall results correspond roughly to our earlier

Table 1.7   OLS Regressions. Fiscal Concentration Measure on Selection of Independent Variables by Year, 1902 to 1982 (absolute t-statistic)

	1902	1913	1922	1932	1942
LAND AREA	4.09E − 08	− 1.14E − 07	− 2.06E − 08	− 2.10E − 07	− 3.84E − 07
	(1.99)*	(.37)	(.07)	(.79)	(1.36)
POPULATION	− 1.08E − 05	− 8.38E − 06	− 1.27E − 04	− 9.96E − 06	− 3.66E − 06
	(1.93)*	(1.29)	(2.22)**	(1.85)*	(.65)
PERCENTAGE	− 0.2139	− 0.3637	− 0.0922	− 0.3881	− 0.6506
URBAN	(2.03)**	(2.64)**	(.66)	(2.47)**	(3.55)***
PER CAPITA	− 5.27E − 05	− 1.10E − 04	7.04E − 05	6.98E − 05	− 2.41E − 05
INCOME	(1.05)	(1.41)	(.84)	(1.28)	(.44)
HOMOGENEITY	0.2753	0.5569	− 0.2164	− 0.1137	0.7401
FARM	(1.15)	(1.61)	(.56)	(.24)	(1.22)
HOMOGENEITY	0.8875	− 0.154	− 1.404	− 0.3403	− 0.8996
WHITE	(2.01)*	(.23)	(1.83)*	(.38)	(.89)
PERCENTAGE	0.2356	− 0.2117	− 0.0988	− 0.1183	− 0.3778
FARM	(2.31)**	(1.15)	(.51)	(.57)	(1.30)
PERCENTAGE	− 0.6444	0.147	0.5052	0.0436	0.5309
WHITE	(3.61)***	(.49)	(1.31)	(.09)	(.92)
SOUTHERN	0.0261	− 0.043	− 0.025	0.0371	0.0359
DUMMY	(.64)	(.79)	(.52)	(.75)	(.70)
Constant	0.8056	0.4787	0.1031	0.5157	0.5139
	(6.5)***	(2.12)**	(.35)	(1.49)	(1.18)
R_2	0.67	0.35	0.37	0.60	0.46

findings, a cursory examination of the table indicates that the results vary considerably from one period to the next; the estimated coefficients on many of the variables exhibit substantial changes in their magnitude and the values of their *t*-statistics from one period to the next. The population and percentage urban variables, however, are consistently negative (with only one exception) and often statistically significant.

In summary, our econometric results, while admittedly somewhat mixed, do provide support for several of the hypotheses. We find that the extent of fiscal centralization varies inversely and significantly with both population size and urbanization (although not significantly with land area). In addition, we have found a positive relationship (at least in the multivariate error-components analysis) between fiscal centralization and the level of per capita income. This is consistent with the view that higher-income states will have a more pronounced inclination to engage in redistributive activities which tend to have a disproportionately large role for the state government. As suggested by the historical discussion, we have found that southern states (at least until quite recently) have relatively centralized state and local fiscs. Finally, we obtained quite mixed (and often puzzling) results with our racial

Table 1.7   (continued)

	1952	1962	1972	1982
LAND	$-3.01E-07$	$2.25E-07$	$-9.90E-08$	$-2.70E-07$
	(1.07)	(1.04)	(.44)	(1.33)
POPULATION	$-5.97E-06$	$-9.55E-06$	$-5.77E-06$	$-4.80E-06$
	(1.15)	(3.19)***	(2.18)**	(2.15)**
PERCENTAGE	-0.8729	-0.4959	-0.1905	-0.1493
URBAN	(3.8)***	(3.42)***	(1.56)	(1.29)
PER CAPITA	$1.62E-05$	$-3.68E-05$	$-8.45E-05$	$-2.65E-05$
INCOME	(.35)	(.94)	(2.39)**	(.97)
HOMOGENEITY	1.467	1.396	3.297	11.201
FARM	(1.61)	(1.24)	(1.81)*	(2.37)**
HOMOGENEITY	-0.9271	0.0621	0.4963	-0.2163
WHITE	(.74)	(.05)	(.39)	(.16)
PERCENTAGE	-0.1491	0.33	2.037	9.262
FARM	(.29)	(.45)	(1.48)	(2.32)**
PERCENTAGE	0.7064	0.0631	0.0424	0.2931
WHITE	(.93)	(.09)	(.05)	(.33)
SOUTHERN	0.0697	0.0291	0.0493	0.0276
DUMMY	(1.35)	(.78)	(1.49)	(1.00)
Constant	0.277	0.4959	-0.0389	-2.3211
	(.48)	(.98)	(.06)	(1.74)*
R^2	0.53	0.66	0.66	0.54

Notes: The dependent variable in all regressions is the state share of combined state and local expenditures.
N = 48 for all regressions.
*** = 1% significance.
** = 5% significance.
* = 10% significance.

and farm variables. Although they often have significant explanatory power in the regression equations, they do not provide clear support for hypothesis six and present formidable problems of interpretation.

1.5   Some Reflections on Future Trends in Fiscal Centralization

As we have seen, the twentieth century has been a period over which the state and local sector has exhibited a strong tendency toward increased fiscal centralization. Is this a trend that is likely to continue? This is not an easy question to answer, but we would like to offer some thoughts. At the turn of the present century, the fiscal role of state governments was a very modest one. However, various developments brought an increased demand for important new public services, notably highways, higher education, and public assistance programs, that were appropriately placed in the domain of state government. As a result, the fiscal share of state government in the state and local sector rose dramatically. But, as we saw, this rise in the extent of fiscal centralization was primarily a phenomenon of the first half of the century. The trend toward further fiscal centralization has slowed dramatically (if not ceased altogether). From this perspective, it would appear that the forces behind the trend toward centralization are largely history now; without some new thrust for state-level intervention, there would seem to be little reason to expect further centralization of the state and local sector.

On closer examination, there appear to be some such centralizing forces still at work—at least to a modest degree. The primary force is a continuing concern with so-called fiscal equalization: the more equal access of all socioeconomic groups to "satisfactory" levels of public services. This concern (although by no means new) has been reinforced by court decisions on public education and various restrictions on local finances, and is no doubt partly responsible for the continuing tendency toward heavier reliance on intergovernmental aid to local governments. Equalizing grants from the states have provided a means for reducing the fiscal disparities between wealthier and poorer localities.

At the same time, there are some reasons to expect the potential welfare gains from decentralized finance to remain substantial and perhaps to grow over time. A basic mechanism for the realization of these gains is the mobility of individuals, permitting the formation of communities that are relatively homogeneous in their demands for local services. The development of metropolitan areas in which individuals work in one locality (perhaps the central city) but reside in a nearby residential community provides a setting well suited to the realization of the gains from local finance. Rising incomes, improved transportation, and the increasing mobility of individuals would suggest that the potential gains from decentralization should remain substantial.

Our overall econometric results point to these divergent forces. If population and urbanization continue to grow, this will create pressures for more decentralized government. However, the positive effect of income growth on fiscal centralization should continue; indeed the concern with equalization may be the manifestation of a kind of income effect. But the other major source of centralization, the declining number of farmers, cannot be expected to contribute much to centralization in the future.

There are thus forces at work, some of which favor increased centralization, but others of which increase the relative gains from decentralized finance. Any prediction of outcomes is thus extremely precarious. However, we would venture the conjecture that the local sector is unlikely, at least in terms of expenditure responsibilities, to experience much further diminution in its relative fiscal role over the next few decades. The local provision of services promises important welfare gains that will not go unnoticed.

Appendix

The variables used in this paper are taken from a variety of Commerce Department sources and are, for the most part, exactly what they seem. Problems arose occasionally from gaps in the available series. This appendix describes how the gaps where bridged.

The fiscal variables, revenues and expenditures by state for state and local governments, were taken from the decennial Census of Governments. This census was taken in 1902, 1913, 1922, 1932, 1942, 1962, 1972, and 1982 (with additional censuses taken in 1927, 1957, 1967, and 1977). A census was contemplated, but not taken, in 1952. Coverage of local governments in the 1902, 1913, and 1922 censuses varied slightly. And the 1922 census did not include a complete enumeration of local government expenditures. These gaps were filled by several interpolation techniques.

The 1902 census of governments recorded complete information on public revenues and expenditures for all levels of government.[9] The 1913 Census of Governments included all governments except for places with population less than 2,500.[10] The 1922 Census of Governments included information on receipts for all levels of government, and expenditures for state governments only.[11]

To account for the exclusion of governments in places with less than 2,500 population, we utilized the breakdown of government expenditures by population size in the 1902 census. The 1902 returns reported fiscal totals for cities with population of 8,000 to 25,000 and all minor subdivisions. The 1913 Census reported fiscal totals for all cities with population of 2,500 to 8,000 but for no smaller units. Both censuses reported totals for larger cities and counties. We calculated revenues and expenditures of minor subdivisions (cities with under 8,000 population) as a percentage of revenues and expenditures for cities with over 8,000 population and counties in 1902. Then revenues and expenditures for cities with over 8,000 population and counties in 1913 were multiplied by the 1902 shares to generate an estimate of "all minor subdivision" revenues and expenditures for 1913.

The revenue data for 1922 were fairly complete. We were able to collect total revenue and expenditure data for state governments, as well as local tax revenues and local revenue from state grants. The census department estimated a nationwide total for local revenues in 1922 at $4,148 million.[12] We assumed that the ratio of local nongrant total revenues to tax revenues was the same in each state as it had been in 1913, and calculated an estimated nongrant total revenue figure for 1922. The estimated nationwide total was slightly higher than the census estimate, and therefore every state was adjusted by a common factor (.927469) to bring our total revenues in line with the census total. Finally, we estimated local expenditure by assuming that the ratio of expenditures to revenues in each state was the same as the nationwide estimates made by the census.[13]

Complete state level data were available for 1953, but no local data were collected. Information on local revenues was collected in 1953 and that information was used to construct estimates of local revenues and expenditures for 1952. Specifically, the census department estimated that nationwide local revenues in 1952 were .91 of the total local revenue in 1953. We simply adjusted the 1953 revenue figures by .91 to obtain our 1952 estimates. The census also estimated that local expenditures in 1952 were 1.2 times greater than revenues, and we calculated local expenditures by multiplying our revenue estimate by 1.2.

The control variables where comparatively easy to assemble. From *Historical Statistics* it was possible to collect population, land size, racial composition, and urban population for each decade. Note that the census data refer to census years (years ending in 0), while the financial variables refer to the relevant Census of Government years. The one variable that caused a problem was per capita income.

Per capita income is available in *Historical Statistics* from 1929 on. Before 1929 the state level income estimates of Richard Easterlin (1957) are available for the years 1900 and 1920. Nationwide GNP per capita was $246 in 1900, $382 in 1910, and $860 in 1920. Of the total growth in income between 1900 and 1920, therefore, .2215 occurred between 1900 and 1910. We took 22.15 percent of the income growth in each state between 1900 and 1920, and added it to the 1900 income figure from Easterlin to estimate per-capita income in each state for 1910.

Notes

1. The years are mainly those during which there was a Census of Governments in the United States (see the appendix).

2. For a more rigorous treatment of the determinants of the optimal degree of decentralization, see Oates (1972, appendix to chapter 2).

3. We also have information on the age structure of the population, but including variables on age structure had no measurable effects on the results; these variables were not statistically significant in the regression analysis.

4. Including a measure of the share of whites in the population along with our racial homogeneity variable in the same equation raises some tricky issues

of interpretation. There is the question of whether this specification is any different than one which enters the white share variable in a nonlinear form with both linear and square terms. If one believes that the homogeneity of the population (as measured by the squared deviation from one-half of the fraction of the population that is white) influences fiscal centralization, then the specification including both PC and (PC − .5)^2 is appropriate. However, this is admittedly a restrictive specification; in particular, it imposes a symmetry condition on the effects of homogeneity (i.e., 55 percent white has the same effect as 45 percent white). If our specification is not the correct one, then of course there may well be some confounding of measured effects between the share and homogeneity variables. We have examined some other (and more complicated) specifications, but they have not altered the main empirical findings in the paper (these results are available from the authors). The interpretation of the homogeneity measure depends upon the particular specification, but not always in a way that is easily characterized. Since the results for these variables are quite sensitive to specification, we are reluctant to place much weight on them in this paper. But as the results in the next section indicate, there does seem to be something here that merits further investigation. This discussion applies as well to our treatment of the farm variables, where we include in the regression equations measures of both the share of the farm population and a farm homogeneity variable.

5. In a cross-sectional study of fiscal decentralization using data for 1969–70, Giertz (1976) finds that the Gini coefficient is positively and significantly associated with the extent of fiscal centralization, suggesting that a higher degree of inequality in the distribution of income is associated with a more centralized state and local sector. This finding runs counter to our hypothesis five. Giertz argues that this result reflects the greater need for income redistribution in states with more inequality.

6. In an earlier cross-sectional study using data for 1962, Litvack and Oates (1970) likewise found population size and percentage urban to be negatively and significantly associated with fiscal centralization in the state and local sector. Giertz (1976) found, in addition, a negative and significant relationship between fiscal centralization and land area.

7. Giertz (1976) found such a relationship in his cross-sectional study.

8. The results using the revenue version of the dependent variable do not differ in any important ways from those reported in table 1.7.

9. U.S. Bureau of the Census (1907). Receipt and Expenditure data taken from Table 10, pp. 982–93.

10. U.S. Bureau of the Census (1914). Receipt and expenditure data for states taken from Table 6, pp. 36–37, Table 8, pp. 40–41. Table 10, pp. 44–45; for counties Table 3, pp. 122–23 and Table 5, pp. 210–11; for incorporated places Table 3, pp. 462–69 and Table 5, pp. 560–67.

11. U.S. Bureau of the Census (1924). Receipts for local governments taken from Table 1, pp. 12–16. Receipts and expenditures taken from Table 2, p. 17, Table 3, pp. 52–53, and Table 4, p. 54.

12. The census estimates for local finances were based on information gathered by the census from a sample of large cities and scattered data collected by the census bureau. Estimates of local government finances were built up from these partial samples. We have used these estimates to fill in missing data in 1922 and in 1952.

13. Local Expenditures = 1.101013 · Local Revenues

References

Bahl, R. W., and S. Nath. 1986. Public expenditure decentralization in developing countries. *Environment and Planning C: Government and Policy* 4:405–18.

Brown, Charles C., and Wallace E. Oates. 1987. Assistance to the poor in a federal system. *Journal of Public Economics* 32:307-30.

Easterlin, Richard A. 1957. State income estimates. In *Population, redistribution, and economic growth, United States, 1870–1950, vol. 1*, ed. Everett Lee. Philadelphia: American Philosophical Society.

Giertz, J. Fred. 1976. Decentralization at the state and local level: An empirical analysis. *National Tax Journal* 29:201–10.

Kee, Woo Sik. 1977. Fiscal decentralization and economic development. *Public Finance Quarterly* 5:79–97.

Litvack, James M., and Wallace E. Oates. 1970. Group size and the output of public goods: Theory and an application to state-local finance in the United States. *Public Finance* 25:42–60.

Martin, Alison, and W. Arthur Lewis. 1956. Patterns of public revenue and expenditure. *Manchester School of Economic and Social Studies* 24:203–44.

Oates, Wallace E. 1972. *Fiscal federalism*. New York: Harcourt, Brace, Jovanovich.

———. 1985. Searching for leviathan: An empirical study. *American Economic Review* 75:748–57.

Schmandt, H. J., and G. R. Stephens. 1960. Measuring municipal output. *National Tax Journal* 13:369–75.

U.S. Bureau of the Census. 1907. *Wealth, debt, and taxation*. Washington, D.C.: U.S. Government Printing Office.

U.S. Bureau of the Census. 1914. *Wealth, debt, and taxation*. Washington D.C.: U.S. Government Printing Office.

U.S. Bureau of the Census. 1924. *Wealth, debt, and taxation*. Washington D.C.: U.S. Government Printing Office.

U.S. Bureau of the Census. 1935. *Financial statistics of state and local governments*. Washington, D.C.: U.S. Government Printing Office.

U.S. Bureau of the Census. 1948. *Revised summary of state and local government finances in 1942*. State and Local Special Studies no. 26. Washington, D.C.: U.S. Government Printing Office.

U.S. Bureau of the Census. 1954. *State government finances*. Washington, D.C.: U.S. Government Printing Office.

U.S. Bureau of the Census. 1964. *Census of governments, 1962*. Vol. 4, no. 4. Washington, D.C.: U.S. Government Printing Office.

U.S. Bureau of the Census. 1974. *Census of governments, 1972*. Vol. 4, no. 5. Washington, D.C.: U.S. Government Printing Office.

U.S. Bureau of the Census. 1984. *Census of governments, 1982*. Vol. 4, no. 5. Washington, D.C.: U.S. Government Printing Office.

Wallis, John Joseph. 1984. Birth of the old federalism. *Journal of Economic History* 94:139–60.

———1987. The political economy of new deal fiscal federalism. Unpublished manuscript.

Wheare, Kenneth C. 1964. *Federal government*. 4th ed. London: Oxford University Press.

Comment   James R. Hines, Jr.

John Wallis and Wallace Oates present an intriguing analysis of twentieth-century trends in state and local public finance. As its title suggests, their paper focuses on the pattern and causes of public sector decentralization, where the authors understand "centralization" to mean the extent to which state governments account for total state and local spending or revenues. As their table 1.1 illustrates, the striking feature of recent state and local fiscal relations is the sharp rise around World War II in state spending and revenues relative to local spending and revenues. Hence, the subnational public sector is more centralized now than it was in the first three decades of this century.

Wallis and Oates seek to understand whether this pattern represents an economically efficient adjustment by different levels of government to changing underlying factors. The seven hypotheses they specify and test capture in part the intuition that public sector centralization is more desirable with a homogeneous population. This conclusion follows from assuming the functions of state and local governments to be the provision of substitute public goods. Since additional consumers can enjoy public goods at little (or zero) cost, simple cost-sharing argues for state rather than local provision of most public goods. On the other hand, citizens of a state must all consume the same bundle of public goods, despite their potentially divergent demands for public services. The more divergent these demands are, the more sense it may make for localities to provide a large fraction of the public goods and tailor them to local needs.

It is hard to know quite what to make of this efficient-response approach to public expenditures and the tests Wallis and Oates employ to evaluate it. One difficulty is the absence of a formal model, with the result that it is not easy to tell whether the data confirm or reject the theory. Presumably, the model requires the public services provided by different levels of government to be imperfect substitutes, since otherwise it is always most efficient for state (or national) governments to provide all the services. If public parks are all perfect substitutes, then it is not efficient for cities to build parks and exclude nonresidents from them; instead, states should pay for them. The nature of the efficient division of fiscal responsibility depends crucially on the substitutability or complementarity of different public services, as well as crowding, scale economies, and other size variables. As a result, most

James R. Hines, Jr., is assistant professor of economics and public affairs at the Woodrow Wilson School, Princeton University, and a faculty research fellow of the National Bureau of Economic Research.

behavioral responses are consistent with the simple hypothesis that governments divide responsibilities efficiently.

A second difficulty is that even the desirability of disparate multilevel government expenditure levels does not require the "decentralization" of the state-local sector. Suppose that some jurisdictions within a state demand extensive subsidized public transportation while other parts of the state do not need such services. There is nothing statutory which prevents state governments from adjusting tax and spending levels to local tastes and needs. Of course, there may be strong political reasons for state governments not to favor some jurisdictions with services or light tax burdens at the expense of others. But it is easy to cite many examples of state (or national) governments doing exactly this.

Since the heterogeneity of local demands for public services plays such an important role in Wallis and Oates's explanation of decentralization patterns, it is worth considering whether state governments may feel compelled to equate tax or spending levels across jurisdictions for reasons other than a vague political desire for equality. Another reason why states may feel constrained to divide taxes and public services among jurisdictions to an inefficient degree is that information on local tastes for public services is not always available to state governments. If asked, localities would always claim to need extensive services and to possess fiscal characteristics (such as a real estate sector which responds elastically to local property taxes) which make it desirable to tax them lightly. The state government's problem then is to elicit truthful revelation of local preferences. Naturally, an extreme resolution of this problem is to decentralize the public sector by making localities rely on their own resources. Localities then have no incentives to distort their fiscal choices and in addition bear tax burdens which are generally (assuming no incidence spillovers) matched to the services they receive. But states need rely on decentralization only when they cannot obtain the information necessary to refine their tax and spending plans — and then only when characteristics differ among local jurisdictions. Note, however, that if characteristics differ systematically on the basis of observable features then state governments can target tax and spending programs based on those features.

A third reason why state governments may impose equal tax and benefit levels across communities is that population is mobile within a state (as well as across states) and the state government may fear excessive Tiebout shifting in response to unequal treatment of substate jurisdictions. While there is little conclusive evidence that taxpayers move in response to fiscal changes, it is possible that state governments perceive such movement to be a potential problem and respond by smoothing taxes and expenditures across jurisdictions.

One limitation of the empirical work Wallis and Oates present is that it is not capable of identifying changes in the desirability of decentralization based on the second or third of these reasons. Wallis and Oates regress the degree of centralization on variables such as income, urbanization, population, and racial homogeneity, all of which are intended to capture the heterogeneity of local demands for public expenditures. But if these characteristics are in fact related to desired expenditure levels, then state governments can infer from demographic variables desired spending levels throughout the state and the problem of demand revelation need not affect the degree of centralization. If, on the other hand, state governments have legitimate fears of population movements in response to fiscal changes, then Wallis and Oates's regression strategy of assuming population characteristics to be exogenous is flawed and the model is not identified.

Another limitation of Wallis and Oates's regressions is that they measure public services by expenditures rather than by true service flow. Of course, this problem is ubiquitous in public finance analysis, since there are no reliable measures of public sector output. This problem becomes important whenever there are large changes in the cost of public services. If one thinks of public services as effective services per capita, then an increase in the heterogeneity of demands for public services raises their cost. But the response of total expenditures to a price change is ambiguous in sign: if the price rises and the demand elasticity is less than one, then total expenditures increase; if elasticity is greater than one expenditures fall. Thus, state-level expenditures may rise in response to a change in population characteristics that makes local expenditures relatively more desirable. This is not to say that local expenditures might not rise relative to state expenditures in such a scenario. But the sign and magnitude of the relative change will depend on specific price and income elasticities.

There is an empirical issue which is closely related to this theoretical ambiguity. The question has to do with the choice of an appropriate scale variable with which to measure centralization. Wallis and Oates choose as their index the ratio of state to total state/local taxes or expenditures. This ratio has been rising over time, but there are many possible sources of this change. Table C1.1 indicates that both the state and local sectors have been growing relative to GNP over this century, though the state sector has been growing at a faster rate. Since most variables of economic importance exhibit secular growth, the growth of state expenditures relative to local expenditures could be explained by a greater state spending elasticity with respect to income, population, other government spending, or many other variables.

It is noteworthy in this context that Wallis and Oates get much stronger results when they pool the data as reported in their table 1.6 than in the cross-sectional results reported in table 1.7. What this suggests is that rising income and other variables have been correlated with a rise in centralization, but that secular trends of unknown origin

Table C1.1   **State and Local Direct Expenditures, as a Percentage of GNP, Selected Years**

Year	Direct State Expenditures/GNP	Direct Local Expenditures/GNP
1902	0.63%	4.44%
1913	0.75	4.95
1922	1.46	6.15
1932	3.48	10.93
1942	2.25	4.64
1952	3.10	5.77
1962	4.51	7.97
1972	6.11	9.95
1982	6.89	10.15

Source: Author's calculations from data in Tax Foundation (1986).

may be driving this correlation since the data do not support the theory in the cross sections. The variables that do not change over time, land area and the southern effect, are not significant. On the other hand, the authors find the predicted sign for the population variable, which would not be expected just on the basis of secular drift, and the urbanization variable is significant in both the cross-sectional and panel regressions.

Fundamentally, the analysis of subnational fiscal centralization must concern itself with the political forces driving state and local relations, and it seems that Wallis and Oates's results should be interpreted as throwing some light on these forces. It is difficult to attach too strong an economic interpretation to their findings, since the best economic explanation still requires state governments to feel politically obliged to equalize spending and tax levels among different groups in the population. The degree to which economic and political considerations interact is very much an open question. More generally, political considerations may affect the extent to which state-level fiscal activity is "centralized" and local-level activity is "decentralized." Central Park in New York City is likely enjoyed by a larger and more heterogeneous group of people than is Taconic State Park in New York State; does this make it more "centralized"? A fuller understanding of the nature of state-local fiscal relations may have to wait for more complete interpretations of the political and economic consequences of taxing and spending.

References

Tax Foundation, Inc. 1986. *Facts and figures on government finance. 23d ed.* Washington, D.C.: Tax Foundation.

2 Federal Assistance and Local Services in the United States: The Evolution of a New Federalist Fiscal Order

Robert P. Inman

2.1 Introduction

From its beginnings, the fiscal system of the United States has been committed to the principle that multiple layers of government is the preferred structure for the financing and provision of government services. The U.S. Constitution through the Tenth Amendment expressly protects the rights of states to pursue their own fiscal agendas provided those agendas do not conflict with clearly legislated federal objectives or constitutionally protected individual rights.[1] Most state constitutions through charters for the creation of local governments offer similar protections for the fiscal activities of cities, counties, and special districts.[2] While the rules for defining the domains of fiscal decisions are reasonably clear, the exact contents of these domains are not. Our federalist fiscal structure is an evolving structure, changing in response to the demands upon it for the provision of public goods. This paper will examine the most recent phase of this evolutionary process: the recent centralization in the financing of the state and local provision of public services.[3]

Robert P. Inman is a professor of finance, economics, and public management at the University of Pennsylvania and a research associate of the National Bureau of Economic Research.

The ideas in this paper were originally presented in a series of classes given at the University of Pennsylvania Law School in a research seminar taught jointly with Professor Michael Fitts, and sponsored by the Law School's Institute of Law and Economics. An initial draft of the paper was given at the NBER Conference on Fiscal Federalism; the comments of my discussant, Tom Romer, and other participants at the conference were most helpful in preparing this current version. I wish to thank the NBER and the Mellon Foundation (through the PARSS grant to the University of Pennsylvania) for financial support and Mr. David Albright for providing his usual high level of research assistance.

Table 2.1   **The Growth of All Government Spending Federal plus State plus Local Government Spending on:[a]**

Year	Total	(% of Personal Income) (1)	Defense (2)	Transfers to Persons (3)	Goods and Services (4)
1902	$ 195.49	(7.74)	$ 23.87	$ 3.10	$ 103.30
1913	272.22	(9.04)	31.62	3.20	137.50
1922	369.18	(12.78)	46.71	5.70	209.00
1932	560.09	(22.14)	44.54	17.40	397.30
1940	830.28	(24.31)	66.19	70.10	420.40
1950	1405.78	(28.70)	290.22	176.50	412.00
1960	1651.31	(34.67)	569.94	217.20	542.10
1970	1834.62	(37.82)	498.72	405.60	809.40
1980	2057.02	(37.78)	346.09	702.70	958.90
1985	2223.12	(39.13)	459.90	662.89	953.01
Annual Rate of Growth, 1902 to 1985	2.96%		3.61%	6.65%	2.70%

Sources: All government spending data for the period 1902 to 1970 are from Bureau of Census, 1975, *Historical Statistics of the United States,* Series Y605–637, Y682–709; data for the year 1980 are from Bureau of Economic Analysis, 1984, *National Income and Product Accounts* (NIPA), 1929–1982, Tables 3.2 and 3.1; data for the year 1985 are from Bureau of Economic Analysis, July 1986, *Survey of Current Business,* Tables 3.2 and 3.3. The price deflator for government goods and services, for defense spending, and for total government spending is the implicit price deflator for all government. Sources are the Bureau of Census, 1975, *Historical Statistics* for the period 1932–1970, Series E1-22; the Bureau of Economic Analysis, 1984, *NIPA,* 1929–1982, Table 7.6, for 1980; and the Bureau of Economic Analysis, July 1986, *Survey of Current Business,* Table 7.6, for 1985. For the period 1902–1932, the GNP price deflator for government services was assumed to have the same rate of change as the "all items" CPI, from *Historical Statistics,* p. 211. The price deflator for transfers to persons was the implicit GNP price deflator, available from *Historical Statistics* for 1902–1970, Series E1-22, from the *NIPA* for 1980, Table 7.6, and from the *Survey of Current Business,* July 1986, Table 7.6, for 1985.

[a]1972 dollars per capita.

Tables 2.1–2.3 reveal the basic trends. Three central facts stand out. First, total federal, state, and local government spending has been increasing steadily over this century, both in real dollars and as a percentage of national income (table 2.1). The major components of this growth are federal outlays for defense (growing at 3.61 percent per annum since 1902), government direct transfers to persons (growing at 6.65 percent per annum), and governments' direct provision of goods and services (growing at 2.70 percent per annum). Second, state and local governments are the main producers of nondefense, nontransfer public goods (Table 2.2). Finally, there is a decided trend towards the centralized financing of these state and local services (table 2.3). At both the state and local levels the trend is to move the revenue decision upward to a higher level of government. Note however, that at the same time we have centralized the financing of state and local services the spending and production decisions have remained at the state and local level. While financing has become centralized, provision decisions have remained localized.

The move of our fiscal system towards the centralized financing of local services is not a new phenomenon. The federal government has always provided aid to the states, and states have always given fiscal assistance to their localities.[4] What is new—at least since 1960—is the dollar volume of such assistance and its rapid growth. The story behind

Table 2.2   **Federal and State-Local Governments' Provision of Nondefense Public Goods and Services[a]**

Year	Total (1)	Federal (2)	State-Local (3)	(State-Local's % of Total)
1902	$103.30	$ 29.96	$ 73.34	(71)
1913	137.50	35.89	101.61	(74)
1922	209.00	73.15	135.85	(65)
1932	397.30	139.05	258.25	(65)
1940	420.40	130.32	290.08	(69)
1950	412.00	45.32	366.68	(81)
1960	542.10	86.19	455.91	(84)
1970	809.40	121.41	687.99	(85)
1980	958.90	160.14	798.76	(83)
1985	953.01	159.95	793.06	(83)
Annual Rate of Growth	2.70%	2.03%	2.89%	

Sources: Expenditure data for 1902–1970 are from the Bureau of Census, 1975, *Historical Statistics of the United States,* Series Y605, Y682–709; for 1980 from the Bureau of Economic Analysis, 1984, *National Income and Product Accounts,* Tables 3.2 and 3.3; for 1985, Bureau of Economic Analysis, July 1986, *Survey of Current Business,* Tables 3.2 and 3.3. The price deflator is the implicit price deflator for all government; see Table 2.1 for references.

[a]1972 dollars per capita.

this important change is both economic and political. Economic in that fundamental demographic and economic changes have acted to increase the demand for state and local services in this period. Political in that local officials have argued, and Congress has eventually agreed, that it would be politically advantageous to finance this expansion by means of federal grants-in-aid. Growing economic pressure for local services and the political attractiveness of centralized financing are the root causes of our new federalist fiscal order.

2.2   The Evolving Structure of Federal Assistance

Historically, the federal government has always supported state and local governments: federal aid is not a new idea. The early land grants to states for purposes of education, railway expansion, and public infrastructure development were sizeable, often constituting 20 percent or more of the land area of the recipient state.[5] Dollar grants appeared for the first time as a significant transfer to states with the passage of the Federal Aid Road Act of 1916 and the approval of the Smith-Hughes Act of 1917.[6] The 1930s marked the next major expansion of federal assistance for state and local governments. The largest single source of these new monies was a variety of federal public relief programs including the first federal program for unemployment relief.[7] Each of these new relief programs contained (sometimes implicit) matching provisions which rewarded states with more assistance as they spent more on public welfare.

Yet each of these two previous periods of aid expansion pale in comparison to the growth in federal assistance for state and local governments from 1960 to 1980. During this period real federal aid to the states more than doubled in dollar amounts and by 1980 had become almost 27 percent of all state revenues (see table 2.3, columns 3 and 4). Just as importantly, direct federal to local assistance—virtually nonexistent before 1960—became a major source of local government dollars accounting for just under 14 percent of all local revenues by 1980. The 1960–80 aid explosion had an important impact on the federal budget as well. Federal assistance to state and local governments amounted to only 10.5 percent of all federal nondefense spending and 6.96 percent of all federal spending on goods and services in 1950, but by 1980 those percentages had risen to 19.75 percent of all nondefense spending and 31.27 percent of all federal goods and service spending.[8] By 1980 all levels of government in our federalist fiscal system had an important stake in the structure of federal aid for state and local governments.

What has caused this fundamental transformation of our fiscal system? We might well hope that it was done by design and for a compelling

Table 2.3   Financing State and Local Government[a]

	State Governments				Local Governments				
Year	Total Revenue (1)	Own Revenue (2)	Federal Aid (3)	Federal Aid as % of Total Revenue (4)	Total Revenue (5)	Own Revenue (6)	Federal Aid (7)	State Aid (8)	Federal + State Aid as % of Total Revenue (9)
1902	$ 15.00	$ 14.76	$ .24	1.6	$ 106.81	$ 99.81	$ .50	$ 6.50	6.5
1913	21.25	20.91	.34	1.6	146.30	137.63	.54	8.13	5.9
1922	61.90	57.01	4.89	7.9	180.98	166.03	.42	14.53	8.3
1932	77.83	70.67	7.16	9.2	286.75	245.88	.50	40.37	14.3
1940	105.13	89.15	15.98	15.2	305.39	220.35	12.24	72.80	27.8
1950	189.01	150.83	38.18	20.2	300.90	205.82	4.53	90.55	31.6
1960	262.03	201.24	60.79	23.2	384.19	266.63	6.90	110.76	30.6
1970	431.77	324.69	107.08	24.8	471.91	299.72	15.19	157.00	36.5
1980	535.90	392.28	143.62	26.8	560.36	313.45	50.95	195.96	44.1
1985	626.22	472.09	154.13	24.6	607.09	370.41	37.23	199.44	38.9

Sources: All aid and revenue data for the three period 1902–1970 are from Bureau of Census, 1975, *Historical Statistics of the United States*, pp. 1129–1132. Data for the period 1971–1985 are from various issues of Bureau of Census, *Governmental Finances*, published annually. The price deflator is the implicit price deflator for all government; see Table 2.1 for references.

[a]1972 dollars per capita.

public purpose, and, indeed, there are good reasons for federal assistance to the state and local sector. Four separate arguments for intergovernmental grants-in-aid have been offered in the literature, three of which make the case for assistance from the perspective of economic efficiency and one of which argues for governmental aid to insure increased economic equity.

First, to achieve efficiency, grants-in-aid may be necessary to induce state and local governments to provide the appropriate level of a *national public good;* national public infrastructures or a minimum level of public education to insure a literate citizenry are examples. Such goods may be financed and produced by the central government or they may be financed centrally and then (via aid) produced by the state or local government. Second, federal government grants to local governments may be necessary to encourage the efficient level of local public goods when those goods display a *significant level of spillovers*— positive or negative—beyond the boundaries of the local political jurisdiction. Third, grants-in-aid can be used to induce a ruling political coalition (e.g., the median voter or a protected agenda-setter) to expand or contract its preferred level of a locally provided public good to more closely approximate that level required to achieve *within-community allocative efficiency.* Finally, federal aid to state and local units can be used to insure a more equitable distribution of economic resources. While most economists agree that income redistribution across households should be a federal function, redistributive grants can still be used to insure a more *equitable distribution of meritorious,* or ethically "primary," *local public goods.* Education is the leading example of such a commodity, and recent court decisions in California, New Jersey, and New York have embraced this argument and have explicitly required their states to redesign their school aid formulas to encourage a more equitable provision of this public good. Each of these efficiency and equity arguments offers a potentially compelling case for federal to state-local grants.[9] If national needs, spillovers, political inefficiencies, or local service inequities have grown over the past thirty years, then so too should the level of federal to state-local aid.

It is instructive, therefore, to examine the actual distribution of federal grants against the standards implied by these typical public finance arguments for federal assistance. Does the distribution of federal aid conform to the dictates of the normative theory for fiscal assistance?[10] Table 2.4 attempts to answer this question for each of the major categories of federal-to-state and federal-to-local grants-in-aid.

The results in table 2.4 show the correlation of the level of aid in each of five benchmark years to variables which might reasonably approximate an efficiency or equity argument for federal assistance. Each regression includes at least one variable which might plausibly be argued to proxy for each of the three efficiency arguments; the

Table 2.4   Federal Aid to State-Local Governments, 1950–1984[a]

(1) Federal Aid to States: ln(Education)

Year	Mean ($)	Coeff. of Variation	National Purpose % ≥ HS	Spillovers %OutM	Within-Government Allocative Efficiency			Equity		Own Spending	R^2
					%OLD	PuKids	PrKids	CVY	lnY		
1952	3.40	.507	.632	(n.a.)	-2.137	.016*	(n.a.)	.441	.486	—	.612
			(1.217)		(4.893)	(.003)		(.306)	(.478)		
			[−.28*]		[−.55*]	[.76*]		[.22]	[−.45*]		
1962	6.16	.589	3.301	(n.a.)	-3.059	.008*	(n.a.)	-.067	.019	—	.262
			(2.447)		(5.713)	(.004)		(.593)	(.802)		
			[.24]		[.02]	[.29*]		[−.16]	[−.02]		
1972	28.55	.325	-1.712*	.564	-.643	.005	-.005	.181	-.985*	—	.620
			(.912)	(1.027)	(2.787)	(.004)	(.004)	(.213)	(.429)		
			[−.39*]	[.28*]	[−.30*]	[.54*]	[−.56*]	[.18]	[−.62*]		
1977	28.16	.268	-1.293	2.44	-1.770	.004	-.005	.035	-.958*	—	.441
			(.94)	(1.068*)	(2.811)	(.004)	(.004)	(.224)	(.479)		
			[−.33*]	[.19]	[−.22]	[.44*]	[−.48*]	[.13]	[−.54*]		
1984	22.92	.221	-.601	-1.26	-3.350*	.001	.002	.455	-1.082*	—	.426
			(.438)	(1.097)	(1.917)	(.003)	(.004)	(.303)	(.355)		
			[−.27*]	[−.05]	[−.29*]	[.43*]	[−.22]	[−.20]	[−.54*]		

For an explanation of column headings, see key to table 2.4, p. 45. Notes follow table on p. 45.

Table 2.4 (continued)

(2) Federal Aid to States: ln(Highways)

Year	Mean ($)	Coeff. of Variation	National Purpose		Spillovers %Metro	Within-Government Allocative Efficiency %OuM	Equity		Own Spending ln(Hwy)	R²
			MPay	VAMin			CVY	lnY		
1952	6.14	.803	(n.a.)	(n.a.)	-2.867* (.850) [-.33*]	(n.a.)	0.72 (.422) [.03]	1.239* (.675) [.02]	.479* (.185)	.415
1962	26.41	.707	.000 (.001) [.07]	-.000 (.001) [.42*]	-.569* (.202) [-.65*]	(n.a.)	-.799 (.260) [-.20]	.169 (.263) [-.14]	1.023 (.119)	.852
1972	30.44	.652	-.0006* (.0003) [-.41*]	.0002 (.00014) [.52*]	-.185 (.276) [-.54*]	5.667* (1.172) [.67*]	.028 (.304) [.05]	-.492 (.487) [-.35*]	.696* (.120)	.854
1977	24.89	.617	-.0001 (.001) [-.16]	.000 (.000) [.52*]	-.209 (.339) [-.58*]	3.291* (1.467) [.64*]	.077 (.356) [.13]	-.113 (.642) [-.25*]	.634* (.126)	.773
1984	20.86	.491	-.001 (.001) [-.03]	-.000 (.000) [.52*]	-.329 (.363) [-.62*]	2.459 (2.103) [.51*]	-.043 (.650) [.11]	-.218 (.687) [-.34*]	.539* (.179)	.548

Table 2.4 (continued)

(3) Federal Aid to States: ln(Welfare)

Year	Mean ($)	Coeff. of Variation	National Purpose % ≥ HS	Spillovers %Pov	Within-Government Allocative Efficiency %Blk	Equity CVY	Equity lnY	Own Spending ln(Wel)	R²
1952	11.14	.492	−.439	(n.a.)	.268	.097	−.469*	.837*	.893
			(.572)		(.316)	(.152)	(.154)	(.049)	
			[−.21]		[.10]	[−.06]	[−.28*]		
1962	17.24	.498	1.735*	3.051*	−.879*	−.402*	.407	.848*	.937
			(.774)	(.660)	(.287)	(.204)	(.320)	(.045)	
			[−.40*]	[.53*]	[.30*]	[.02]	[−.46*]		
1972	45.05	.373	−1.284	−1.469	.369	.164	−.846*	.729*	.788
			(1.027)	(1.105)	(.640)	(.213)	(.482)	(.064)	
			[−.21]	[.14]	[.20]	[.29*]	[.03]		
1977	45.90	.339	−.689	1.079	−.005	.301	−.907	.490*	.620
			(1.325)	(2.285)	(.696)	(.261)	(.614)	(.063)	
			[−.01]	[.01]	[−.07]	[.21]	[−.05]		
1984	49.70	.362	−2.725*	−1.475	−.193	.935*	−1.138*	.490*	.656
			(.896)	(2.448)	(.582)	(.453)	(.567)	(.061)	
			[−.15]	[−.03]	[.03]	[.17]	[.12]		

Table 2.4 (continued)

(4) Federal Aid to States: ln(Other)

Year	Mean ($)	Coeff. of Variation	National Purpose PDen	Spillovers NHouse	%OutM	Within-Government Allocative Efficiency GDen	YGrow	Equity CVY	lnY	Own Spending	R²
1952	4.51	1.393	-.273 (.587) [-.17]	(n.a.)	(n.a.)	-8.122* (2.397) [-.25*]	-4.386 (3.115) [.10]	-.291 (.429) [-.15]	1.505* (.506) [.15]	—	.303
1962	6.96	1.176	-.014 (.567) [-.18]	(n.a.)	(n.a.)	-5.593* (2.972) [-.27*]	-3.430 (5.889) [-.27*]	-.556 (.642) [-.14]	.294 (.574) [-.08]	—	.162
1972	16.12	.684	-1.213 (.847) [.21]	-.127 (.096) [-.24*]	7.659* (1.482) [.59*]	-2.474 (2.488) [-.27*]	-11.323* (4.729) [.07]	.497 (.438) [.10]	-1.294* (.597) [-.20]	—	.552
1977	29.01	.643	.264 (1.047) [-.18]	.017 (.195) [-.21]	6.779* (1.641) [.59*]	-.573 (2.681) [-.23]	.571 (4.015) [.02]	.535 (.427) [.11]	-1.504* (.691) [-.15]	—	.436
1984	25.06	.957	.261 (.997) [-.11]	-.012 (.136) [-.13]	3.167 (2.341) [.41*]	1.857 (3.194) [-.13]	-9.085 (5.933) [-.44*]	.761 (.787) [.25*]	-1.231 (.844) [-.08]	—	.239

Table 2.4 (continued)

(5) Federal Aid to States: ln(Revenue-Sharing)

Year	Mean ($)	Coeff. of Variation	National Purpose TElas	Spillovers %OutM	Within-Government Allocative Efficiency			Equity		Own Spending	R²
					PDen	VAMin	SLExp	CVY	lnY		
1972	7.19	.220	-.033 (.080) [.16]	-1.485* (.703) [-.02]	.018 (.122) [-.19]	.000 (.000) [.21]	.0011* (.0003) [-.01]	.405* (.153) [.35*]	-1.615* (.301) [-.51*]	—	.552
1977	6.37	.171	-.034 (.054) [.25*]	-2.259* (.487) [-.29*]	.048 (.082) [.05]	.000 (.000) [-.01]	.0010* (.0002) [.17]	.228* (.105) [.36*]	-1.437* (.212) [-.43*]	—	.663
1984	0	0	—	—	—	—	—	—	—	—	—

Table 2.4 (continued)

(6) Federal Aid to Local: ln(All Categorical)

Year	Mean ($)	Coeff. of Variation	National Purpose			Spillovers	Within-Government Allocative Efficiency	Equity		Own Spending	R²
			%Urb	%DetH	Age	GDen	%OutM	CVY	lnY		
1957	2.69	.793	5.370* (1.249) [.08]	3.187* (1.405) [-.12]	-.004 (.003) [-.21]	-13.927* (2.706) [-.43*]	(n.a.)	-.157 (.606) [-.12]	.673 (1.017) [.02]	—	.498
1962	5.22	.517	1.209 (.975) [.15]	-1.309 (2.279) [-.18]	-.001 (.002) [-.27*]	-6.435* (2.712) [-.34*]	(n.a.)	.951 (.781) [-.05]	-.324 (1.203) [.12]	—	.242
1972	16.59	.374	1.921* (.483) [.34*]	2.185 (1.679) [-.11]	-.000 (.000) [-.14]	-2.592 (1.933) [-.16]	.949 (1.719) [.17]	.942* (.390) [.06]	.175 (.827) [.16]	—	.392
1977	28.63	.348	1.654* (.419) [.52*]	-.726 (1.366) [-.31*]	-.001 (.001) [-.16]	-1.285 (1.624) [.21]	-2.312 (1.529) [-.22]	.438 (.334) [-.14]	-.801 (.695) [.29*]	—	.424
1984	24.04	.289	.415 (.383) [.39*]	-3.919 (4.451) [-.32*]	.001 (.001) [.07]	-1.306 (1.322) [-.13]	-1.659 (1.440) [-.08]	.535 (.463) [.26*]	.047 (.561) [.31*]	—	.223

Table 2.4 (continued)

(7) Federal Aid to Local: ln(Revenue-Sharing)

Year	Mean ($)	Coeff. of Variation	National Purpose TElas	Spillovers %OutM	Within-Government Allocative Efficiency			Equity		Own Spending	R²
					PDen	VAMin	SLExp	CVY	lnY		
1974	15.12	.198	−.109	−2.027*	−.064	−.000	.0011*	.257*	−1.426*		.522
			(.072)	(.633)	(.110)	(.000)	(.0002)	(.38)	(.272)	—	
			[.09]	[−.13]	[−.16]	[.12]	[.07]	[.31*]	[−.41*]		
1977	12.24	.152	−.006	−2.179*	−.022	.000	.0008*	.239*	−1.201*		.644
			(.046)	(.415)	(.069)	(.000)	(.0002)	(.089)	(.181)	—	
			[.30*]	[−.32*]	[−.02]	[−.02]	[.17]	[.39*]	[−.43*]		
1984	7.17	.155	.029	−1.553*	.158	.000	.0006*	.354	−1.014*		.537
			(.061)	(.601)	(.097)	(.000)	(.0002)	(.215)	(.198)	—	
			[.19]	[−.08]	[−.05]	[.28*]	[.37*]	[.07]	[−.38*]		

[a]The table reports the mean (in 1972 dollars per capita) and coefficient of variation of federal aid to states and local governments as well as the regression coefficients, standard errors (within parentheses), and zero-order correlation coefficients (within brackets) for the effect of each variable on the corresponding level of aid spending within states for the reported year.

An asterisk (*) indicates statistical significance at the .1 level or higher against the null hypothesis that the regression coefficient or zero-order correlation coefficient is equal to zero.

(n.a.) indicates data were not available to test the hypothesis for this fiscal year.

Key for Table 2.4

National Purpose

%≥HS: Percentage adults over 25 with four or more years of high school in the state.
MPay: Military payroll per capita in the state.
VAMin: Value-added in mining per capita in the state
PDen: Population density, population per square mile in the state.
TElas: Elasticity of state and local taxes with respect to income.
%Urb: Percentage of state population living in urban areas.
%DetH: Percentage of housing deteriorated in the state.
Age: Years since statehood.

Spillovers

%OutM: Percentage of state residents who have left the state within the past year.
%Pov: Percentage of households below poverty level in the state.
NHouse: New housing starts per capita within the state.
GDen: Number of local governments per square mile in the state.

Within-Government Allocative Efficiency

%OLD: Percentage population over 65 in the state.
PuKids: Public school children per capita in the state.
PrKids: Private school children per capita in the state.
%OutM: Percentage of state residents who have left the state within the past year.
%Blk: Percentage of state residents who are black.
GDen: Number of local governments per square mile in the state.
YGrow: Annual rate of growth in state income in previous 4 years.
PDen: Population density, population per capita in the state.
SLExp: State and local expenditures per capita in the state.

Equity

CVY: Coefficient of variation of real state income per family.
ln Y: log of real state income per capita.

Own Spending

ln(Hwy): log of real state own expenditures on highways.
ln(Wel): log of real state own expenditures on welfare.

efficiency variables (denoted by the vector **X**) will differ across aid categories as the efficiency rationale differs. Further, two variables— income per capita in the state (denoted as Y) and the coefficient of variation in family income within the state (denoted by CVY)—are included to test for the presence of an equity rationale for federal aid. Equalizing aid should be negatively related to average state income and positively related to the coefficient of variation of income within the state.[11] Each aid regression is of the general form:

(1) $$AID = \{e^{\beta \mathbf{X}} + {}^{\sigma CVY}\} Y^{\epsilon} e^{u},$$

where β, σ, and ϵ are coefficients to be estimated, and u is a randomly distributed error term.

The resulting regression coefficients will measure the separate influences of the efficiency arguments—via the **X** variables—and the equity rationale—via *CVY* and *Y*—on the distribution of federal aid across states, for each aid category in each sample year. In effect, these estimates of the *AID* equation describe the *de facto* aid formulas which allocate federal aid dollars to state and local governments within each aid category. Each year's sample includes the 48 mainland states. Estimation is by ordinary least squares. To minimize problems of simultaneity, all **X** variables, *CVY*, and *Y* are measured so as to predate the year in which *AID* is given. Table 2.4 also reports the simple correlations of *AID* with each efficiency and equity proxy as well as the means and the coefficients of variation of *AID* itself for each aid category for each of the five sample years.

Two results are immediately apparent from table 2.4. First, the historical growth in total real aid per capita observed in tables 2.1–2.3 is also observed for each of the individual aid categories specified in table 2.4: federal-to-state education aid has grown nearly seven-fold over the last three decades, welfare aid by a factor of five, "other" federal-to-state aid shows a six-time increase, and federal-to-local government categorical aid has increased by almost an order of ten. Only federal-to-state highway aid seems to have moderated its growth path, declining from a peak of $30.44 per capita in 1972 (a five factor increase from its 1952 level of $6.14 per capita) to $20.86 per capita by 1984. But that fall was more than offset by the introduction of federal general revenue sharing. Second, and just as important, such assistance is becoming more equally distributed across the 48 mainland states receiving aid. Table 2.4 reports the coefficient of variation in the distribution of aid across states for each aid category for each of the five sample years, and without exception the coefficient of variation of aid declines through time. At the same time that federal aid is growing, it is also becoming more equally distributed across states.

Is there an *economic* or *public purpose* logic to this growth and distribution of federal grants-in-aid? Table 2.4 reports both the simple, zero-order correlations of the state characteristics with *AID* (within brackets) and the partial regression coefficients of the characteristics and *AID* (with standard errors within parentheses). The resulting regression equations are a summary of the federal government's *de facto* aid formula and a direct test of how well the efificiency and equity arguments do in describing the actual distribution of aid. In the case of federal welfare and highway aid—both open-ended matching grants where the level of *AID* increases with state-local spending—the log of spending on the aided service is also included in the regressions as a characteristic which determines the log of *AID*. Thus, for these aid programs, the state characteristics other than own spending describe the implicit matching rate.[12] A key for the variables in table 2.4 defines the list of explanatory variables used in *AID* equation.

How descriptive of federal aid is the *national purpose* argument? The results are mixed at best. In the case of federal aid for education, the variable thought to measure a possible national purpose for educational aid is the percentage of adults over the age of 25 with four or more years of high school education (%>*HS*). States with a low percentage of educated adults might be allocated more federal education aid to promote the national objective of an educated citizenry. If so, the variable %>*HS* ought to have a significant and negative regression coefficient. The simple correlations are often significantly negative; however, the partial regression correlations are not. Federal education aid seems to find the less educated states on average, but not on the margin.

For highway assistance, the often-stated national purpose is the development of an efficient interstate transportation system for times of national emergencies, e.g., wars. To test this hypothesis the level of military payrolls within the state and the value-added from mining (the need for natural resource deployment) are included to explain highway assistance. A positive relationship is expected, but it is observed for only the simple correlations.

For welfare assistance to states, %>*HS* is again used to proxy for a national purpose, the argument here being that in states with less educated adults, income transfers can substitute for human capital and perhaps minimize the antisocial consequences often associated with abject poverty. The regression coefficients and simple correlations should be negative; they are, but only rarely significantly so.

"Other" federal-to-state assistance is primarily for state infrastructures such as sewers, dams, and hospital beds. To insure that all states have such an infrastructure even when it may not be feasible to provide it competitively, the federal government might offer national assistance. If so, aid ought to go to the more rural states, measured here by the state's population density. A negative relationship is expected, but never observed. Direct federal aid to local governments is also primarily for infrastructures and one might invoke a "save the cities" argument in the spirit of Jane Jacobs (1961) as a possible national purpose rationale for such assistance. Three variables are used to measure the possible importance and status of a state's urban environment: the percentage of the population that lives in urban areas, the percentage of housing that is listed as deteriorated, and the age of the state measured since its date of statehood. There is some evidence that urban states get more federal-to-local government assistance, but it is not the older states and it is not those states with deteriorated housing stocks. Again, the evidence for the economic argument is mixed at best.

Finally, general revenue-sharing aid (*GRS*) was first introduced under the banner of correcting the microeconomic and macroeconomic consequences of stagnant state and local tax bases. If this is the purpose of *GRS*, then aid ought to be allocated to those states with the least income-responsive tax structures, measured here by the elasticity of state and local revenues with respect to state income. The *GRS* regression coefficients and the simple correlations do not show the expected negative relationship between *GRS* and the elasticity of the tax structure. On balance, the national purpose arguments do not support the observed structure of federal assistance.

The *spillover rationale* is no more compelling as a basis for federal aid. As an increasing percentage of a state's population out-migrates (measured by *%OutM* in table 2.4) one can argue that across-state spillovers from education, health care, and state and local services generally may increase. Thus, states may tend to underprovide such services when beneficiaries are planning to leave; grants can correct the resulting inefficiency. We should therefore observe more federal education aid and more general revenue-sharing assistance to states with higher rates of out-migration; we do not.

Within-state spillovers or congestion problems resulting from increased metropolitanization may also be a problem, particularly in transportation. Increased highway aid might correct this problem. But again the observed distribution of aid is in the wrong direction; as the percentage of the state's population living in metropolitan areas increases, federal highway aid per capita in fact declines. To minimize the adverse spillover effects of low-income households relocating to find higher welfare payments, welfare matching aid should be allocated to the states where the poor now reside. The matching rate for welfare aid ought to increase with the percentage of the state's population below poverty; surprisingly perhaps, except for 1962, it does not.

Federal assistance for states in the category "other" is primarily infrastructure aid; such assistance might best be allocated to those high-growth states where environmental spillovers might be most worrisome. The variable *NHouse*—new housing per square mile in the state—shows there is no such relationship. In the same spirit, federal aid to local governments should be allocated to those states with many local governments per square mile (*GDen*) so as to overcome the propensity of a highly decentralized fiscal system to ignore across-community spillovers. In fact, federal categorical assistance to local governments is allocated to states with less decentralized fiscal structures. On balance, the spillover rationale for aid does little to help us understand the actual distribution of federal assistance.

The final efficiency argument for federal aid would use grants-in-aid to correct for a perceived *failure of the local political process* to equate the community's marginal public benefits (i.e., ΣMRS) to the marginal costs of producing the local public good (MC); see, for example, Barlow (1970). Such problems can arise for a variety of reasons. Collective inaction by the larger majority may allow a better organized minority to dictate the local outcomes—for example, a tax-conscious coalition of elderly residents and private school parents might be able to influence local school boards to hold spending below the majority's preferred outcome. Federal education aid might then be given to those states and school districts where these coalitions are most influential and where the perceived need for public education is the strongest. From the results in table 2.4, however, we see federal education aid is not so allocated; states with relatively more elderly ($\%Old$) and more private school enrollments ($PrKids$) get less aid on average and on the margin.

In other political settings, minorities may not be able to organize. Federal aid might then be used to induce the controlling majority to be more responsive to the needs of the weakened minority. For example, previous research on welfare allocations (e.g., Orr 1976) has shown blacks are often discriminated against in the distribution of transfers. Thus, more federal welfare assistance might be allocated to states whose population has a larger percentage of black residents, all else equal. Table 2.4 shows that there is no such pattern.

The mobility of voters often creates special problems for the politically efficient allocation of state and local public goods. Infrastructure allocations—highways, sewers, sanitation facilities, dams—might well be underprovided in those states and localities from which households are most likely to relocate, under the rationale of consume now and let the new residents pay later. Federal aid can be used to offset such a beggar-thy-neighbor strategy, with more aid allocated for infrastructure development in those states with the highest rates of out-migration ($\%OutM$); see, for example, Inman and Albright (1987). Table 2.4 does show such an allocation pattern for highway aid and "other" federal to state aid but not for federal to local categorical aid. Two other variables which measure the need for infrastructures aid—income growth ($YGrow$) and the number of local governments per square mile ($GDen$)—always show an insignificant or an unexpected negative relationship.

Finally, the new theory of efficient interregional grants (see Boadway and Flatters 1982) suggests how aid can be used to correct another problem of resident mobility—the propensity of individuals to respond to the average gains from relocation while ignoring the marginal effects such moves may have on overall regional welfare. The result may be inefficiently congested public goods facilities in some communities and underutilization in others, or overpopulated regional labor markets elsewhere. To correct for these inefficient relocations, aid should be given: (1) to those regions which have lower natural resource rents per capita to help equalize average rents; and then given average rents, (2) to those regions which have fewer people so as to induce labor in-migration from the other regions; and (3) to those regions which provide relatively more of still uncongested public goods.[13] To test this hypothesis, revenue-sharing aid was regressed on value-added in mining in a state (to approximate for natural resource rents), on the state's population density, and on the level of state-local spending. Revenue-sharing aid is positively related to state and local spending as expected but not significantly related to the value-added in mining or to population density. The evidence is weak at best for this efficiency rationale for general revenue sharing.

It seems safe to conclude, therefore, that if one is to find a compelling public purpose logic to the present structure of federal aid to state and local governments it will have to be on the grounds of economic equity not economic efficiency. In fact, table 2.4 does show an equalizing intent to federal assistance, particularly for achieving across-state equity. While aid is occasionally allocated more heavily to states with larger within-state income variations (*CVY*, to achieve within-state service or tax equity), federal aid is almost always inversely related to the level of state income. Education aid, highway aid, and federal "other" aid in the 1950s and 1960s are the only exceptions. By 1972, almost all federal aid is equalizing.

With this observed equity bias to federal aid, we need to ask the next question: How well does such aid do in equalizing across-state/ variations in the distribution of meritorious state-local public goods? Are the aid programs' equalizing intentions realized? Table 2.5 provides evidence on this point. For each aid category, the marginal effect of another dollar of state income on spending is calculated based upon demand studies for state-local public goods (column 1). In all cases, as residents' incomes rise, states and localities spend more on state and local public services. But so too do states and localities which receive more federal aid; see column 2. If the poorer income states receive more federal aid, then perhaps the increase in federal aid more than offsets the propensity of lower-income states to spend less on state and local services.

Column 3 of table 2.5 shows the effects of one dollar of additional income on the receipt of federal aid; a negative coefficient indicates equalizing federal assistance. Column 4 of table 2.5 predicts the effects on spending of this additional amount of federal aid. If this equity-based federal aid does neutralize the expenditure effects of private income, then the total effect of a dollar more of income—equal to the own spending effect (column 1) plus the aid offset effect (column 4)—should be zero; see column 5.[14] If there is more than a full offset to the spending effects of income—Arrow (1971) provides some arguments why this might be desired—then the total effects of income plus

Table 2.5 The Fiscal Equity Performance of Federal Aid, 1952–1984

Federal Aid to	State-Local "Merit" Good	Spending Effects of $1 of Income (1)	Spending Effects of $1 of Aid (2)	Change in Aid with $1 of Income (3)	Spending Effects of Income via Aid (4)	Total Effect of $1 of Income (5)
States						
1) Education						
1952		.023	.865	+.001	+.001	.024
1962	Education	.023	.865	+.000	+.000	.023
1972		.023	.865	−.007	−.006	.017
1984		.023	.865	−.005	−.004	.019
2) Highways						
1952		.019	1.170	+.003	+.004	.023
1962		.019	1.170	+.002	+.002	.021
1972	Infrastructures	.019	1.170	−.004	−.005	.014
1984		.019	1.170	−.001	−.001	.018
3) Welfare						
1952		.008	1.350	−.002	−.003	.005
1962		.008	1.350	+.003	+.004	.012
1972	Welfare	.008	1.350	−.010	−.014	−.006
1984		.008	1.350	−.013	−.017	−.009
4) "Other"						
1952		.019	1.170	+.001	+.001	.020
1962		.019	1.170	+.000	+.000	.019
1972	Infrastructures	.019	1.170	−.006	−.007	.012
1984		.019	1.170	−.007	−.008	.011

		(1)	(2)	(3)	(4)	(5)
5) Revenue-Sharing						
1974	Infrastructures	.023	.865	−.004	−.0034	.020
1984		.023	.865	(n.a.)	(n.a.)	(n.a.)
Locals						
1) Categorical						
1957		.019	1.170	+.001	+.001	.020
1962		.019	1.170	−.001	−.001	.018
1972	Infrastructures	.019	1.170	+.000	+.000	.019
1984		.019	1.170	+.000	+.000	.019
2) Revenue-Sharing						
1974	Infrastructures	.023	.865	−.006	−.005	.018
1984		.023	.865	−.002	−.002	.021

Notes:

Column 1: The spending effects of $1 of additional state income are from estimates contained in Craig-Inman (1982, tables 1 and 2) for education; Craig-Inman (1986, p. 207) for infrastructures; and Craig-Inman (1986, table 7.1) for welfare.

Column 2: The spending effects of $1 of additional federal aid are from estimates contained in Craig-Inman (1982, table 3) for education; Craig-Inman (1986, table 7.2) for infrastructures, and Craig-Inman (1986, table 7.2) for welfare. The fact that the marginal effect of $1 of aid is greater than $1.00 for highway and welfare aid is due to the matching provisions implicit in such assistance.

Column 3: Calculated from the elasticity estimates (ê) in table 2.4, where $dAID/dY = (ê) \cdot (AID/Y)$. Calculations for 1972 use the 1972 estimates of ê and the 1972 (AID/Y) ratio; calculations for 1984 use the 1984 estimates of ê and the 1984 (AID/Y) ratio.

Column 4: Column (2) × Column (3).

Column 5: Column (1) + Column (4).

The notation (n.a.) for state revenue sharing in 1984 reflects the absence of such assistance in that year.

aid should be negative in column 5. In only one case does federal aid fully neutralize the prospending effects of state income; that case is welfare spending since 1972. For the other aid programs and "merit" goods considered here—education and public infrastructures—federal aid is sometimes equalizing but never so equalizing as to neutralize the original effects of income. At best, the current federal aid structure reduces 25 percent of the income generated inequities in state-local spending on education or infrastructures; compare the differences between columns 1 and 5 in table 2.5. While federal aid is a useful step toward state-local fiscal equity, table 2.5 suggests it would be hard to rationalize the present aid system as a grant structure designed solely to promote fairness.

The final impression left by this dissection of contemporary federal grants to state and local governments is that the actual pattern of federal aid does not map closely the usual economic or public purpose arguments advanced for such assistance. Perhaps this conclusion is not surprising.[15] But if it is not good public policy reasoning which describes the recent major increase in federal aid for the state and local sector, what does? Section 2.3 argues that the answer is to be found not in the logic of normative economics but in the workings of behavioral politics.

2.3   The Political Economy of Federal Grants

The pressure to use government to redistribute economic resources is endemic to stable democratic societies. Coalitions inevitably form around institutions with the power to tax and transfer incomes, and in stable democracies that institution is government.[16] Federal grants-in-aid are a prime vehicle for such redistributions. It is my hypothesis, to be tested here, that the most recent growth of federal assistance to state and local governments can be best explained as an exercise in redistributive politics.

The argument proceeds in two steps. First, with the growth of the urban public economy following World War II there emerged a new and substantial demand for state and local public services. The process of suburbanization and the baby boom of the 1950s and early 1960s created the need for more schooling and more public infrastructures, historically the concerns of the state and local sectors. Further, suburbanization created unique fiscal difficulties for our older central cities placing additional pressure on the state and local fisc. The net result was a growing demand for public services from the state and the local sector. Second, as demand increased it was natural to look for new sources of income. The state and local sector was no different, and the representatives of that sector—the mayors, the governors, and other locally elected officials—turned to the only source they could: Washington. Washington responded, but not immediately. It took an important shift in institutional structure before additional aid started flowing to the state and local sector. That institutional shift was the decentralization of congressional decision making over the period 1969–72. By 1975, our new federalist fiscal structure was firmly in place. It was built by a growing demand for local services and by a decentralized congressional fiscal process that had discovered the political advantages of redistributive, centralized financing.

2.3.1   The Growing Demand for State and Local Services

Tables 2.2 and 2.3 reveal the growth in resources allocated by the state and local public sector over this century. The trend has been steadily upward. From 1902 to 1950 the real (1972 dollars) level of state and local government own revenues grew at an annual rate of 2.23 percent, from \$115 per capita in 1902 (= \$14.76 + \$99.81) to \$357 per capita (\$150.83 + \$205.82) by 1950; see Table 2.3. Since 1950, growth has continued at an even faster rate; own real revenues of the state and local sector have increased at an annual rate of 2.50 percent, rising from \$357 to \$842 dollars per capita (= \$472.09 + \$370.41) by 1985. Federal aid has also grown dramatically over this period, from \$43 per capita (= \$38.18 + \$4.53) in 1950 to \$191 per capita (= \$154.13 + \$37.23) by 1985 for an annual rate of growth of 4.26 percent. The joint effect has been to increase total revenues to the state-local sector by 2.70 percent per year since 1950, from \$400 per capita (= \$357 + \$43) to \$1033 per capita (= \$842 + \$191).

The driving force behind this growth in revenues has been the increasing demand by residents for services from the state and local sector. Equation (2) describes this growth in demand for state and local activities for the period 1948–85. Specified as a demand relationship, total state-local government spending per capita (= state-local government expenditures on goods and transfers plus the annual fiscal surplus, $E + S$, measured in 1972 dollars) is seen to depend positively on last year's real income (Y_{-1}), the previous year's exogenous (nonmatching) real federal aid per capita (Z_{-1} = total federal aid minus welfare and highways aid), the level of new housing starts per capita ($NHouse_{-1}$), the number of school-age children per capita ($Kids_{-1}$), and the crime rate ($Crime_{-1}$) in the previous year. Expenditures are also inversely related to the net price of state-local spending, defined here as 1 minus the average federal matching rate for the previous year [(= $\bar{m}$ = (welfare aid + highway aid)/$E)_{-1})$] multiplied by 1 minus the average effective federal tax rate of the median income taxpayer, $(1 - \tau)$, to allow for the federal deductibility of state and local taxes.[17]

(2) $\ln(E + S) = 1.619 + .243 \ln(Y)_{-1} + .039 \ln(Z)_{-1}$

   (.395)* (.067)*   (.017)*

   $- .421 \; \ln\{(1 - \bar{m})(1 - \tau) + .042 \ln(NHouse)_{-1}$

   (.176)*   (.017)*

   $+ .145 \ln(Kids)_{-1} + .186 \ln(Crime)_{-1}$

   (.049)*   (.022)*

$\bar{R}^2 = .996$ D.W. $= 1.98$

(Standard errors of coefficient estimates are within parentheses; an * indicates the coefficient is statistically different from 0 at least at the .1 level of significance.)

While the growth in real income has been an important determinant of the growth in state and local spending since 1948, the central causes behind the increase are to be found in the demographic and structural changes that reshaped the local public economy. Estimates of the relative contribution of each demand variable to the growth in state-local spending reveal that the baby boom (measured by the increase in school-aged children per capita), the added difficulties of urban living (measured by the growth in the crime rate), and the growth in personal income were the prime forces behind the growth in state-local spending during the period 1948–70. Since 1970 income and urban needs have remained important determinants of spending growth, but the baby-boom has disappeared as a driving force and has been replaced in relative importance by the increase in federal grants-in-aid.[18] The end result of these local fiscal dynamics has been a rising state-local tax rate (= own state-local revenues/income) and a growing number of state and local public employees per capita.[19] The demand for state and local services has been rising but at a rate faster than a simple—and politically, accommodating—income effect might justify. Further, those with the most direct vested interest in satisfying these rising demands—state and local public employees—have been growing too. In such instances, it is always easiest for political leaders to look elsewhere for financial support to ease the growing fiscal pressure. Elected officials from the state and local sector have proved themselves to be no different. Washington was the obvious place to turn.

2.3.2 Congressional Decentralization and the Growth of Federal Grants

Congress as an institution for fiscal policy underwent a major transformation in structure from 1969 to 1972, evolving from a legislative body dominated by a few major decision-makers with firm control over fiscal affairs to a largely decentralized forum of individual deal-makers each required to maximize his or her own net gain from legislative decisions. A variety of factors contributed to this transition: the declining influence of political parties, the increasing sophistication of voters and their willingness to vote off the party line to favor their own interests, and congressional redistricting favoring suburban and urban interests to balance the previous rural influence in Congress.[20] For each of these reasons, the congressional leadership found itself less and less able to dictate fiscal allocations, and more and more pressured to be responsive to the demands of all the members.[21] These demands were often couched in very simple terms: bring home "the bacon." In this new political environment, to get anything approved often meant approval for everything.

The consequences of this changing congressional structure for fiscal policy—and more specifically for federal grants funding—can be specified more formally in a model of representative decision-making within alternative legislative structures. An elected representative to Congress is assumed to derive political benefits from the provision of federal government project dollars to his or her constituents (denoted by x, paid for example by federal aid), where the level of benefits enjoyed will depend on a set of exogenous characteristics of the constituents (denoted by the vector $\mathbf{P}$): $B = B(x; \mathbf{P})$. The representative bears a political cost, however, whenever dollars flow from the district to support federal expenditures elsewhere. Those dollars will typically be paid as federal taxes (T) and are assumed to equal the representative's district's (s's) share (denoted as ϕ_s) of all taxes needed to support all project dollars allocated to all of N districts:

$$T_s = \phi_s \sum_{i \neq s}^{N} x_i = T(x_s; \phi_s, \sum_{i \neq s}^{N} x_i).$$

The representative's net political benefits (NPB) from the allocation of federal dollars financed by taxes is therefore:

$$(3) \qquad NPB = B(x_s; \mathbf{P}) - T(x_s; \phi_s, \sum_{i \neq s}^{N} x_i).$$

The representative is assumed to lobby for a preferred level of x_s for the district and to support any legislative coalition which can deliver on that preferred allocation.

Exactly what that preferred allocation will be, however, depends fundamentally on how Congress conducts its budgetary business. Three alternative legislative regimes—and the effects of each on a representative's preferred budget—can be specified. The first, called the fully decentralized regime, assumes that each legislator selects the district's preferred project size x_s under the assumption that marginal changes in x_s will have no implications for the level of spending preferred by other legislators. Each legislator then submits his preferred budget—denoted $x^*_s(D)$ for the decentralized regime—and all representatives vote to simply approve each other's preferred $x^*_s(D)$'s, where each individual $x^*_s(D)$ is specified from equation (3) by

$$\partial NPB/\partial x_s = 0 ,$$

or alternatively as

$$\partial B/\partial x_s = b(x_s, P) = \phi_s = \partial T/\partial x_s ,$$

where ϕ_s is the district's share of the national taxes in the decentralized legislative regime. Figure 2.1 illustrates the preferred district project size under the decentralized legislative regime in the very simple case where ϕ_s equals $1/N$—that is, when each of the N legislative districts contributes an average amount to national taxes.[22] Since each district pays only a small fraction ($\simeq 1/N$) of its own project's costs, the incentive is to prefer a much larger project than if the district were responsible for the full marginal costs of the added project spending ($= \$1$): $x^*_s(D) > x^*_s(C)$ in figure 2.1. The fiscal behavior of such decentralized legislatures is typically called "pork barrel" budgeting.

The second legislative regime, called a majority-controlled legislature, limits pork barrel spending to some extent. Here a single political party or majority coalition has sufficient control to insure passage of

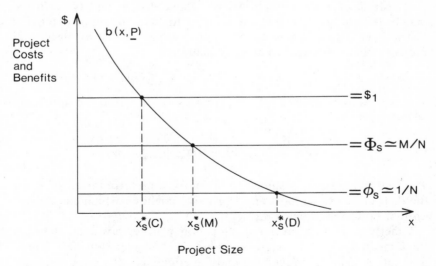

C = Cooperative Legislative Regime
M = Majority-Rule Legislative Regime
D = Decentralized Legislative Regime

Fig. 2.1   Project allocations under alternative legislative regimes.

a budget without granting the excluded minority any unwanted favors. Only those legislators in good standing within the majority are certain to have their districts' preferred projects included within the budget. In addition, the dominant majority is run by a strong leadership capable of setting majority policy and enforcing that policy on coalition members; in effect, the leadership selects each district's preferred project size based upon the district's revealed NPB schedule. The district's allocation is again set so as to maximize NPB, but now subject to the leadership's realization that each district's project's costs will spill over onto taxpayers from other districts within the majority coalition. (Project costs which fall on taxpayers represented by the minorities are ignored by the majority leadership.)

The preferred district project is again defined by maximizing equation (3):

$$\partial NPB/\partial x_s = 0$$

but now

$$\partial B/\partial x_s = b(x_s, P) = \Phi_s = dT/dx_s$$

defines the optimal project size, where Φ_s ($= dT/dx_s$) is the relevant marginal tax cost of a new project dollar and allows for the spillover effects of spending across districts within the majority coalition. In the simple case in which all districts pay equal taxes, Φ_s will equal M/N or the percentage of majority member districts (of size M) in the full legislature (of size N).[23] The size of each project in a majority member district declines from what it might have been in a fully decentralized legislature because of the partial internalization of project costs achieved by strong majority coalition leadership; see Figure 2.1 where $x_s^*(M) < x_s^*(D)$ because $\Phi_s > \phi_s$.[24]

The final legislative regime, called a cooperative legislature, employs a single political leader, representing a coalition of the whole, to set each district's allocation for x_s. The cooperative regime fully internalizes all fiscal spillovers that result from centralized financing. In this regime, each district receives that project size which equates the marginal political benefits of x_s to the full marginal costs of x_s: $b(x, P) = 1$. The resulting project size in each district is $x_s^*(C)$ in Figure 2.1; $x_s^*(C)$ is each legislator's preferred budget if he or she can be certain that all other legislators will cooperate. To achieve the fully cooperative budget, the political leader of the coalition of the whole must be capable of punishing those individual legislators who seek to deviate from this allocation by free riding on the system of centralized financing and setting their own $x_s > x_s^*(C)$. Such punishment might entail branding the renegade a "budget-buster" and then working for his defeat in the next legislative election. Only when the leader has sufficient resources—financial or otherwise—to make this punishment credible can the fully cooperative allocation be sustained.

The size of the total project budget (denoted G) will be equal to the sum of all district allocations and can be specified for each of these three legislative regimes. In the case of the fully decentralized legislature, each district receives its preferred project of size $x_s^*(D)$; the total budget will therefore equal $G(D) = \sum_{s=1}^{N} x_s^*(D)$. In the case of the fully cooperative regime each district receives its cooperative allocation $x_s^*(C)$; the final budget is therefore $G(C) = \sum_{s=1}^{N} x_s^*(C)$. For the majority rule regime the overall project budget will equal the sum of all majority members' projects—$\sum_{s \in M} x_s^*(M)$, where M is the size of the majority—plus any project spending allocated by the majority to minority districts. Allocations to the minority for projects of type x need not be zero. But any minority spending which does occur will only occur if it improves the welfare of the majority. This may well be the case if there are policies of interest to the fiscal majority which demand the cooperation of a minority for approval—e.g., filibuster overrides or treaty approvals that require a super-majority. Cooperation can be purchased by granting the minority a level of spending on projects of type x. The most cost-effective bribe is that which maximizes the political surplus to a minority member *without imposing political costs on the majority*. This will be a project of size $x^*(C)$, the allocation of which maximizes the political surplus available in trade to the majority coalition. If we assume such trades do in fact occur, then the budget for expenditure on projects of type x will be the sum of all projects given to majority members plus the sum of all projects supplied to minority members or $G(M) = \sum_{s \in M} x_s^*(M) + \sum_{s \in (N-M)} x_s^*(C)$. Together the three legislative regimes define three alternative budgets for project spending. Specified in increasing order of total outlays they are

(4) $$G(C) = \sum_{s=1}^{N} x_s^*(C),$$

$$G(M) = \sum_{s=1}^{N} x_s^*(C) + \sum_{s \in M} [x_s^*(M) - x_s^*(C)],$$

and

$$G(D) = \sum_{s=1}^{N} x_s^*(C) + \sum_{s \in M} [x_s^*(M) - x_s^*(C)]$$
$$+ \sum_{s \in M} [x_s^*(D) - x_s^*(M)] + \sum_{s \in (N-M)} [x_s^*(D) - x_s^*(C)].$$

As characterized above, the recent transformation of congressional decision-making in the early 1970s marks a shift from majority-controlled fiscal politics to fiscal allocations based upon fully decentralized budgeting. No longer are budgets packaged in a dictatorial fashion by the majority's chosen chairmen of the Ways and Means, Finance, and Appropriations Committees. In the new Congress, it has been argued, budgets emerge from the process of give and take in the numerous subcommittees and caucuses of the House and Senate. The behavioral implications of such a change are threefold: (1) the aggregate level of project spending should expand from $G(M)$ to $G(D)$; (2) spending across congressional districts and the states should become more equalized as previous minority districts receive more project support; and (3) the absolute number of legislated projects and programs should expand to accommodate the specific needs of each legislative district.

Federal grants to state and local governments provides one case study in which to look for these consequences of the congressional transformation. At least on the surface the evidence is supportive. First, the aggregate level of federal grants to state and local governments showed a noticeable upturn around 1970, particularly in federal aid paid directly to local governments; see table 2.3. Second, the overall distribution of aid has become more equal across states as measured by the decline in the coefficient of variation in the distribution of aid; see table 2.4. Further, 1972 seems to stand as a key turning point in this downward trend.[25] Finally, the simple number of aid programs passed by Congress increased dramatically in the late 1960s and the early 1970s, rising from 160 programs in 1962 to 412 by 1976.[26] It seems clear that the structure of congressional decision making has had an important influence on the level and structure of our grants system.

We can make these observations more precise and estimate quantitatively the influence of congressional structure on the level of federal support for the state-local sector. The three-regime legislative model specified in equation (4) can also be written in "nested" form as

$$(5) \qquad G = \sum_{s=1}^{N} x_s^*(C) + \mu \sum_{s \in M} [x_s^*(M) - x_s^*(C)]$$

$$+ \delta \sum_{s=1}^{N} + \delta \sum_{s=1}^{N} [x_s^*(D - x_s^*(C)] \, ,$$

where the dummy variable $\mu = 1$ if the legislature is majority-rule and 0 otherwise and the dummy variable $\delta = 1$ if the legislature is decentralized and 0 otherwise. The default regime ($\mu = \delta = 0$) is the fully cooperative model of budgeting. Estimation of equation (5) requires a specification of $x_s^*(C)$ and the increments $[x_s^*(M) - x_s^*(C)]$ and $[x_s^*(D) - x_s^*(C)]$. Each can be defined from knowledge of the marginal political benefit schedule and from district tax shares under the fully cooperative

($= 1$), the majority rule ($= \Phi_s$), and the decentralized ($= \phi_s$) legislative regimes; see Figure 2.1.

The marginal political benefit schedule for grants in aid, $b(x, \mathbf{P})$, is assumed to depend upon the demand for state-local public goods within the district. The political benefits from grants is expected to increase with the effective burden of state and local own revenues on income (R/Y), new housing starts in the district (*NHouse*), the number of school-age children (*Kids*), the crime rate in the district (*Crime*), and the number of state-local employees per capita. The burden represents fiscal pressure on the state-local sector while housing starts, school-age children, and the crime rate each indicate a special need which might engender added assistance. State-local employees per capita (*SLEmp*) measure the size of the most likely organized lobby which can express these needs in Washington.[27] Together the variables (R/Y, *NHouse, Kids, Crime,* and *SLEmp* define the vector $\mathbf{P}$ of $b(x,\mathbf{P})$. The marginal benefits of grants are assumed to increase with each variable.

District tax shares under the majority rule and the decentralized legislative regimes are assumed to equal M/N ($= \phi_s$) and $1/N$ ($= \phi_s$) respectively, where M/N is the percent of the legislature in the majority coalition and N is the total size of the legislature. For this analysis, the majority coalition's share is taken to be the percentage of the House of Representatives controlled by the dominant party, whether Republican or Democrat. While these measures of tax shares are not precisely correct for each district,[28] the degree of error in this approximation is likely to be small, and certainly of second order importance when defining the relevant increments, $[x_s^*(M) - x_s^*(C)]$ and $[x_s^*(D) - x_s^*(C)]$.

Assuming that the marginal benefit schedule is a linear function of the vector $\mathbf{P}$ ($= R/Y$, *NHouse, Kids, Crime, SLEmp*), then $x_s^*(C), x_s^*(M)$, and $x_s^*(D)$ will also be linear functions of $\mathbf{P}$ and their corresponding tax shares—1, M/N, and $1/N$ respectively.[29] Assuming further that the political benefit schedules are structurally identical across districts except for variations in $\mathbf{P}$ and that elected representatives define all benefits and costs in per capita ($\simeq$ per vote) units, then the aggregate spending equation in (5) can be respecified in per capita units as

$$(6) \qquad g = x^*(1, \overline{\mathbf{P}}) + \overline{\Delta x}(M)[\mu \cdot (M/N)] + \overline{\Delta x}(D) [\delta] + v \ ,$$

where g is federal aid per capita, $x^*(1,\overline{\mathbf{P}})$ is the per capita demand for aid when the district tax share is 1 and when the elements of $\mathbf{P}$ assume their national average values [$= x^*(1, \overline{\mathbf{P}}) = x_s^*(C; \overline{\mathbf{P}})$], $\overline{\Delta x}(M)$ is the average increase in per capita grants spending in districts within the majority coalition as the legislative regime shifts from cooperative to majority-rule, and $\overline{\Delta x}(D)$ is the average increase in per capita grants spending in all districts as the legislative regime shifts from a cooperative to a decentralized structure.[30] With the addition of an assumed additive error term [denoted as v in (6)], equation (6) becomes the basis for an econometric analysis of recent federal grants spending.

Parameter estimates from equation (6) will define the coefficients of the linear political benefit schedule as well as the marginal effects of any congressional regime shifts, from cooperative to majority rule $[\overline{\Delta x}(M)]$ or from cooperative to fully decentralized $[\overline{\Delta x}(D)]$. From the coefficient estimates of $\overline{\Delta x}(M)$ and $\overline{\Delta x}(D)$ we can also estimate the effects on grants spending of the shift from a majority rule to a decentralized Congress. It is necessary, however, to specify a priori the periods which define the alternative legislative regimes (i.e., μ and δ). Congressional scholars generally describe the period from 1948 to 1968 as an example of strong party leadership in fiscal affairs; see Fenno (1966) and Manley (1970). The period from 1972 to today is generally characterized by decentralized legislative decision-making; see Shepsle and Weingast (1984). The years 1969–72 marked the period of transition; see Ornstein (1975). For this analysis, the majority rule dummy variable μ is assigned a value of 1 for the years 1948–71, and a value of 0 otherwise. The decentralized legislative regime is represented by a value of δ equal to 1 for the years 1972 onward; for all previous years $\delta = 0$. To minimize problems of simultaneity all elements of the vector $\mathbf{P}$ are lagged one year. Estimation of equation (6) also allows for the possibility of first-order serial correlation in the additive error terms (represented by ρ, the correlation coefficient between v_t and v_{t-1}). Estimation is based upon data for the period 1948–85. Results are reported in table 2.6.

The initial specification in equation (a) of table 2.6 assumes that Congress has been uniformly responsive to constituent demands over the period 1948–85; the specification in equation (b) tests for the additional effects of congressional structure on aid spending. In both specifications the individual coefficients measuring the political benefits of aid—vector $\mathbf{P}$—show that federal aid increases as the fiscal burden of state-local finance increases, as the number of school-aged children increases, and as state-local employees per capita rise. The crime rate and new housing starts are never significant, at least beyond their influence on fiscal pressure, $(R/Y)_{-1}$; see equation (2) above. What is particularly impressive is the statistically significant and quantitatively important role that state-local public employees play in the determination of federal aid; congressional spending is quite responsive to the growing size of this interest group. The elasticity of aid with respect to $(SLEmp)_{-1}$ is 2.16, more than twice the elasticities of aid with respect to $(R/Y_{-1} (= .51)$, $NHouse_{-1} (= .07)$, or $Kids_{-1} (= .86)$.

As important as constituent demand and interest group representation has been to the recent growth in federal aid, so too has been the

Table 2.6   The Political Economy of Federal Aid

Model	Intercept	(R/Y)₋₁	NHouse₋₁	Kids₋₁	Crime₋₁	SLEmp₋₁	μ(M/N)	δ	Year	ρ	Root MSE	R̄²
				Constituent Demand				Congress	Reagan			

Constituent Demand columns: Intercept, $(R/Y)_{-1}$, $NHouse_{-1}$, $Kids_{-1}$, $Crime_{-1}$, $SLEmp_{-1}$
Congress columns: $\mu(M/N)$, δ
Reagan columns: Year, ρ

Model	Intercept	$(R/Y)_{-1}$	$NHouse_{-1}$	$Kids_{-1}$	$Crime_{-1}$	$SLEmp_{-1}$	$\mu(M/N)$	δ	Year	ρ	Root MSE	$\bar{R}^2$
Total Aid												
a.	−313.33	286.07	.003	.608	.052	4.826				.43	8.27	.932
	(81.27)*	(133.12)*	(.001)*	(.196)*	(.002)	(1.217)*				(.12)*		
b.	−332.73	304.50	.001	.464	−.005	6.158	51.56	61.42		.43	7.88	.938
	(85.04)*	(128.53)*	(.001)	(.203)*	(.004)	(1.354)*	(44.44)	(31.13)*		(.12)*		
c.	−213.59	185.28	.000	.063	−.004	6.346	45.41	59.01		.21	6.38	.988
	(65.96)*	(99.43)*	(.001)	(.198)	(.004)	(1.184)*	(33.31)	(23.18)*		(.19)		
1982									−28.69			
									(7.87)*			
1983									−32.40			
									(8.56)*			
1984									−34.48			
									(8.24)*			
1985									−43.03			
									(8.97)*			
Total Aid Less GRS and Welfare												
d.	−130.86	54.63	−.001	.074	−.001	3.579	40.57	69.53		.02	8.73	.965
	(81.58)	(125.09)	(.001)	(.265)	(.005)	(1.573)*	(28.97)	(41.76)*		(.20)		
1982									−33.74			
									(11.15)*			
1983									−35.34			
									(11.25)*			
1984									−38.31			
									(10.71)*			
1985									−43.48			
									(11.70)*			

Note: An (*) indicates the coefficient is significantly different from 0 at the .1 level or better.

structural shifts in congressional fiscal politics; see equations (b) and (c) in table 2.6. Equation (b) is the basic specification of the budget model; equation (c) extends that specification to test for a "Reagan-Stockman" effect on aid spending. An F - test for the joint significance of the two congressional variables—$\mu(M/N)$ and δ—rejects the null hypothesis of no effect at the 10 percent level of significance in both equations. Further, the congressional structure variables influence federal aid as predicted. The coefficients on $\mu(M/N)$—$\overline{\Delta x}(M) = \$51.46$ in equation (b) and \$45.41 in equation (c)—measure the average increase in per capita aid in a *majority rule* district as Congress moves from a fully cooperative to a majority rule regime. The coefficients on δ—$\overline{\Delta x}(D) = \$61.42$ in equation (b) and \$59.01 in equation (c)—measure the average increase in the preferred level of aid spending in *every district* as Congress shifts from the cooperative to the decentralized regime.

Figure 2.2 illustrates the effects of these congressional structures on federal grants spending, based upon the econometric estimates of $\overline{\Delta x}(M)$ and $\overline{\Delta x}(D)$ from equation (c) and actual federal aid expenditures for calendar 1974, one of the first aid budgets to be decided by the newly decentralized Congress. Total grants spending in 1974 in an average congressional district equalled \$179 per capita, an estimate of $x^*(D)$ for that year. The estimate of $\overline{\Delta x}(D) \simeq \$59/capita$ from equation

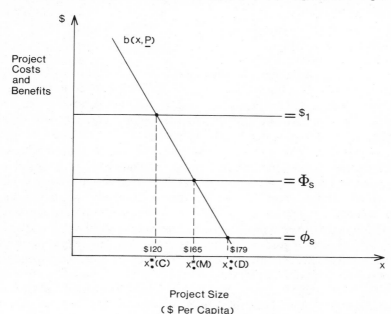

Project Size
($ Per Capita)

Fig. 2.2   1974 aid allocations under alternative congressional regimes.

(c) implies the level of the cooperative budget in the average district would have been $120 per capita ($=x^*(C) = x^*(D) - \overline{\Delta x}(D)$). The estimate of $\overline{\Delta x}(M)$ from equation (c) implies that the average district's majority-rule budget—if a member of the majority—would have exceeded its cooperative budget by $\simeq$ $45 per capita; therefore the majority-rule budget for a majority coalition district would have been $165 per capita ($=x^*(M) = x^*(C) + \overline{\Delta x}(M)$). Together these estimates imply that the shift from majority-rule to decentralized fiscal politics increased the size of the federal grants budget in an average majority coalition district by $14 per capita.

The real dollar gains from decentralization accrue to those districts previously excluded from the majority coalition. In 1974 the Democrats controlled 55 percent of the House seats and, for this analysis, are assumed to constitute the majority coalition. Under decentralized budgeting, the remaining 45 percent of congressional districts now move alongside the original majority to capture $x^*(D)$ as well. As assumed under the model's original specification, these minority districts would have received initially only $x^*(C)$ from the majority. The effect of the decentralization of budgetary politics is to therefore allocate an additional $59 per capita in federal aid ($= \overline{\Delta x}(D) = x^*(D) - x^*(C)$) to the average minority district. Overall, the econometric model predicts that under decentralized budgeting grants-in-aid spending rose by an average of $34 per capita ($= .55 \times $14 + .45 \times 59), or by 24 percent, over what it might have been had Congress remained a strong majority-rule fiscal institution ($= $145 = .55 \times x^*(M) + .45 \times x^*(C) = .55 \times $165 + .45 \times 120).

This trend towards increased aid spending continued throughout the 1970s and into 1981, but the period 1982 to 1985 showed another significant break in the pattern. Now the trend turned downward; see equation (c). The explanation lies in the Reagan-Stockman budgets of those years.[31] As fashioned by David Stockman, the 1982–85 Reagan budgets were an effort to internalize the fiscal externalities created under decentralized congressional budgeting and to move, if possible, towards the cooperative allocation, $x_s^*(C)$, based upon a coalition of the whole. The strategy was to join across-the-board spending cuts with a general reduction in taxes—just what the cooperative budget would require.[32] Reagan provided the leadership—and the political arm-twisting—needed to guide such budgets through a Congress committed to decentralized fiscal politics.[33] For each of the first four Reagan budget years—represented by a year dummy variable in equation (c)—real aid spending was reduced from what it might have been had full decentralized congressional budgeting prevailed. Aggregate aid spending was reduced initially by $28 per capita in 1982 and finally by $43 per capita in 1985, a 15 percent to 22 percent reduction when compared to the

1981 aid expenditures of $194 per capita, the last pre-Reagan budget. The Reagan budgets appear to have returned us to just about where we would have been in total aid financing had Congress remained under firm majority-rule leadership.

This analysis of the budgetary effects of congressional reform is complicated however by one important fact. While 1972 was the operative date of transition to decentralized fiscal politics within Congress, it also marks the date of passage of a major new aid program, the State and Local Fiscal Assistance Act of 1972. Also known as General Revenue Sharing (GRS), this program infused into the state and local public sector an average of $22 per capita in new grants; see table 2.4. Given the coincidence of GRS funding and the emergence of decentralized budgeting, it could well be that the results in equations (b) and (c)—which have been attributed to the new structure of fiscal politics—are in fact due to the passage of GRS. A "clean" test of the structural reform hypothesis would reestimate equations (b) and (c) using all aid other than GRS assistance as the dependent variable.

A further refinement of the analysis should also be considered. As large formula grants tied to state and local spending, federal welfare aid via AFDC and Medicaid grants may also obscure the true effects of reforms in congressional structures. A preferred test for the effects of reform might omit these grants from the dependent variable as well. What will remain are all the many small grant programs which provide assistance to the state-local sector for education, health care, and public infrastructures—programs which together still totalled $125 per capita or more in grants in the 1970s. Equation (d) provides this refined test and reestimates the structural aid model using as the dependent variable total aid less GRS and welfare grants. The results are nearly identical to those achieved earlier, and, if anything, are slightly stronger.[34] The basic conclusion remains in force: the new, decentralized structure of congressional fiscal politics has been an important stimulus to the level of federal grants spending.

2.4   Conclusion

From its inception, the U.S. public economy has been committed to the principle of fiscal decentralization. Appropriately designed, such a system can make a significant contribution to the twin goals of economic efficiency and economic equity. A potentially important part of that structure are intergovernmental grants-in-aid. This paper has examined the recent evolution of our federal grants system from two perspectives. First, can the present system of federal assistance to state and local governments be rationalized by the usual normative economic arguments for efficency and equity in the provision of local public services: Does such aid provide national public goods, or internalize externalities across jurisdictions, or overcome internal failings of local fiscal choice, or insure a more equitable provision of meritorious public goods? Second, if not, then what does explain the structure of our federal aid system?

Against the usual efficiency arguments for aid, there is little evidence in the present structure of federal assistance that current aid is motivated from that perspective. There is more evidence to support an equity foundation for federal grants, at least to equalize the across-state distribution of meritorious public services. Yet with the possible exception of welfare aid, such assistance has had only a marginal effect on the final distribution of state-local public goods. If we are to rationalize the present structure of federal grants, therefore, it would appear that we should look to arguments other than those based on achieving economic efficiency or equity.

An alternative rationale, based upon a model of redistributive politics, was advanced and tested for the period 1948–85. The observed growth in federal grants-in-aid over this period proved consistent with the underlying structure of this model. Aid has grown with increasing fiscal pressure on the state and local sector. The baby boom, the process of suburbanization, and the emergence of the fiscally troubled central city have all contributed to the demand for federal assistance. Congress has been responsive to these demands; particularly so, following the institutional reforms of 1969–72. Those reforms have opened the process of congressional budgeting to decentralized negotiations and deal-making. When coupled with a national tax system which shares the costs of local expenditures across all legislative districts, the result is a budgeting process for federal grants which is potentially biased towards over-spending. The empirical results presented here (see figure 2.2) suggest that the present congressionally determined aid budgets may be inflated by as much as $34 per person, or 24 percent, over what they might have been had strong majority-rule leadership remained in force, and they may be as much as $59 per capita, or 50 percent, larger than what all legislators might prefer were they capable of achieving a fully cooperative fiscal allocation.

What can be done to control this apparently excessive aid spending? Short of a constitutional amendment to limit grants spending, there is really only one solution: stronger and more effective fiscal leadership in Congress. The Reagan-Stockman budgets of 1982–85 revealed the potential influence such leadership could have on spending, but the resulting cuts seem to have been a unique, and perhaps short-lived event. Attempts to institutionalize such reductions by means of Reagan's New Federalism reforms never received serious consideration by Congress; the passage in the winter of 1987, over Reagan's veto, of new highway and clean water grants only underscores the point.[35] The basic message of this analysis is clear: as long as congressional budgeting remains a decentralized fiscal process, the incentives to finance centrally, and to spend locally, will remain as well. Our current system of federal grants to state and local governments is just one logical outcome of this process.

Notes

1. While the Tenth Amendment is clear on the point that the states are to retain some policy role within our fiscal system, exactly what that role is to be is not exactly specified by the Constitution. The Supreme Court has found it difficult to draw the lines of responsibility without this guidance; see *National League of Cities v. Usery* (426 U.S. 833 [1976]) and then the recent Supreme Court opinion in *Garcia v. San Antonio Metropolitan Transit Authority* (105 S. Ct. 1005 [1985]).

2. See, for example, Michelman and Sandalow (1970, chapter 2).

3. The early phases of the evolution of federal relations with the state and local sector are described in Scheiber (1966) and in Beer (1973).

4. For the history of federal support for state and local governments, see Gates (1968), Bitterman (1938), and more recently Wallis (1984) and Wright (1974). For analysis of state aid for local services, see Craig and Inman (1986).

5. See Gates (1968, appendix C, p. 804).

6. See Bitterman (1938) for the history of these early aid programs.

7. See Wallis (1984).

8. In 1950 the federal government spent $403.89 per capita (1972 dollars) on nondefense goods and services and on transfers to households and governments. Federal aid to state-local governments in 1950 was $42.72 per capita (see table 2.3) or 10.5 percent of this total. Nondefense spending on just goods and services totaled $265 per capita in 1950; federal aid other than welfare aid totaled $18.43 per capita (tables 2.3 and 2.5) or 6.96 percent (= $18.43/$265) of all federal spending on nondefense goods and services. By 1980, total federal aid had become $194.57 per capita or 19.75 percent of the $985 per capita of all federal nondefense spending in that year. Federal aid other than welfare aid was $126 per capita in 1980 which was 31.72 percent of all federal nondefense, nontransfer expenditures in 1980 (= $126/$397).

9. For good introductions to the efficiency theory of grants-in-aid, see Oates (1972) and Boadway and Flatters (1982). For a discussion of grants-in-aid to achieve public service equity, see Feldstein (1975), Inman (1978), and Inman and Rubinfeld (1979).

10. Political scientists have raised this same question, but in slightly different terms, asking: Do grants-in-aid provide significant "general benefits, those collective goods that people value because they believe everyone profits, including themselves?" See Arnold (1981, p. 253).

11. Since local service levels are determined in part by local income levels, a large variation in personal income within a state (high CVY) is likely to imply a large variation in the distribution of local services. Federal aid can provide additional resources which may—state politics permitting—be allocated towards narrowing public service inequities.

12. For services supported by matching aid, total aid will be defined by AID = $m(\mathbf{X}, CVY, Y)$. (Own Spending), where $m(\mathbf{X}, CVY, Y)$ defines the program's matching rate.

13. See Boadway and Flatters (1982), particularly at p. 627.

14. Feldstein (1975) interprets the school finance court decisions in these terms.

15. This result has been noted as well for earlier periods in the history of federal assistance for state-local governments; see Wright (1974) for a discussion of federal grants during the depression period, and Monypenny (1960) for an analysis of federal aid in the 1950s.

16. Olson (1982) and North (1985) develop their theories of government economic performance around this idea.

17. Information on the actual levels of deductions for state and local taxes are available from *Statistics of Income*, Department of the Treasury, Internal Revenue Services, but only for the years 1972–85. The ratio of actual deductions to the level of actual state and local taxes is an estimate of the average rate of deductibility implicit in the federal tax code. A comparison of this ratio for the available years with the average effective tax rate of the median income voter for the same years shows the two series to be very close.

18. Estimates of the relative contribution of each demand variable to the growth in total state-local spending were calculated using the estimated elasticities from equation (2) multiplied by the percentage changes in each demand variable for the time periods 1948–70, 1970–80, and 1980–85. Annual growth rates in state-local spending due to these changes were then calculated and compared to the actual annual rate of growth in state-local spending. For the period 1948–70, the actual rate of growth in $(E + S)$ was 2.64 percent per year. Had only real income increased, the growth rate would have been only 0.66 percent per year. The increase in aid and the fall in the tax price (the federal subsidies) by themselves would have increased $(E + S)$ by 0.49 percent per year. Together, the increase in school-aged children (0.22 percent per year) and the crime rate (1.30 percent per year) were the major contributors to the growth in $(E + S)$ for the periods 1948–70. For the period 1970–80, $(E + S)$ grew at a rate of 2.19 percent per year. Income growth alone would have increased $(E + S)$ by 0.33 percent per year, the crime rate alone would have increased $(E + S)$ by 2.34 percent and federal aid alone would have increased $(E + S)$ by 0.36 percent per year. The fall off in housing starts and the baby bust from 1970 onward were negative influences on $(E + S)$. Since 1980, the decline in real aid, the fall in the crime rate, and the fall in number of school-aged children have all acted to reduce $(E + S)$ while the growth in real income has increased $(E + S)$; the net effect has been to hold real $(E + S)$ constant over the past six years.

19. The ratio of state and local own revenues to state-local residential income rose from 0.151 in 1950 to 0.167 in 1960, remained stable at that rate to 1980, and then rose again to 0.183 by 1985. The number of state-local employees per 1,000 residents grew steadily from 26 per 1,000 in 1950 to 58 per 1,000 by 1980, but then fell slightly to 57 per 1,000 by 1985.

20. On the declining influence of political parties, see Burnham (1975) and Sundquist (1973). On the new independence of the American voter, see Nie, Verba, and Petrocik (1979). On the effects of congressional redistricting on congressional policy-making, see McCubbins and Schwartz (1987).

21. The classic presentation of the argument is now in Fiorina (1977).

22. A district's share of tax-financed expenditures on projects of type x will be $\phi_s = T_s / \Sigma x_i$, or as $\Sigma x_i = \Sigma T_i$, then $\phi_s = T_s / \Sigma T_i$. If all districts contribute an average amount to national taxes $(= \overline{T})$, then $\phi_s = \overline{T} / N.\overline{T} = 1/N$.

23. While an individual district tax share of new expenditures on projects of type x will be $\phi_s = T_s/\Sigma x_i = T_s/\Sigma T_i$, a coalition's tax share of such expenditures, inclusive of all coalition members' taxes, will be $\Phi_s = \sum_{s \in M} T_s/\Sigma x_s$, or as $\Sigma x_i = \Sigma T_i$, $\phi_s = \sum_{s \in M} T_s/\Sigma T_i$. If all districts contribute an average amount ($= \bar{T}$) to national taxes, then $\phi_s = M \cdot \bar{T}/N \cdot \bar{T} = M/N$.

24. The fact that $x^*(M)$ is less than $x^*(D)$ does not mean that districts in the majority coalition are worse off than they would be as members of a decentralized legislature. In fact, it is easy to see from figure 2.1 that they are better off. They save the inefficiency associated with the over-provision of x under decentralization (the approximate triangle from $x_s^*(C)$ to $x_s^*(D)$ above $b(x, \mathbf{P})$ but below the full marginal cost line at \$1), and they receive a tax subsidy from the minority coalitions of $(1 - M/N) \cdot x_s^*(M)$. Further, to the extent the majority can extract a fiscal transfer from the minority through the provision of $x_s = x_s^*(C)$ to the minority, then they benefit again. This result is simply an example of the general principle that it is always best to be in a majority coalition of minimum size in a redistribution game, if you are in any coalition at all. The problem for any individual legislator is, of course, knowing if he or she will be in the majority coalition. Redistribution games are very unstable, and legislators may be in a winning majority one moment and out the next. When legislators are at all uncertain as to whether they will be in or out of the winning coalition, they may prefer a legislative structure which gives them a smaller, but more certain net political benefit. This preference for a lower, but more certain pay-off in legislative redistribution games has been offered as a rationale for the currently decentralized nature of congressional fiscal politics; see initially Weingast (1979) and more recently Niou and Ordeshook (1985) and Epple and Riordan (1986).

25. The bias towards equal aid spending across all districts in a decentralized congressional setting is discussed in Arnold (1981), particularly at pp. 265–279.

26. See ACIR (1978) for a summary of the growth in aid programs.

27. Perhaps the most prominent of the state-local employee associations is the National Education Association (NEA), a teacher union which played an important role in the presidential election of Jimmy Carter. They were rewarded with the establishment of the Office of Education as a new cabinet level department. Elected state-local officials have also organized as lobby groups in Washington, and perhaps more than any other organizations were responsible for the passage of General Revenue Sharing; see Beer (1976).

28. To be so, all districts must pay the same amount in federal taxes; see n. 23 above.

29. A linear marginal benefit schedule of the form $b(x,P) = \alpha_0 - \alpha_1 x_s + \Sigma\beta_i P_{is}$ defines a linear demand curve for x when $b(x, \mathbf{P})$ is set equal to the marginal tax cost of x under the alternative legislative regimes. For the fully cooperative regime, $b(x, \mathbf{P}) = 1$ defines $x_s^*(C)$ as $x_s^*(C) = (\alpha_0/\alpha_1) - (1/\alpha_1)1 + \Sigma(\beta_i/\alpha_1)P_{is}$; for the majority rule regime: $x_s^*(M) = (\alpha_0/\alpha_1) - (1/\alpha_1)\phi_s + \Sigma(\beta_i/\alpha_1)P_{is}$; and for the decentralized regime: $x_s^*(D) = (\alpha_0/\alpha_1) - (1/\alpha_1)\phi_s + \Sigma(\beta_i/\alpha_1)P_{is}$.

30. More formally, the specification in equation (6) implies $\overline{\Delta x}(D) = \sum_{s=1}^{N} \overline{\Delta x_s}(D) (Pop_s/\Sigma Pop_s)$ and $\overline{\Delta x}(M) = \sum_{s \in M} \overline{\Delta x_s}(M)(Pop_s/\sum_{s \in M} Pop_s)(\overline{Pop^M}/\overline{Pop^N})$, where $\overline{\Delta x_s}(D) x_s^*(D) - x_s^*(C)$, $\overline{\Delta x_s}(M) = x_s^*(M) - x_s^*(C)$, Pop_s is the population in district s, and $\overline{Pop^M}$ and $\overline{Pop^N}$ are average population sizes for majority districts and all districts respectively. For most purposes it seems reasonable

to assume $(\overline{Pop^M}/\overline{Pop^N}) \simeq 1$; thus $\overline{\Delta x}(M)$ is an estimate of the average increase in per capita aid in majority coalition districts.

31. Aid spending in calendar year 1982 was defined largely by the budget for fiscal year 1982, ending on 30 September 1982. The FY 1982 budget was approved during the calendar year 1981 and reflects the policies of the first year of the Reagan administration.

32. The Reagan-Stockman budget strategy is well described in Stockman (1986), particularly chapter 5.

33. The important role of the president in the passage of the Reagan budgets is described in Stockman (1986), particularly chapter 6.

34. The results for a regression of total aid minus only GRS funding are similar to those in equations (c) and (d) of table 2.6, though the estimates for the congressional coefficients are not as precise. While it is reasurring that all these alternative specifications give the same conclusion, there are good reasons to embrace equation (c) using total aid expenditures as the preferred specification. Beer's (1976) review of the passage of GRS makes clear that it was largely decentralized congressional fiscal politics which defined the aid formula and the levels of assistance. Stockman's discussion of the attempts to trim welfare and Medicaid assistance show that the same incentives dominate these programs as well; see Stockman (1986) at the index references for AFDC and Medicaid and at p. 442, particularly.

35. For a discussion of the political fate of the New Federalism, see the *National Journal* (1982). In the appendix to his book on Reagan budget policies, Stockman reviews the final record of his efforts to trim the federal aid budget and concludes that while some progress has been made, it may not be permanent: "Every big program and every piddling program that marched out of the Cutting Room dead or bleeding in February 1981 lived to tell about it." And both Republicans and Democrats in Congress were on the "first-aid team." Stockman (1986, p. 442). The recent veto overrides suggest a revival may be coming.

References

ACIR. 1978. *Categorical grants: Their role and design.* No. A-52. Washington, D.C.: U.S. Government Printing Office.

Arnold, R. D. 1981. The local roots of domestic policy. In *The new congress,* ed. T. E. Mann and N. J. Ornstein. Washington, D.C.: American Enterprise Institute.

Arrow, K. J. 1971. A utilitarian approach to the concept of equality in public expenditures. *Quarterly Journal of Economics* 85: 409–15.

Barlow, R. 1970. Efficiency aspects of local school finance. *Journal of Political Economy* 78: 1028–40.

Beer, S. 1973. The modernization of american federalism. *Publius: The Journal of Federalism* 3: 49–95.

———. 1976. The adoption of general revenue sharing: A case study in public sector politics. *Public Policy* 24: 127–96.

Bitterman, H. J. 1938. *State and federal grants-in-aid.* New York: Mentzer, Bush and Company.

Boadway, R., and F. Flatters. 1982. Efficiency and equalization payments in a federal system of government: A synthesis and extension of recent results. *Canadian Journal of Economics* 15: 613–33.

Burnham, D. 1975. American Politics in the 1970s: Beyond party? In *The american party systems,* ed. W. N. Chambers and W. D. Burnham. New York: Oxford University Press.

Craig, S., and R. Inman. 1982. Federal aid and public education: An empirical look at the new fiscal federalism. *Review of Economics and Statistics* 64: 541–52.

———. 1986. Education, welfare and the new federalism: State budgeting in a federalist public economy. In *Studies in state and local public finance,* ed. H. Rosen, 187–22. Chicago: University of Chicago Press.

Epple, D., and M. Riordan. 1986. Cooperation and punishment under repeated majority voting. Paper presented at the Carnegie Conference on Political Economy, Carnegie-Mellon University, Pittsbugh, Pa.

Feldstein, M. 1975. Wealth neutrality and local choice in public education. *American Economic Review* 65: 75–89.

Fenno, R. 1966. *The power of the purse.* Boston: Little, Brown and Company.

Fiorina, M. 1977. *Congress: Keystone of the washington establishment.* New Haven: Yale University Press.

Gates, P. 1968. *History of public land law development.* Washington, D.C.: Government Printing Office.

Inman, R. P. 1978. Optimal fiscal reform of metropolitan schools: Some simulation results. *American Economic Review* 68: 107–22.

Inman, R. P., and D. Albright. 1987. Central policies for local debt. Working Paper no. 2166, National Bureau of Economic Research.

Inman, R. P., and D. Rubinfeld. 1979. The judicial pursuit of local fiscal equity. *Harvard Law Review* 92: 1662–1750.

Jacobs, J. 1961. *The death and life of great american cities.* New York: Vintage Books.

McCubbins, M., and T. Schwartz. 1987 (forthcoming). Congress, the courts, and public policy consequences of the one man, one vote rule. *American Journal of Political Science* 31.

Manley, J. F. 1970. *The politics of finance.* Boston: Little, Brown and Company.

Michelman, F., and T. Sandalow. 1970. *Materials on government in urban areas.* St. Paul: West Publishing Co.

Monypenny, P. 1960. Federal grants-in-aid to state governments: A political analysis. *National Tax Journal* 13: 11–16.

National Journal. 1982. The New Federalism. Vol. 14, February 27, 1982.

Nie, N. S., S. Verba, and J. Petrocik. 1979. *The changing American voter.* Cambridge: Harvard University Press.

Niou, E., and P. C. Ordeshook. 1985. Universalism in congress. *American Journal of Political Science* 29: 246–58.

North, D. 1985. The growth of government in the United States: A historian's perspective. *Journal of Public Economics,* 28: 383–99.

Oates, W. 1972. *Fiscal federalism.* New York: Harcourt Brace Jovanovich, Inc.

Olson, M. 1982. *The rise and decline of nations.* New Haven: Yale University Press.

Ornstein, N. 1975. *Congress in change.* New York: Praeger.

Orr, L. 1976. Income transfers as a public good: An application to AFDC. *American Economic Review,* 66: 359–71.

Scheiber, H. 1966. The condition of American federalism: An historian's view. Subcommittee on Intergovernmental Relations to the Committee on Government Operations, U.S. Senate, 89th Congress, 2d session.

Shepsle, K., and B. Weingast. 1984. Legislative politics and budget outcomes. In *Federal budget policy in 1980s,* ed. G. B. Mills and J. L. Palmer. Washington, D.C.: Urban Institute Press.

Stockman, D. 1986. *The Triumph of Politics: The Inside Story of the Reagan Revolution.* New York: Harper and Row.

Sundquist, J. L. 1973. Whither the American party system? *Political Science Quarterly* 88: 559–81.

Wallis, J. J. 1984. The birth of the old federalism: Financing the New Deal, 1932–1940. *Journal of Economic History* 44: 139–59.

Weingast, B. 1979. A rational choice perspective on congressional norms. *American Journal of Political Science* 23: 245–62.

Wright, G. 1974. The political economy of New Deal spending: An econometric analysis. *Review of Economics and Statistics* 56: 30–38.

Comment   Thomas Romer

The central message of Inman's paper is that, as with other types of government spending, pork barrel considerations have played an important—perhaps dominant—role in the development of federal grants to state and local governments. This would not surprise political scientists (who, if anything, have overemphasized "distributive politics" as the basis of government spending), but may come as a mild shock to some economists.

Part of the empirical support for Inman's claim rests on a series of cross-sectional estimates for various types of grants (table 2.4 in the paper). These results reveal only sporadic association between real per capita federal aid to lower-level governments in each state and variables that might plausibly capture efficiency-based motivations for such grants. One might argue that a more convincing analysis would use more disaggregated data and a wider range of explanatory variables, but these findings are intriguing and pose a clear challenge to those who would propose efficiency as the basis of a positive theory of grant structure.

Inman ties much of his discussion of the growth of aid to a claim that a structural shift in Congress was central to a major shift in the structure of federalism and, in particular, led to a dramatic increase in federal grants after 1972.

Looking at the time series on federal grants in a bit more detail than that given in the paper is helpful here. Table C2.1 shows year-to-year growth in real per capita federal grants to states and localities. The

Thomas Romer is professor of economics and political economy at the Graduate School of Industrial Administration, Carnegie-Mellon University.

Table C2.1   **Federal Grants to State and Local Governments, Year-to-Year Percentage Changes, 1948–1983[a]**

Fiscal Year	%Change From Prior Year	Fiscal Year	%Change From Prior Year	Fiscal Year	%Change From Prior Year
1948	29.4	1960	5.8	1972	12.4
1949	− 0.7	1961	− 2.6	1973	16.0
1950	23.3	1962	5.1	1974	− 4.3
1951	− 4.1	1963	6.0	1975	1.7
1952	− 6.0	1964	11.3	1976	9.7
1953	7.6	1965	6.0	1977	3.7
1954	− 0.9	1966	12.2	1978	2.5
1955	1.4	1967	9.5	1979	− 1.9
1956	− 0.3	1968	5.0	1980	− 1.0
1957	8.0	1969	3.0	1981	− 0.9
1958	21.6	1970	4.5	1982	− 10.6
1959	26.0	1971	10.5	1983	− 3.8

Sources: Computed from U.S. Department of the Treasury Office of State and Local Finance, 1985, *Federal-State-Local Fiscal Relations,* Table III.10, p. 65.
[a] 1972 dollars per capita.

pattern is not so much one of steady growth followed by an explosion after 1972 as it is one consisting of a series of explosions. The major episodes correspond to what might be viewed as innovations in the use of federal grants. The late 1950s' boom is largely due to funding pursuant to the 1956 Interstate Highway Act. In the next decade there is the use of federal grants to fund the programs associated with the Great Society, especially transfer programs but with a liberal sprinkling of public works projects thrown in. There was indeed another explosion in the early 1970s, culminating in the advent of General Revenue-Sharing, but by the second half of the Carter administration real per capita federal grants began to decline—before the advent of the newest "new federalism."

Each of these explosions represents substantial real increases in federal outlays. My strong hunch is that, given the dynamics shown in my table, the linear specification in Inman's table 2.6 is unlikely to capture correctly the political effects he is looking for. Rather than pointing to a dramatic shift of spending after 1972, the estimated coefficients of δ reported in table 2.6 reflect the cumulative upward shift of the intercept of these linear specifications over the previous 15 years. An indication that the quantitative results should be viewed with some skepticism is evident from figure 2.2. The coordinates indicated there clearly cannot all lie on a linear marginal benefit schedule. Taking the project sizes and costs corresponding to $x^*(C)$ and $x^*(M)$ as given would suggest that $\phi_s \approx .41$ if we agree that $x^*(D) = \$179$. This, in turn, seems not very different from what might emerge from the simple pork barrel model under a modest decentralization. (In a way, my calculated value of ϕ_s is somewhat reassuring, since $\phi_s \approx 1/435$ along this linear marginal benefit function would require $x^*(D) \approx \$220$ per capita!)

All the same, I think more detailed investigation of the political economy of federalism will bear out Inman's central message. Here, even more than with the work on efficiency aspects of grants, more disaggregation and attention to the dynamics of grant amounts and types is likely to be revealing. Some tantalizing evidence about the "Christmas tree" aspects of federal grants comes from data reported in Inman's table 2.4. There we see that across states, for each type of grant, the coefficient of variation in real per capita federal grants decreases over time, at least up to the 1980s. This is equally true for categories where the mean was increasing (as with "other" grants to states) and those where the mean flattened out or declined by 1977 (welfare or highways).

For the most part, this tendency toward more equal distribution of federal grants across states (and, as more detailed data show, across congressional districts) has been accomplished by the shift from mostly categorical grants toward greater reliance on broad-based block grants using formulas carefully calibrated to provide for "equitable" distribution across states. It is this shift, rather than an especially dramatic change in the volume of grants, that I think is the hallmark of the move toward the congressional decentralization that figures so prominently in Inman's account.

The 1980s have witnessed a substantial retrenchment in the use of federal grants. The real declines shown in table C2.1 and implicit in the Reagan dummies of table 2.6 are part of an even more striking development. Grants-in-aid as a proportion of total nondefense outlays by the federal government rose steadily from 1950 to about 22 percent in 1970, and hovered around that figure through 1978. From then, grants became the most expendable part of the domestic budget. By the end of the first Reagan term, grants-in-aid to state and local governments represented only 16 percent of federal domestic budget outlays—a lower fraction than the corresponding 1960 figure. (Aronson and Hilley 1986, table 3-1, p. 49.)

The cuts in the first Reagan term reflect the fact that, for the most part, these grants were "budget items . . . subject to discretionary reductions by the president and Congress without changes in existing law, and thus [were] exceptionally vulnerable to a president determined to cut federal spending." (Palmer 1984, 53.) Nonetheless, the congressional incentives discussed by Inman are, if anything, stronger now than they were in the early '70s. Moreover, federal grants (the fewer strings attached the better) are a politically delightful revenue source from the viewpoint of state and local governments. (Much better than indirect gains from reductions in federal taxes, for example.) These considerations suggest that the next "new" federalism will also be the next "explosion" in grants-in-aid.

References

Aronson, J. R., and J. L. Hilley. 1986. *Financing state and local governments.* 4th ed. Washington: Brookings Institution.
Palmer, K. T. 1984. The evolution of grant policies. In *The changing politics of federal grants,* ed. L. D. Brown, J. W. Fossett, and K. T. Palmer. Washington: Brookings Institution.
U. S. Department of the Treasury. Office of State and Local Finance. 1985. *Federal-state-local fiscal relations.* Washington: U.S. Government Printing Office.

3   The Effects of Jurisdiction Types and Numbers on Local Public Finance

Jeffrey S. Zax

3.1   Introduction

Local government in the United States is a multitiered structure. The purpose of this study is to investigate the effects of alternative local government structures on aggregate local public debt and expenditures. These effects are dominated by two opposing principles of efficiency. First, larger—and, therefore, fewer—governments may capture economies of scale in the production and distribution of local public goods. Second, smaller and more plentiful governments may provide a greater variety of public good bundles, and, therefore, healthy competition for each other.

Both of these principles have implications for the optimal structure of local government. Unfortunately, the implications of each have become, for the most part, competitive rather than complementary prescriptions. The first principle has been compelling to specialists in public administration, the second to economists. In consequence, the public administration program for local government reform consists of local government consolidation. The economists' program consists of fragmentation.

This study demonstrates that both principles are operative in the determination of aggregate county public debt and expenditure (the sums of debt and expenditures for all governments within a county, including the county itself) as shares of total county personal income.

Jeffrey S. Zax is an assistant professor of economics at Queens College and at the Graduate Center of the City University of New York, and a research economist at the National Bureau of Economic Research.

The Project in State and Local Government Finance of the National Bureau of Economic Research graciously supported the research presented in this paper. Only I am responsible for the content.

Aggregate debt and expenditures are positive functions of jurisdictions per capita, suggesting that small jurisdictions are inefficient. However, they are negative functions of jurisdictions per dollar of government expenditure, suggesting that when jurisdictions have large average "market shares," they use their monopoly power to expand the local public sector. In addition, agggregate debt and expenditures are negative functions of the absolute number of governments. For the most part, these results also characterize the effects of surrounding jurisdictions on city government debt and expenditures.

The structure of local government within counties is less important than the number of units. The income share of local government debt is, in general, sensitive to the number of local jurisdictions but not to their types. However, the income share of government expenditures is significantly more sensitive to the numbers of municipalities than to the numbers of single-purpose school and special districts.

These results imply, unsurprisingly, that neither consolidation nor fragmentation is unambiguously superior. In a system of general-purpose local governments, neither the extreme of jurisdictions which are many, small, competitive, and inefficient nor that of jurisdictions which are few, large, efficient, and monopolistic will minimize debt and expenditures.

As policy, both consolidation and fragmentation may be inferior to a third strategy in which single-purpose governments are more prominent. Both programs, implicitly, advocate fewer tiers of local government. Under consolidation, tiers are subsumed into a single county- or metropolitan-area-wide government. Under fragmentation, multiunit single-purpose districts are decomposed into single units. However, the intermediate tier of single-purpose jurisdictions may be essential to the best compromise between economies of scale and competitive supply.

3.2   Consolidation and Fragmentation

The 50 states of America are, with few exceptions, divided into counties which in aggregate exhaust state territory. These counties are the top tier of local government. County territory is, in turn, exhausted by jurisdictions which provide primary and secondary education. These jurisdictions are most often single-purpose school districts. Within counties, centers of population are incorporated as general-purpose municipalities. They occasionally include primary and secondary education among their functions. Sewerage, water, transit, and other services may be provided by single-purpose special districts, usually within counties, but to areas which include more than one general-purpose government (ACIR 1982).

For the most part, the positive theory of this system addresses the number and types of jurisdictions separately. Multiple jurisdictions are beneficial because they restrict the opportunities for monopoly behavior by local government officials. However, they also restrict the opportunities to take advantage of returns to scale in government production and to redistribute wealth. Single-purpose jurisdictions are beneficial because they reduce the power of general-purpose governments. However, they increase the complexity of local government, which may create fiscal illusions under which citizens accept higher debt levels than they would if the costs and benefits of government were more readily calculable.

Fragmented local jurisdictions are beneficial because they offer citizens choice among different collections of local public goods. If few alternative jurisdictions are available, inefficient jurisdictions need not fear the sanctions which could potentially be imposed by taxpayer and tax base emigration. Public officials, whose personal objectives are served by bigger government (Niskanen 1975), can expand government activity beyond levels which would be acceptable to voters if the "market" in local public services were more "complete."

If the variety of available jurisdictions is sufficient, citizen mobility may render inconsequential the geographic monopoly held by each jurisdiction within its own borders (Tiebout 1956). In the absence of intrajurisdictional politics (citizen voice), the monopoly power of individual jurisdictions is inversely related to the number of jurisdictions. However, with fixed jurisdictional boundaries (land is immobile), citizen exit will not entirely deprive local governments of monopoly power, regardless of the number of alternative jurisdictions (Epple and Zelenitz 1981).

The advantages of sufficient jurisdictional choice are relevant to many issues in government organization. For example, annexations reduce the potential alternatives to the annexing jurisdiction, and may therefore permit higher expenditures (Mehay 1981). Municipal incorporations dilute the monopoly power of existing municipalities. This effect is explicitly recognized in the statutes of 18 states, where new municipalities are prohibited within specified distances of existing municipalities (ACIR 1982). Where existing municipalities can prevent new incorporations, incorporations may be less frequent and expenditures by existing municipalities higher (Martin and Wagner 1978). Revenue- or tax-base-sharing reduces competition among jurisdictions by insulating individual jurisdictions from changes in their tax base. Here again, expenditures may increase (McKenzie and Staaf 1978).

Despite the appeal of competition through multiple jurisdictions, the case for fragmentation is not conclusive. Large jurisdictions may capture economies of scale or coordination that are lost to smaller units

(Rothenberg 1975; ACIR 1975). In addition, small jurisdictions cannot effectively redistribute wealth, since intrajurisdictional variation in wealth would be small and adverse selection easy (Reschovsky 1980). If large units of local government are more efficient than small units, consolidation, rather than fragmentation, will reduce the size of local government.

Though recent theoretical considerations of local government predominantly present arguments in favor of fragmentation,[1] the arguments in favor of consolidation are consequential. Presentations for either position do not so much contradict as ignore each other. For example, most models of local government monopoly assume constant or decreasing returns to scale (Epple and Zelenitz 1981; Wagner and Weber 1975).

Studies which consider the advantages of both small- and large-scale local government are rare and speculative: Martin and McKenzie hypothesize that citizens will not benefit from the efficiencies available through consolidation because the bureaucracy, whose monopoly power is enhanced by consolidation, will appropriate all the gains. Mullen hypothesizes that fragmentation is a luxury good, "bought" by wealthier citizens at the cost of inefficiency in order to enjoy local autonomy. Empirically, local government debt and expenditures must be minimized for a given level of services when local jurisdictions strike a careful balance between the efficiency of large units and the competitive vulnerability of small units.

Similarly, within the system of local governments, single-purpose jurisdictions may either reduce or expand local government activity. To the extent that they increase the numbers of local governments, they contribute to the competitive pressures all face. In this role, they reduce aggregate local government expenditures for a given level of services (Wagner and Weber 1975; Mehay 1984).

However, single-purpose governments also complicate the structure of local government. If this creates a fiscal illusion among citizens as to the true tax price of the local services they receive, single-purpose jurisdictions may allow aggregate government activity to expand beyond the limits that would be set by an electorate which fully understood their effects (DiLorenzo 1982). The principle purpose of special districts may be to circumvent statutory limits on general obligation debt of general-purpose governments (Copeland 1961; Wagner 1976; Eppel and Spatt 1986).

The arguments for and against consolidation are also relevant. If single-purpose jurisdictions obtain economies of scale that are unattainable by the general-purpose governments they serve (ACIR 1982), they reduce the size of local government. If they are so big as to replace the geographic monopolies of general-purpose governments with functional monopolies, bureaucratic self-interest may lead to an expansion of the local public sector. This danger is enhanced by the structure of many special districts, whose officials are appointed by the general purpose governments they serve and are, therefore, isolated from the electorate.

Arguments in favor of both reductions and expansions of local government through single-purpose jurisdictions are appealing. Empirically, they present a challenge to identify both the competitive, efficient, and the monopolizing, illusory effects of single-purpose jurisdictions.

3.3   Numbers and Types of Local Jurisdictions

Government hierarchies within county-level jurisdictions provide comparisons which test for the public finance effects of differences in local government organization. Comparisons across counties are appropriate for three reasons. First, counties are large enough to contain structures of smaller jurisdictions. Second, they are small enough to permit Tiebout-style sorting by potential residents. Third, and most important, the aggreggate of services provided by counties and the jurisdictions they contain typically make up the complete array of local services available to county residents. Comparisons across counties, within states, can conveniently account for differences in service arrays.

There are approximately 3,130 county-level governments in the United States.[2] Among them are examples of almost all degrees of local government fragmentation and consolidation. Seventeen counties contain no local governments.[3] Five counties contain more than 200. Cook County, Illinois, is the most fragmented in terms of jurisdiction counts, with 513 local jurisdictions.

However, Cook County also has more than five million residents, or approximately one jurisdiction per 1,000. In per capita terms, at least 25 percent of all counties are more fragmented. Residents in Slope County, North Dakota, are most generously endowed, with 27.6 jurisdictions per 1,000 residents. Slope County also has the smallest average jurisdictions, in financial terms: 27.1 jurisdictions per $1,000,000 in aggregate local government expenditures.

In contrast, the greatest geographic densities are in eastern states. Bergen and Hudson, counties in New Jersey directly across the Hudson river from New York City, both have more than 0.6 jurisdictions per square mile. Table 3.1 presents the entire distribution of jurisdictions per county, per square mile, per 1,000 county population, and per $1,000,000 aggregate expenditure.

Table 3.2 presents distributions of cities and towns per county, special districts per county, and school districts per county. Seventy-six counties contain only cities or towns. Eighty-five percent of counties have

Table 3.1   **Distribution of Counties by Jurisdictions, Jurisdictions per Square Mile, Jurisdiction per 1,000 Capita, and Jurisdictions per $1,000,000 Expenditures**

Local Jurisdiction per County		Local Jurisdictions per Square Mile	
Number	Percent	Number	Percent
0	.5	0	.5
1– 10	34.6	0–.005	8.1
11– 20	21.8	.005–.015	22.1
21– 30	13.7	.015–.025	18.8
31– 50	17.0	.025–.05	22.2
51–100	10.2	.05–.1	20.9
> 101	2.1	> .1	7.4

Local Jurisdictions per 1,000 Capita		Local Jurisdictions per $1,000,000 Expenditures
Number	Percent	Percent
0	.5	.5
0– .2	15.5	16.3
.2– .5	23.5	22.5
.5–1.0	23.2	25.0
1.1–2.0	19.4	20.8
2.1–5.0	13.3	11.7
> 5.1	4.5	3.2

Notes: Jurisdictions and expenditures are measured as of 1982. Population is measured as of 1980.

N = 3,129 counties.

Table 3.2   **Distribution of Counties by Number of Cities and Towns, Special Districts, and School Districts**

Number	Cities and Towns per County %	Special Districts per County %	School Districts per County %
0	2.0	5.4	12.2
1– 2	21.9	23.1	35.0
3– 5	23.9	28.2	25.8
6–10	17.5	18.5	16.7
11–20	15.1	14.1	7.6
21–50	17.8	9.0	2.5
> 51	1.8	1.8	.3

Note: N = 3,129 counties.

governments of all three types. Cook County has the most cities and towns, 150, and the most special districts, 152. Harris County, Texas, has 348 school districts. Slope County, again, has the most cities and towns per 1,000 capita, with slightly over 20. Loving County's one special district amounts to 10.9 special districts per 1,000 capita. McPherson County, Nebraska, has 13.4 school districts per 1,000 capita.

As tables 3.1 and 3.2 demonstrate, few counties match these extreme jurisdiction numbers, by any measure. However, by any measure, the variation in jurisdiction numbers across counties is striking. Furthermore, counties vary dramatically in the mix of municipalities, special districts, and school districts they contain. They therefore provide an appropriate sample in which to investigate the effects of the tier-structure of local government on the size of the local public sector.

3.4   Local Jurisdictions and Aggregate County Public Finance

Comparisons of aggregate debt levels, debt changes, and expenditure levels across counties reveal the effects of local government structure on agggregate local public finance. If small, competitive jurisdictions are most efficient, counties with many jurisdictions will have smaller aggregate local public sector debt and expenditure levels than counties with few, for any level of public services. If large-scale government is efficient, their debt and expenditure levels will be higher.[4] Though the theories which support fragmentation and consolidation are not explicitly dynamic, the relationship between efficiency and growth in aggregate local public sector debt may also be negative.

Following Gordon and Slemrod (1986), debt is measured here as a fraction of aggregate county personal income, both gross and net of sinking, bond, and insurance funds. Their econometric specification for debt determination also forms the basis for tests of government structure effects. In their regression model, debt is a linear function of imputed marginal tax rates, the proportion of adults aged 25 to 44, the proportion of adults greater than 60 years old, the percentage of households which changed housing units between 1975 and 1980, the percentage of households which changed county of residence between 1975 and 1980, the percentage of housing units with renter occupants, the percentage of housing units constructed between 1975 and 1980, and dummy variables for state. Gordon and Slemrod use these variables to capture variations in population characteristics and in tastes for local public goods across counties. Here, a variable measuring the interquartile range of the 1980 within-county family income distribution provides additional controls for heterogeneity in county populations.

Gordon and Slemrod apply this model to a sample consisting of municipalities in New England in order to determine the effects of federal income taxation on arbitrage through the local public sector. This study applies it to a sample of 3,129 observations, each representing aggregate local governmental activity within the borders of a single county-level government, to determine the effects of government structure on government size. Accordingly, a dummy variable representing counties in Standard Metropolitan Statistical Areas (SMSA's), a vector of dummy variables representing local provision of 22 different services,[5] and measures of the number and type of within-county jurisdictions augment the Gordon/Slemrod specification.[6]

The same specification is used here for equations which estimate county aggregate local public expenditures and the 1982 fiscal year change in long-term debt, as proportions of aggregate county personal income. This is a convenient specification for debt changes, as a comparison to equations for debt levels. It is also similar to the canonical expenditure specifications of Borcherding and Deacon (1986) and Bergstrom and Goodman (1973) though not identical.[7]

In this specification, coefficients on the jurisdiction measures test the effects of consolidation and fragmentation. In principle, finance measures and jurisdiction counts may be mutually dependent. The decision to create new or combine old jurisdictions can depend on the expected effects of these changes on local public services and finance.

Unfortunately, the effects of finance choices on jurisdiction structure are ambiguous. For example, a population with strong tastes and high expenditures for local public services may fragment their county so as to provide many specialized bundles of public goods, or consolidate so as to efficiently provide large quantities of "commodity" public services.

In practice, this issue is occasionally important. In some periods jurisdictional structures have been quite flexible. Between 1962 and 1972, the number of local jurisdictions in the United States fell by 14.2 percent, from 91,186 to 78,218. This reduction was confined entirely to school districts, whose numbers fell by 54.5 percent. Numbers of counties, cities, and townships were virtually constant, while numbers of special districts grew by 30.4 percent (ACIR 1982).

Local government structure has recently been less malleable. Since 1972 local government numbers have changed little, growing by only 5.2 percent. Municipality counts have grown by only 3.0 percent, township counts have fallen by 1.5 percent, school district counts have fallen by 5.9 percent, and special district counts have grown by 19.7 percent (ACIR 1982; U.S. Bureau of the Census 1984).

Despite the theoretical connection, effects of public finance on jurisdiction structure are certainly negligible in the sample studied here. Jurisdictional counts by county in 1982, the year under study, are almost perfectly predictable by 1977 counts alone. Regressions of 1982 on 1977 counts achieve R^2s of .95 for special districts, and greater than .99 for cities, towns, and school districts.[8] Given 1977 jurisdiction counts, there is very little variance left to 1982 counts which could depend on public finance choices in all the intervening years, much less in 1982.

Table 3.3 presents equations for gross and net debt levels, debt changes and expenditure shares in aggregate income as functions of the number and squared number of jurisdictions in the county.[9] Increases in juris-

Table 3.3   **Equations for Aggregate County Debt and Total Expenditure Shares in Total Personal Income with Jurisdiction Counts**

Independent Variable	Gross County Debt	Net County Debt	Change, County Long-term Debt	Total County Expenditure
Number of local jurisdictions in county	−.00370 (3.05)	−.00284 (2.60)	−.00238 (3.70)	−.00101 (4.18)
Number of local jurisdictions in county, squared	.00000681 (1.84)	.00000523 (1.57)	.00000492 (2.50)	.00000174 (2.36)
Interquartile range, family income distribution	.0000463 (7.74)	.0000483 (8.97)	.0000244 (7.68)	−.00000211 (1.78)
Marginal federal income tax rate	−4.15 (1.51)	−3.01 (1.22)	−1.45 (.992)	−1.47 (2.70)
Marginal federal income tax rate, squared	5.72 (1.45)	3.78 (1.06)	1.74 (.827)	2.16 (2.76)
Marginal state income tax rate	−13.0 (1.06)	−11.9 (1.08)	−10.2 (1.57)	−3.59 (1.47)
Marginal state income tax rate, squared	92.9 (1.57)	73.7 (1.38)	79.2 (2.51)	19.2 (1.63)
Percentage of adult population aged 25–44	−1.15 (1.26)	−.484 (.590)	−.546 (1.13)	−.533 (2.94)
Percentage of adult population aged 61 or more	−1.26 (1.39)	−.676 (.828)	−.590 (1.22)	−.526 (2.92)
Percentage in same house as 1975	.0852 (.284)	−.0217 (.0805)	−.204 (1.28)	.413 (6.94)
Percentage in same county, different house as 1975	.847 (2.23)	.686 (2.00)	.526 (2.60)	.167 (2.21)
Percentage in rental units	.0292 (.102)	−.203 (.787)	−.229 (1.50)	.441 (7.75)
Percentage structures built since 1975	1.10 (2.83)	.770 (2.20)	.202 (.977)	.540 (6.98)
Included in an SMSA	−.105 (2.42)	−.0947 (2.43)	−.0442 (1.92)	−.0224 (2.60)
Intercept	.565 (.600)	.0733 (.0865)	.537 (1.07)	.395 (2.11)
R^2	.104	.0977	.0757	.230
Means of Dependent Variables	.184	.111	.0504	.199

Note: t-statistics are in parentheses. All equations have 3,043 degrees of freedom.

dictions per county reduce levels of all four dependent variables with 1 percent significance. In terms of jurisdiction counts, fragmentation reduces the aggregate size of the local public sector. This result is consistent with the hypothesis that monopolizing bureaucrats have greater power in larger jurisdictions.[10]

This effect diminishes as jurisdiction numbers increase. Quadratic terms in jurisdiction counts are positive, significant at 5 percent for total expenditures and the change in long-term debt, and at 10 percent for gross debt. Together, the linear and quadratic terms imply that, within state, and with given functions and population characteristics, the income share of total local government expenditures is minimized with 290 jurisdictions per county. Holding these factors constant, this share is 12.2 percentage points smaller with 290 jurisdictions per county than with 25, the average value across counties. All other explanatory variables constant, gross debt is minimized with 272 jurisdictions and the change in long-term debt is minimized with 242. As noted above, few counties actually contain this many local jurisdictions.

Section 3.3 introduced three measures of jurisdiction density in addition to absolute jurisdiction counts. Table 3.4 presents the coefficients

Table 3.4   Coefficients for Various Jurisdiction Measures in Equations for Aggregate County Debt and Total Expenditure Shares in Total Personal Income

Jurisdiction Measure	Gross County Debt	Net County Debt	Change, County Long-term Debt	Total County Expenditure
Jurisdictions per $1,000,000 expenditures	−.124	−.107	−.0464	−.0239
	(5.33)	(5.09)	(3.72)	(5.15)
Jurisdictions per $1,000,000 expenditures, squared	.00459	.00381	.00164	.000928
	(3.21)	(2.95)	(2.15)	(3.26)
R²	.111	.104	.0762	.232
Jurisdictions per square mile	−1.16	−.958	−.927	−.166
	(1.78)	(1.64)	(2.68)	(1.29)
Jurisdictions per square mile, squared	1.30	1.11	1.15	.122
	(1.31)	(1.24)	(2.18)	(.615)
R²	.102	.0963	.0735	.225
Jurisdictions per 1,000 capita	−.0152	−.0280	−.0123	.0212
	(.690)	(1.41)	(1.05)	(4.86)
Jurisdictions per 1,000 capita, squared	−.000255	.000227	.000159	−.000916
	(.194)	(.192)	(.227)	(3.51)
R²	.102	.0970	.0721	.231

Note: t-statistics are in parentheses. All equations have 3,043 degrees of freedom.

estimated for jurisdictions per 1,000 capita, per square mile, and per $1,000,000 government expenditures, when each replaces absolute jurisdiction counts in the specification of table 3.3.[11]

Regression equations achieve higher explanatory power with jurisdictions measured per $1,000,000 expenditures than with any of the other three "normalizations." All linear terms and three quadratic terms are significant at 1 percent, the remaining quadratic term at 5 percent. Consistent with the results in table 3.3, increasing jurisdictions per $1,000,000 expenditures—in effect, reducing jurisdictional "market share"—reduces the income share of local public debt and expenditures at a diminishing rate.

Jurisdictional normalizations with land area are less successful, but consistent. In all four equations, the linear coefficient on jurisdictions per square mile has a negative, and the quadratic term a positive sign. However, only two of these coefficients are significant at 5 percent, with a third significant at 10 percent.

Linear coefficients on jurisdictions per 1,000 capita are similarly negative in all debt equations, but insignificant. Two of three quadratic terms in these equations are positive, but again all three are insignificant. Both coefficients are significant in the expenditure equation, but here signs are reversed. The income share of local government expenditures appears to increase at a diminishing rate as the number of governments per capita increases. In effect, increases in the population served reduce the local government share in income.

This last result is the only indication in the equations of tables 3.3 and 3.4 that jurisdiction numbers may have efficiency as well as monopoly effects. Equations which contain only one measure of jurisdiction density cannot identify both. Equations which contain linear and quadratic terms for two or more measures suggest that both effects are important in the determination of public finance income shares.

Among the four measures of jurisdiction density, there are eleven different combinations of two or more. Each measure performs consistently in all equations which include combinations of which it is a part. Linear coefficients on absolute jurisdiction numbers and jurisdictions per $1,000,000 are invariably negative and usually significant. Quadratic coefficients on these two are significantly positive. Linear and quadratic coefficients on jurisdictions per 1,000 capita are positive and negative, respectively, and often significant. In combination with other measures, linear and quadratic coefficients on jurisdictions per square mile are rarely significant.

Table 3.5 presents equation estimates for the specification which best represents these effects. It includes linear and quadratic terms for all measures of jurisdiction density with the exception of jurisdictions per square mile. Linear and quadratic terms for jurisdictions per square mile are insignificant when added to this specification.

Table 3.5   Equations for Aggregate County Debt and Total Expenditure Shares in Total Personal Income with Multiple Jurisdiction Measures

Independent Variable	Gross County Debt	Net County Debt	Change, County Long-term Debt	Total County Expenditures
Number of local jurisdictions in county	−.00213 (1.73)	−.00148 (1.33)	−.00185 (2.81)	−.000672 (2.86)
Number of local jurisdictions in county, squared	.00000338 (.908)	.00000223 (.664)	.00000376 (1.88)	.00000107 (1.50)
Jurisdiction per 1,000 capita	.274 (6.52)	.185 (4.89)	.0769 (3.42)	.132 (16.5)
Jurisdictions per 1,000 capita, squared	−.0147 (4.97)	−.0105 (3.94)	−.00407 (2.57)	−.00618 (11.0)
Jurisdictions per $1,000,000 expenditures	−.357 (8.14)	−.264 (6.66)	−.107 (4.54)	−.139 (16.6)
Jurisdictions per $1,000,000 expenditures, squared	.0186 (5.80)	.0138 (4.77)	.00534 (3.11)	.00687 (11.2)
Interquartile range, family income distribution	.0000465 (7.84)	.0000482 (9.00)	.0000245 (7.70)	−.00000175 (1.55)
Marginal federal income tax rate	−5.13 (1.88)	−3.49 (1.41)	−1.69 (1.16)	−2.23 (4.29)
Marginal federal income tax rate, squared	6.51 (1.66)	4.01 (1.13)	1.90 (.904)	3.01 (4.02)
Marginal state income tax rate	−10.7 (.878)	−11.0 (.999)	−9.70 (1.49)	−1.53 (.659)
Marginal state income tax rate, squared	76.8 (1.30)	66.0 (1.24)	75.2 (2.38)	6.68 (.594)
Percentage of adult population aged 25–44	−.705 (.775)	−.218 (.265)	−.423 (.869)	−.274 (1.58)
Percentage of adult population aged 61 or more	−.635 (.701)	−.234 (.286)	−.402 (.830)	−.263 (1.52)
Percentage in same house as 1975	−.0233 (.0782)	−.0859 (.319)	−.231 (1.45)	.346 (6.09)
Percentage in same county, different house as 1975	.637 (1.64)	.448 (1.28)	.440 (2.12)	.207 (2.80)
Percentage in rental units	−.150 (.527)	−.321 (1.25)	−.281 (1.84)	.347 (6.39)
Percentage structures built since 1975	.927 (2.39)	.607 (1.73)	.139 (.669)	.520 (7.02)
Included in an SMSA	−.0966 (2.25)	−.0902 (2.32)	−.0422 (1.83)	−.0165 (2.01)
Intercept	.735 (.786)	.246 (.291)	.599 (1.20)	.402 (2.25)
R^2	.125	.112	.0825	.305

Note: *t*-statistics are in parentheses. All equations have 3,039 degrees of freedom.

The effects of jurisdictions per $1,000,000 are again consistent with those predicted by the competitive model of fragmentation. In all four equations, linear coefficients for jurisdictions per $1,000,000 are negative, quadratic terms are negative, and all coefficients are significant at 1 percent. Minimum debt and expenditure income shares occur in the range of 9.6 to 10.1 governments per $1,000,000 expenditure.

Absolute jurisdiction counts have similar, but weaker effects. The linear coefficient on counts is always negative, significant at 1 percent for the change in long-term debt and total expenditures and at 10 percent for gross debt. Quadratic terms are all positive, but only that for the change in long-term debt is significant, at 10 percent. Accepting point estimates for both linear and quadratic effects, minimum debt and expenditure income shares occur in the approximate range of 250 to 330 governments per county.

As demonstrated in section 3.3, very few counties attain these income-share-minimizing levels of fragmentation. The coefficients on jurisdictions per 1,000 capita indicate that one reason for this failure may be that fragmentation at this level creates inefficiencies in public service production, as well as market efficiencies associated with competition. All linear coefficients for this measure are positive, all quadratic coefficients are negative, and all are significant at 1 percent. With respect to population served, local public debt and income shares are maximized in the range of 8.8 to 10.7 governments per 1,000 capita.[12] With a positive correlation between absolute jurisdiction numbers, county population, and absolute size of the local public sector, jurisdiction densities that minimize public sector income shares along the dimension of jurisdiction counts and market shares maximize them along the dimension of population served.

The results of tables 3.3, 3.4 and 3.5 are robust to many assumptions about local public finance. In particular, they do not depend upon counties of extreme size in the sample. The specifications in these tables produce identical results when applied to the subsample of counties with populations between one thousand and one million.[13]

However, equations calculated on the original sample, with separate measures of jurisdiction density for counties of greater than and less than 10,000 population, suggest that the effects of jurisdiction density may differ between small and large counties. Equations with single measures of jurisdiction density suggest, for example, that fragmentation reduces the income share of total government expenditures in only counties with populations which exceed 10,000.

Table 3.6 presents coefficients on jurisdiction measures from estimates of the specification of table 3.5, with interactions between all three jurisdiction measures and county size class. These coefficients indicate that effects in the two different county size classes are similar

Table 3.6   Coefficients for Jurisdiction Measures Interacted with County Population Size Class

Independent Variable	Gross County Debt	Net County Debt	Change, County Long-term Debt	Total County Expenditure
Counties with more than 10,000 population:				
Number of local jurisdictions in county	−.00212 (1.60)	−.00164 (1.37)	−.00160 (2.26)	−.000674 (2.69)
Number of local jurisdictions in county, squared	.00000358 (.924)	.00000283 (.808)	.00000315 (1.51)	.00000113 (1.54)
Jurisdictions per 1,000 capita	.743 (6.64)	.605 (5.99)	.117 (1.95)	.265 (12.5)
Jurisdictions per 1,000 capita, squared	−.102 (4.63)	−.0851 (4.28)	−.0194 (1.64)	−.0311 (7.43)
Jurisdictions per $1,000,000 expenditures	−.820 (7.70)	−.658 (6.84)	−.173 (3.03)	−.272 (13.4)
Jurisdictions per $1,000,000 expenditures, squared	.107 (5.01)	.0861 (4.46)	.0256 (2.23)	.0327 (8.07)
Counties with less than 10,000 population:				
Number of local jurisdictions in county	.00213 (.329)	.00548 (.937)	−.00277 (.795)	.000340 (.277)
Number of local jurisdictions in county, squared	−.0000483 (.551)	−.0000722 (.912)	.00000616 (.131)	−.0000134 (.806)
Jurisdictions per 1,000 capita	.221 (4.49)	.127 (2.85)	.0824 (3.11)	.119 (12.7)
Jurisdictions per 1,000 capita, squared	−.0110 (3.37)	−.00667 (2.26)	−.00423 (2.41)	−.00520 (8.37)
Jurisdictions per $1,000,000 expenditures	−.314 (6.51)	−.224 (5.15)	−.110 (4.23)	−.127 (13.9)
Jurisdictions per $1,000,000 expenditures, Squared	.0148 (4.36)	.0103 (3.34)	.00538 (2.94)	.00585 (9.06)
R^2	.131	.119	.0839	.317
F-tests and degrees of freedom for equality of effects across county population classes:				
Jurisdictions counts (2,3033)	.221 (.802)	.768 (.465)	.145 (.865)	.398 (.672)
Jurisdictions per 1,000 capita (2,3033)	10.6 (.0001)	10.8 (.0001)	1.26 (.283)	23.3 (.0001)
Juristicion per $1,000,000 expenditures (2,3033)	11.3 (.0001)	9.97 (.0001)	1.74 (.176)	25.7 (.0001)
All three measures of jurisdiction density (6,3033)	3.97 (.0006)	3.80 (.0009)	.740 (.617)	9.00 (.0001)

Note: t-statistics are in parentheses below coefficients. Significance levels are in parentheses below F-tests.

in direction and significance, but of significantly larger magnitude in counties with more than 10,000 residents. F-tests demonstrate that effects of jurisdictions per 1,000 capita and per $1,000,000 expenditure are significantly different across county population classes in all equations with the exception of that for changes in long-term debt. With this exception, effects of all three jurisdiction measures simultaneously differ significantly across classes as well. These results suggest that the interactions between jurisdictional structure and county size are a promising topic for further study.

The results of this section suggest that both fragmentation of market power and consolidation of service provision reduce local debt and expenditure income shares. Within states, holding constant population characteristics and the array of available local services, they suggest that the local public sector expands when governments command enough economic resources to confer some degree of monopoly power on their officials. It contracts when governments with large-scale efficiencies provide local public services.

3.5   Types of Jurisdictions and Aggregate County Public Finance

The results of the previous section describe the effects of jurisdiction numbers on income shares of local public sector debt, debt changes, and expenditures. As noted in section 3.2, local governments are of three types; general-purpose municipalities, single-purpose special districts, and single-purpose school districts. This section describes the differences and similarities between local government types in their effects on local public-sector income shares.

The equation specifications of table 3.3, with linear terms in jurisdiction counts, jurisdictions per 1,000 capita, and per $1,000,000 expenditures for all three jurisdiction types, estimate the effects of local government types on the size of the local public sector.[14] F-tests indicate that the effects of municipalities, special districts, and school districts, as counts or normalized by 1,000 capita or $1,000,000 expenditures, on gross debt, net debt, change in long-term debt, nonguaranteed debt, short-term debt, and fund holdings are statistically indistinguishable.[15]

These similarities imply that special districts are responsible for the recent explosion of nonguaranteed local public debt only through their numbers, and not through any special facility. Municipalities have been successful at issuing nonguaranteed debt on their own accounts, without the intervention of a special district. Furthermore, the recent growth of special districts has probably not increased total debt income shares by more than would have similar growth in municipalities.

However, F-tests in table 3.7 demonstrate that effects of jurisdiction types on guaranteed debt, fiscal-year changes in short-term debt, and

Table 3.7   Coefficients for Jurisdiction-Type Measures

Independent Variables	Guaranteed Debt	Change Short-Term Debt 1982 Fiscal Year	Total Expenditures
Cities and towns in county	− .000287 (.457)	.0000757 (1.80)	− .000803 (2.00)
Special districts in county	− .000308 (.693)	− .00000727 (.245)	− .000214 (.753)
School districts in county	− .000275 (.262)	− .0000492 (.701)	− .000485 (.723)
Cities and towns per 1,000 capita	.0650 (4.20)	.00399 (3.85)	.0968 (9.79)
Special districts per 1,000 capita	− .00956 (.635)	− .000649 (.645)	.0245 (2.55)
School districts per 1,000 capita	− .00688 (.282)	− .000392 (.241)	.0535 (3.44)
Cities and towns per $1,000,000 expenditures	− .0684 (4.09)	− −.00466 (4.17)	− .102 (9.51)
Special districts per $1,000,000 expenditures	.0245 (1.29)	.00184 (1.45)	− .0319 (2.63)
School districts per $1,000,000 expenditures	.0124 (.444)	.0000458 (.0245)	− .0662 (3.71)
R²	.108	.0688	.280
F-tests and degrees of freedom for:			
Equality between city and special district effects (3,3036)	3.45 (.0159)	4.08 (.0068)	7.43 (.0001)
Equality between city and school district effects (3,3036)	1.79 (.145)	2.19 (.0853)	2.01 (.109)
Equality between special and school district effects (3,3036)	.108 (.951)	.870 (.458)	.777 (.510)
Equality between city, special, and school district effects (6,3036)	1.95 (.0690)	2.38 (.0267)	3.91 (.0007)

Note: t-statistics are in parentheses below coefficients. Significance levels are in parentheses below F-tests. F-tests test for joint equality between coefficients for number of jurisdictions, jurisdictions per 1,000 capita, and jurisdictions per $1,000,000 across two or three jurisdiction types.

total expenditures differ at significant or near-significant levels.[16] Municipalities are entirely responsible for income shares of full-faith-and-credit debt and for fiscal-year changes in short-term debt. Total expenditures are equally sensitive to numbers of school and special districts, but significantly more sensitive to numbers of municipalities.

Table 3.7 presents the coefficients on jurisdiction counts, jurisdictions per 1,000 capita, and per $1,000,000 expenditures, by type of jurisdiction, from regression models for these three variables. t-statistics for coefficients in equations for guaranteed debt and changes in short term debt demonstrate that neither special nor school districts have any significant effects on either.[17] The effects of cities and towns are similar to the effects of total jurisdictions in table 3.5. Income shares of guaranteed debt increase with municipalities per 1,000 capita, and diminish with municipalities per $1,000,000 expenditures. Effects on changes in short-term debt are similar, with the addition of a positive effect of city numbers.

In contrast, municipalities, special districts, and school districts all have significant effects on the income share of total expenditures. Each type of government has effects similar to those of total jurisdictions in table 3.5. However, F-tests of equality across jurisdictions reject the hypotheses that effects of municipalities are equal to those of special or school districts. Coefficients for municipalities are nearly twice as large as those for school districts, and three times the size of those for special districts.

Where jurisdiction types differ in their effects on the size of the local public sector, the incentives presented by consolidation and fragmentation operate most strongly on general-purpose governments. They may be constitutionally more flexible, because their responsibility for multiple functions gives them an additional dimension along which to adjust to changes in local government structure. They may also be more sensitive to voters, if elections for single-purpose governments attract less voter interest than do municipal elections. Regardless of explanation, the income share of local public expenditures expands most when municipalities have large budgets, and diminshes most when they serve large populations. This is an additional topic which deserves further study.

3.6 Multiple Jurisdictions and City Finances

The previous sections demonstrate that the aggregates of local public debt and expenditures depend on the hierarchical structure of local government. This implies that debt and expenditures in individual jurisdictions should depend on the numbers of surrounding jurisdictions as well. This section presents a preliminary investigation of these spillover effects among cities with populations greater than 10,000. Despite differences in structure and in sample, debt and expenditure income-share regressions for cities yield results which are similar to those for county aggregates.

The *Census of Governments, 1982,* Finance Summary Statistics Tape File A, and the *Census of Population and Housing, 1980,* Summary Tape Files 1C and 3C, report complete data for 2,796 general-purpose governments,[18] each with populations greater than 10,000. Only 1,066 of the counties analyzed above contain cities of this size. The counties represented in this city sample are a subsample of the sample above, comprising, naturally, the biggest counties. The counties in which these cities are located contain, on average, approximately 31.8 cities and towns, 33.7 special districts, and 20.7 school districts.

In principle, comparisons of public finances across these cities are more difficult than across counties, because they should control for differences in service arrays across overlapping special districts, school districts, and counties as well as across the cities under study. The analysis here controls only for differences in the service arrays provided by the cities themselves. It consists of regression equations similar to those of tables 3.3 and 3.5, with city-specific population and housing measures, and various measures of city density within counties.

The regressions of table 3.8 include two measures of city density for each city, the numbers of large and small cities in the same county. Large cities are those in this sample; small cities are all cities not in this sample. The number of large cities is defined as the number of cities in this sample that are located in the same county. The number of small cities is the difference between the number of large cities and the total number of cities in that county.[19]

The debt and expenditure income-share regressions of table 3.8 yield results which are both similar to, and extensions of, those for county aggregates.[20] As with the number of jurisdictions in table 3.3, the number of small cities has negative effects on all debt measures and on total expenditures. These effects are significant at 5 percent for gross debt and total expenditures, at 10 percent for net debt and changes in long-term debt.

In contrast, the number of large cities has positive effects on all three debt measures, though no effect on expenditures. This result is not consistent with the purported advantages of either consolidation or fragmentation. It may well be attributable to uncontrolled differences in the services provided by other levels of local government.

Table 3.9 presents a regression specification similar to that of table 3.5. This specification includes linear and quadratic terms in cities per 1,000 county population and cities per $1,000,000 aggregate local public sector expenditures in the county, as well as counts of large and small

Table 3.8   **Equations for Municipality Debt and Total Expenditure Shares in Total Personal Income with Jurisdiction Counts**

Independent Variables	Gross City Debt	Net City Debt	Change, City Long-term Debt	Total City Expenditure
Number of large cities in county	.000982 (2.36)	.000686 (1.75)	.000490 (2.41)	.0000366 (.508)
Number of small cities in county	−.00101 (2.18)	−.000774 (1.78)	−.000405 (1.80)	−.000172 (2.14)
Interquartile range, family income distribution	.00000101 (.988)	.00000087 (.906)	.00000051 (1.02)	.00000001 (.0593)
Marginal federal income tax rate	1.39 (1.27)	.970 (.944)	.667 (1.25)	−.0969 (.512)
Marginal federal income tax rate, squared	−2.49 (1.82)	−1.87 (1.45)	−1.16 (1.74)	−.0434 (.183)
Marginal state income tax rate	5.49 (1.60)	7.31 (2.26)	2.54 (1.52)	1.32 (2.22)
Marginal state income tax rate, squared	−27.8 (1.53)	−34.0 (1.98)	−12.9 (1.45)	−8.99 (2.85)
Percentage of adult population aged 25–44	−.0884 (.455)	−.0667 (.365)	−.0133 (.140)	−.0555 (1.65)
Percentage of adult population aged 61 or more	−.205 (1.08)	−.168 (.939)	−.0604 (.653)	−.0526 (1.60)
Percentage in same house as 1975	.0576 (.596)	.0824 (.907)	.0170 (.362)	.0793 (4.74)
Percentage in same county, different house as 1975	−.0105 (.122)	−.00628 (.0780)	−.00953 (.228)	.0158 (1.07)
Percentage in rental units	.0482 (.691)	.0412 (.629)	.00471 (.139)	.0989 (8.20)
Percentage structures built since 1975	.229 (2.70)	.216 (2.72)	.0828 (2.00)	.0707 (4.82)
Included in an SMSA	−.00564 (.317)	−.00276 (.165)	.00338 (.389)	−.00823 (2.67)
Intercept	−.112 (.377)	−.138 (.496)	−.0849 (.589)	.0167 (.327)
R^2	.158	.143	.135	.657
Means of Dependent Variables	.0891	.0529	.0229	.0768

Note: *t*-statistics are in parentheses. All equations have 3,043 degrees of freedom.

cities. Coefficients for large and small city measures are similar to those in table 3.8.

Effects of other city density measures replicate the analogous effects in table 3.5. All linear and quadratic coefficients are significant, most at 1 percent and only one at 10 percent. Increasing the number of cities

Table 3.9   Equations for Municipality Debt and Total Expenditure Shares in Total Personal Income with Multiple Jurisdiction Measures

Independent Variables	Gross City Debt	Net City Debt	Change, City Long-term Debt	Total City Expenditure
Number of large cities in county	.000975 (2.22)	.000654 (1.58)	.000450 (2.09)	.0000715 (.954)
Number of small cities in county	−.00130 (2.73)	−.000987 (2.19)	−.000457 (1.95)	−.000294 (3.59)
Cities per 1,000 capita	1.56 (4.46)	1.22 (3.77)	.456 (2.66)	.534 (8.94)
Cities per 1,000 capita, squared	−1.38 (2.97)	−1.07 (2.46)	−.433 (1.91)	−.489 (6.16)
Cities per $1,000,000 expenditures	−1.64 (4.71)	−1.32 (4.02)	−.512 (3.00)	−.518 (8.70)
Cities per $1,000,000 expenditures, squared	1.57 (3.34)	1.29 (2.90)	.523 (2.27)	.483 (6.00)
Interquartile range, family income distribution	.0000011 (1.08)	.0000009 (.972)	.0000005 (1.03)	.00000006 (.331)
Marginal federal income tax rate	1.36 (1.24)	.950 (.926)	.663 (1.24)	−.115 (.618)
Marginal federal income tax rate, squared	−2.45 (1.80)	−1.86 (1.45)	−1.17 (1.76)	−.0124 (.0533)
Marginal state income tax rate	5.46 (1.58)	7.34 (2.26)	2.66 (1.57)	1.24 (2.11)
Marginal state income tax rate, squared	−27.2 (1.48)	−33.7 (1.95)	−13.4 (1.50)	−8.45 (2.70)
Percentage of adult population aged 25–44	−.0644 (.332)	−.0469 (.257)	−.00739 (.0779)	−.0486 (1.47)
Percentage of adult population aged 61 or more	−.190 (.999)	−.153 (.857)	−.0523 (.563)	−.0515 (1.59)
Percentage in same house as 1975	.0707 (.719)	.0907 (.980)	.0152 (.316)	.0871 (5.19)
Percentage in same county, different house as 1975	−.0304 (.353)	−.0236 (.291)	−.0182 (.434)	.0115 (.783)
Percentage in rental units	.0671 (.950)	.0543 (.817)	.00645 (.187)	.108 (8.93)
Percentage structures built since 1975	.230 (2.70)	.216 (2.70)	.0807 (1.94)	.0729 (5.02)
Included in an SMSA	−.00510 (.286)	−.00196 (.117)	.00361 (.414)	−.00839 (2.75)
Intercept	−.108 (.366)	−.133 (.480)	−.0788 (.545)	.0142 (.282)
R^2	.166	.149	.138	.668

Note: *t*-statistics are in parentheses. All equations have 3,043 degrees of freedom.

per capita in the county increases the share of individual city debt and expenditures in the income of its residents at a diminishing rate. Increasing the number of cities per local government expenditure reduces the income share of city debt and expenditures at a diminishing rate.

These results reaffirm the simultaneous advantages of fragmentation and consolidation. The income shares of city finances increase with reductions in the population served, and fall with reductions in city market share. However, they also suggest that spillovers among large cities involve other considerations as well. These spillovers, which may also occur among counties, merit further investigation.

3.7   Conclusion

The recent scholarly literature on jurisdiction numbers has been predominantly hostile towards consolidation and to consolidationist advocacy. This attitude is unfair for two reasons. First, the advocates of consolidation have become relatively inactive. They were most active and influential at a time when school districts were far more numerous, and their position was correspondingly more persuasive.

Second, empirical demonstrations, in selected samples, of the advantages of competitive local governments have not allowed for the possibility that large-scale production and distribution may also be advantageous. The results here demonstrate that, across all counties in the country, jurisdiction numbers have negative effects on size of the local public sector when model specifications do not allow for simultaneous measures of competition and efficiency. These results suggest that, when they do, both the restraining influence of competition among jurisdictions, and the efficiencies of scale play a role in reducing the shares of local government debt and expenditures in aggregate income.

Debt and expenditures are minimized by simultaneously reducing jurisdiction market shares and expanding jurisdiction coverage. A system which depends wholly on general-purpose governments cannot exploit both mechanisms. Fragmentation means more competition and more redundancy, consolidation means more efficiency and more monopoly power.

Though numbers of single-purpose governments have smaller effects on expenditures than do numbers of municipalities, single-purpose governments may still play an important role in minimizing the size of the local public sector. If they are constructed to serve large, though not monopoly, shares of county population, and assigned only small fractions of total government activity, they may at once achieve both efficiency and competition. A complex system of local government which relies on them, judiciously, may provide local public services at less current and future expense than can the simple systems of either consolidation or fragmentation.

Notes

1. Curiously, authors in this tradition perceive it to be the position of a distinct minority. Wagner and Weber (1975), Martin and McKenzie (1975), and Wikstrom (1978) are examples.

2. The *Census of Population, 1980* identifies 3,137. The *Census of Governments, 1982* identifies 3,132. The intersection between these two data sets contains 3,131 county-level governments. Among these are Washington, D.C. and New York City, whose government structures are unique. Omitting them, the sample for this paper is composed of 3,129 counties. For brevity, this paper refers to individual county-level governments as "counties," though a few are legally boroughs, townships, or independent cities.

3. County populations vary widely. The *Census of Population, 1980* reports that 25 counties had fewer than 1,000 inhabitants in 1980. Loving County, Texas, had only 91. At the same time, 25 counties had more than 1,000,000 inhabitants. Los Angeles, with 7,477,503 was the most populous.

4. Gordon and Slemrod (1986) and Mieszkowski (1986) agree that debt is appropriate finance for municipal activities only if municipal debt presents favorable opportunities for arbitrage, relative to combinations of tax financing and private debt. Nevertheless, the structure and number of jurisdictions may affect debt levels. Directly, fragmentation may create homogeneous districts in which electorates are uniform in their preferencs with regard to arbitrage opportunities. This effect may imply either higher or lower debt levels. Under consolidation, monopolizing bureaucrats may take advantage of the opportunities at all margins to enlarge government size. They may therefore issue debt beyond the limits imposed by profitable arbitration.

5. The *Census of Governments, 1982* surveys 31 government functions. Nine functions occur in at least 99 percent of all counties. In the regression equations below, these functions are not represented by explicit dummy variables. Instead, their effects are captured in the intercept term.

6. The *Census of Population and Housing, 1980.* Summary Tape Files 1C and 3C provide the measures of population characteristics, housing characteristics and the SMSA dummy used in this model. The *Census of Governments, 1982,* Finance Summary Statistics Tape File B is the source for the function dummies, the debt and expenditure statistics used here. Tape File A is the source for the jurisdiction counts.

The specific representation of marginal tax rates here differs from that in Gordon and Slemrod. The equations below include linear and quadratic terms in both marginal federal and marginal state income tax rates. Tax Foundation's *Facts and Figures on Government Finance, 1983* is the source for 1982 federal rates. State rates are a linear interpolation of 1982 rates given in Feenberg and Rosen (1986). Rate values are estimated as the marginal rates applicable to median family incomes by county, as reported in the *Census of Population and Housing, 1980.*

7. The Borcherding/Deacon and Bergstrom/Goodman models are linear in logarithms, with expenditures as the dependent variable, and population and

income among the independent variables. Here, population and income appear in the denominator of the dependent expenditure measure. Logarithmic expenditure equations for this sample of counties yield standard values for parameter estimates.

Borcherding/Deacon and Bergstrom/Goodman measure tax-share as the percentage of total property taxes attributable to estimated property taxes on homes of median value. They choose the property tax measure because property taxes constitute more than half of own-source revenue in 1962, the year from which their data are drawn. As they recognize, assumptions that the median voter has median income, and that the median income person owns a home of median value, effectively make their tax-share variable a function of income. In the expenditure models below, tax-share is an explicit function of income. In 1982, all taxes constitute only 49 percent of local government own-source revenue.

8. These regressions include only county-level governments in both the 1977 and 1982 *Census of Government,* with nonzero counts for the relevant government type: 3,108 for cities, 1,169 for towns, 2,843 for special districts, and 3,108 for school districts. Regressions that include all 3,108 available counties achieve identical results. Complete results are available from the author.

9. The performance of these debt equations is similar to those in Gordon and Slemrod (1986), although of lower explanatory power. However, they do not replicate the effects of income taxation on gross and net debt. Both federal and state marginal income tax rates are insignificant in these equations. Federal rates have strongly significant coefficients, and effects similar to those in Gordon and Slemrod, if the specification here omits the interquartile range of the family income distribution. This comparison suggests that the effects estimated by Gordon and Slemrod may be partially attributable to uncontrolled heterogeneity in population demands for public services. State marginal tax rates often have significant effects, similar to those of federal rates, in equations which omit state dummies.

10. Sjoquist (1982) reports a similar negative relationship between jurisdiction numbers and 1972 per capita expenditures for 48 SMSA's in the south, using a logarithmic specification which omits controls for state, function, and population characteristics.

11. Coefficients for the other explanatory variables are virtually invariant to different jurisdiction measures. In the expenditure equation, total expenditures are the denominator of the jurisdictions per $1,000,000 expenditures variable on the right hand side of the equation, as well as the numerator in the dependent variable. Therefore, this equation should be taken as illustrative rather than conclusive. This problem is analogous to that confronting regressions of rates of return on market shares. Jurisdictions measured relative to lagged total expenditures would probably yield similar results.

12. Schneider (1986) reports a contrary result; suburban governments per 100,000 SMSA population have a significant negative linear effect on total 1977 expenditures and 1972 expenditures for common functions. His sample is 757 suburban municipalities in only 46 SMSA's. He uses a linear specification which omits both state and function dummies.

13. The complete equations discussed in this and the next two paragraphs are available from the author.

14. These equations disaggregate the jurisdiction measures of tables 3.3 through 3.6. They omit quadratic terms for the different types of local government in order to simplify comparisons.

15. These equations are available from the author.

16. These tests are weakened by the inclusion of coefficients for jurisdiction counts. They reject equality across the three government types with much greater significance for jurisdictions per 1,000 capita and per $1,000,000.

17. Special districts may be legally prohibited from issuing guaranteed debt.

18. General-purpose governments are, for this analysis, all municipalities and towns in the eleven "strong-township" states (ACIR 1982). For convenience, they are referred to as cities in the rest of this section.

19. Quadratic terms in these variables are omitted because they are invariably insignificant.

20. Function and state dummies contribute substantially more explanatory power in city than in county regressions. In consequence, debt equations for cities have similar explanatory power to those for counties, though population variables appear less significant. Expenditure equations for cities attain substantially higher R^2s than those for counties.

References

ACIR. 1975. *State legislative program.* Vol. 2, *Local government modernization.* Report M-93, Washington, D.C.: U.S. Government Printing Office.

ACIR. 1982. *State and local roles in the federal system.* Report A-88. Washington, D.C.: U.S. Government Printing Office.

Bergstrom, Theodore C., and Robert P. Goodman. 1973. Private demands for public goods. *American Economic Review* 63, no. 3: 280–96.

Borcherding, Thomas E., and Robert T. Deacon. 1972. The demand for the services of nonfederal governments. *American Economic Review* 62, no. 5: 891–901.

Copeland, Morris A. 1961. *Trends in government financing.* Princeton: National Bureau of Economic Research and Princeton University Press.

DiLorenzo, Thomas J. 1982. Utility profits, fiscal illusion, and local public expenditures. *Public Choice* 38, no. 3: 243–52.

Epple, Dennis, and Chester Spatt. 1986. State restrictions on local debt: Their role in preventing default. *Journal of Public Economics* 29, no. 2: 199–221.

Epple, Dennis, and Allan Zelenitz. 1981. The implications of competition among jurisdictions: Does tiebout need politics? *Journal of Political Economy* 89, no. 6: 1197–1217.

Feenberg, Daniel R., and Harvey S. Rosen. 1986. State personal income and sales taxes, 1977–1983. In *Studies in state and local public finance,* ed. Harvey S. Rosen. Chicago: National Bureau of Economic Research and The University of Chicago Press.

Gordon, Roger H., and Joel Slemrod. 1986. An empirical examination of municipal financial policy. In *Studies in state and local public finance,* ed. Harvey S. Rosen. Chicago: National Bureau of Economic Research and The University of Chicago Press.

McKenzie, Richard B., and Robert J. Staaf. 1978. Revenue sharing and monopoly government. *Public Choice* 33, no. 3: 93–97.

Martin, Dolores T., and Richard B. McKenzie. 1975. Bureaucratic profits, migration costs, and the consolidation of local government. *Public Choice* 23 (Fall): 95–100.

Martin, Dolores T., and Richard E. Wagner. 1978. The institutional framework for municipal incorporation: An economic analysis of local agency formation commissions in California. *Journal of Law and Economics* 21, no. 2: 409–26.

Mehay, Stephen L. 1981. The expenditure effects of municipal annexation." *Public Choice* 36, no. 1: 53–62.

―――. 1984. The effect of governmental structure on special district expenditures. *Public Choice* 44, no. 2 339–48.

Mieszkowski, Peter. 1986. Comment: An Empirical Examination of Municipal Financial Policy. In *Studies in state and local public finance,* ed. Harvey S. Rosen. Chicago: National Bureau of Economic Research and The University of Chicago Press.

Mullen, John K. 1980. The role of income in explaining state-local fiscal decentralization. *Public Finance* 35, no. 2: 300–308.

Niskanen, William A. 1975. Bureaucrats and politicans. *Journal of Law and Economics* 18, no. 3: 617–43.

Reschovsky, Andrew. 1980. An evaluation of metropolitan area tax base sharing. *National Tax Journal* 33, no. 1: 55–66.

Rothenberg, Jerome. 1975. Comment: Competition, monopoly, and the organization of government in metropolitan areas. *Journal of Law and Economics* 18, no. 3: 685–90.

Schneider, Mark. 1986. Fragmentation and the growth of local government. *Public Choice* 48, no. 3: 255–63.

Sjoquist, David L. 1982. The effect of the number of local governments on central city expenditures. *National Tax Journal* 35, no. 1: 79–88.

Tax Foundation, Inc. 1983. *Facts and figures on government finance, 1983.* Washington, D.C.: Tax Foundation.

Tiebout, Charles M. 1956. A pure theory of local expenditures. *Journal of Political Economy* 64, no. 5: 416–24.

U.S. Bureau of the Census. 1981. *Census of population and housing, 1980.* Washington, D.C.: U.S. Government Printing Office.

U.S. Bureau of the Census. 1984. *Census of governments, 1982.* Washington, D.C.: U.S. Government Printing Office.

Wagner, Richard E. 1976. Revenue structure, fiscal illusion, and budgetary choice. *Public Choice* 25 (Spring): 45–61.

Wagner, Richard E., and Warren E. Weber. 1975. Competition, monopoly, and the organization of government in metropolitan areas. *Journal of Law and Economics* 18, no. 3: 661–84.

Wikstrom, Nelson. 1978. A reassessment: Metropolitan governmental consolidation. *Growth and Change* 9, no. 1: 2–7.

Comment   Alan J. Auerbach

An important, if overlooked, aspect of fiscal federalism is the impact of local government structure on the level and pattern of local public spending. Jeffrey Zax seeks to improve our understanding in this area by estimating the impact of different measures of jurisdictional fragmentation on the nature of government behavior. Zax's basic unit of

Alan J. Auerbach is a professor of economics at the University of Pennsylvania and a research associate of the National Bureau of Economic Research.

observation is the county, and he tests his hypotheses on a sample that includes essentially every county in the United States, over 3,000 of them in all.

Perhaps the first interesting fact revealed in his analysis is the heterogeneity of the sample. Twenty-five counties had fewer than 1,000 inhabitants in 1980, while the same number of counties had over 1 million people living in them. This leads to my first comment about the paper's logic. In some types of empirical analysis, the unit of measurement is fairly obvious or at least subject to a fairly narrow range of choices. For example, if we were estimating labor supply functions we might choose to concentrate on the family or the individual, and if we were looking at investment behavior we would wish to look at the firm. But what is the appropriate unit of measurement for a study of the effects of governmental fragmentation?

What Zax appears to have in mind is a jurisdiction that is small enough for a type of Tiebout sorting to occur, but still large enough to have lower levels of government within it. But it is not clear that the designation "county" has a very clear or consistent meaning throughout the sample. One would not expect the 91 people in Loving County, Texas, to organize their lower levels of government to achieve the same objectives as the voters of Cook County, Illinois, whose number exceeds 5 million even without the inclusion of the deceased. This also highlights an econometric problem which the paper partially addresses: should these extreme observations be weighted equally, as they currently are, or should some account be taken of their very large size differences. At present, anomalous behavior of a few small governments could lead to estimates that would offer a poor description of the behavior of county governments representing most citizens. Even though the results are reported not to change when very small (population below 1,000) and very large (population above 1 million) counties are omitted, I would have found a comparison of weighted (by size of county) and unweighted regressions informative.

Let me turn now to the theory that underlies the paper. If one were designing a local jurisdictional structure within a county, one would face offsetting costs and benefits of the sort commonly encountered in questions of local public goods provision. On the one hand, the larger the number of governments, the greater their ability to respond to differences in tastes among constituents. On the other hand, such small governments might also face greater costs if their level of operation were below the minimum efficient scale. To this familiar trade-off between the satisfaction of heterogeneous tastes and the efficiency of provision, Zax adds the question of competition, arguing that counties with fewer jurisdictions, per some measure of county size, will lead to greater market power and poorer performance.

While one might attempt to characterize the optimal structure of government in such a model, Zax takes governmental structure as exogenous and instead estimates the impact of such structural variations on public expenditure and debt levels. Because he has not modeled the optimal behavior of governments, I am somewhat confused by the normative terminology he uses in describing his empirical findings. In section 3.1, for example, he equates the minimization of debt and expenditure with superior performance. Since most citizens would desire some positive levels of public spending on education, police, and fire protection, even if provided by inefficient and oligopolistic governments, Zax's comments suggest the view that government is inherently biased toward the overprovision of public goods.

The assumption of exogenous government structure is also a problem when one attempts to interpret the empirical results. For simultaneity bias to be avoided, it is necessary that the variations in governmental structure be independent of the population characteristics. Generally, however, one might expect that counties inhabited by people with a strong taste for public goods might find it sensible to establish more governments per capita in order to supply these goods. This would predict a positive sign if one regressed expenditures on the number of jurisdictions per capita, as Zax indeed finds empirically in the last column of table 3.4, without in any way suggesting inefficiency in the scale of governmental operation, which is the interpretation Zax gives to this result. Zax supports the exogeneity assumption with evidence that jurisdiction counts in 1982 are almost perfectly predictable using 1977 counts alone. If, however, local taste differences are a long-run phenomenon, there may still be a problem of simultaneity bias. I believe this may be a serious problem, but will say no more about it.

Let me turn now to the empirical relations that Zax estimates. There are many results reported, so I must be selective in my comments. He constructs a number of measures of each county's local government characteristics, and includes these along with other demographic variables in cross-sectional regressions to explain the ratios of aggregate government debt and public expenditures to total personal income in the county. I will focus on the equations that explain variations in expenditures, because I am less sure how to interpret the equations for government debt in the context of Zax's model.

There are several variables constructed to characterize government fragmentation. These include the number of all local jurisdictions and different types of such jurisdictions (such as cities and towns and school districts) per county, per thousand residents, and per million dollars of public expenditures, as well as the number of jurisdictions per square mile. Let me first summarize Zax's findings concerning these variables.

In table 3.3, the number of local jurisdictions per county is found over most of the relevant range (the variable also enters in quadratic form so that the overall effect decreases and eventually switches sign with the variable's size) to have a significantly negative effect on expenditures per dollar of income, which Zax interprets as showing that fragmentation leads to competitive behavior. In table 3.4, we find that the number of jurisdictions per capita increases total expenditures while the number of jurisdictions per dollar of expenditure decreases expenditures, which are interpreted as showing that governments with small constituencies are inefficient but that governments with small budgets behave competitively. I see several difficulties with these interpretations.

First of all, why should population be a better measure of scale of operations than budget size? Second, why put one measure of fragmentation in table 3.3 and the others in table 3.4, if all are supposed to matter? Third, since government expenditures enter in the numerator of the dependent variable and the denominator of one of the explanatory variables, one would expect a negative sign on this variable even if jurisdictional structure were totally irrelevant to the determination of public spending levels. Finally, increased inefficiency would lead to higher spending levels only if the price elasticity of demand for the public goods is less than one in absolute value. Likewise, though a less competitive government might increase the price of government services, one might expect total expenditure on public goods to decline; a monopolist, for example, restricts output to the point at which marginal revenue equals a positive marginal cost.

In table 3.7, Zax divides the local jurisdictions into cities and towns, special districts, and school districts and repeats the analysis of table 3.4. He finds the same signs as before for each of the three types of jurisdictions: that the number of jurisdictions per capita increases expenditures while the number per dollar of expenditure decreases expenditures. It is interesting, howver, that the effects are much larger for cities and towns than for the other two measures. Zax does not really come up with a convincing explanation for this finding. I don't have one, either, but would suggest a closer examination of the pattern and frequency of these different forms of government in different parts of the country. My guess is that there is considerable variation in the use of special districts across different parts of the country and according to population density.

There are many other interesting results in this paper. I think that Jeffrey Zax has attacked a very complicated and difficult question. Many of the problems I have suggested are really a necessary byproduct of the decision to undertake such an ambitious task. Nevertheless, I think a tighter theoretical foundation and greater attention to certain econometric difficulties could yield substantial returns in helping us understand the full implications of these interesting and suggestive results.

4 Tax Deductibility and Municipal Budget Structure

Douglas Holtz-Eakin and Harvey S. Rosen

4.1 Introduction

Historically, federal tax law has allowed itemizers to deduct state and local property, income, and general sales taxes on their personal income tax returns. This provision is estimated to have decreased federal tax revenues by about $30.8 billion in 1985. (Executive Office of the President 1986, G-42). The last several years have witnessed a serious public debate about the merits of partially or totally eliminating state and local tax deductibility. The U.S. Treasury recommended complete abolition of deductibility in 1984, as did President Reagan in 1985.[1] The Tax Reform Act of 1986 disallowed state sales tax deductions, but continued those for income and property taxes. More changes in the tax code are likely in the next few years, and state and local tax deductibility is likely to remain a controversial issue.

Those who favor deductibility argue that its elimination would have a disastrous impact on state and local public finance.[2] In this view, if people cannot deduct state and local taxes on their federal tax returns, then state and local government goods and services in effect become more expensive, and the demand for them declines. State and local public officials appear to believe this scenario. When the United States Conference of Mayors convened in 1985, the *New York Times* reported

Douglas Holtz-Eakin is assistant professor of economics at Columbia University and a research economist at the National Bureau of Economic Research. Harvey S. Rosen is professor of economics at Princeton University and a research associate at the National Bureau of Economic Research.

We have received useful comments from participants at seminars at SUNY Stony Brook and the University of Maryland. We are grateful to Ronald Fisher for his suggestions, to Dan Edelstein for assistance with the computations, and to NSF Grant No. SES-8419238 for financial support. This study is part of the National Bureau of Economic Research Project in State and Local Government Finance.

that the meeting "ended with an unusual display of bipartisan unanimity: only one 'no' vote was audible on a resolution urging Congress to amend the [president's] tax plan to keep deductibility of state and local taxes."[3]

This very simple story about the impact of deductibility ignores the fact that subfederal governments have access to nondeductible sources of revenue, such as user charges, license fees, special assessments, etc. It could be that eliminating deductibility would lead only to the substitution of nondeductible for deductible revenue sources, and have no impact on spending. However, econometric studies by Inman (1985), Hettich and Winer (1984), and Noto and Zimmerman (1984) find that a jurisdiction's choice of revenue instruments is not responsive to its "tax price": the effective cost of a dollar of expenditure taking into account federal deductibility. Recently, Feldstein and Metcalf (1986) challenged this result, arguing that these studies employed inappropriate data, incorrect tax price measures, and/or inconsistent econometric techniques. Their examination of 1980 data suggested that if deductibility were removed (1) state and local use of deductible taxes would decline, (2) use of other revenue sources would increase, and (3) net expenditures from local funds would stay about the same. Moreover, because some of the revenue sources that are nondeductible to individuals *are* deductible to businesses, eliminating deductibility on personal tax returns would not increase federal revenues as much as one would expect if one ignored revenue instrument substitution effects. Indeed, federal tax collections might even decrease. Unfortunately, the regression coefficients which form the basis for all these conclusions are estimated imprecisely in the sense that the coefficients are small relative to their standard errors.

At the moment, then, economists' understanding of the empirical impact of deductibility seems to be a bit murky. In this paper we present new evidence based on a rich set of data which tracks the fiscal behavior of 172 local governments from 1978 to 1980. Our goal is to find the effects of deductibility on the mix between deductible and nondeductible revenue sources, and on expenditures. The use of panel data allows us to control for the existence of "individual effects" in our equations for the various fiscal spending decisions, and hence to obtain more convincing estimates of the effects of deductibility. Our main findings are that (1) the elasticity of deductible taxes with respect to their tax price is in the range of -1.2 to -1.6; (2) the tax price has no statistically significant effect on the use of nondeductible revenue sources; and (3) the elasticity of local expenditures with respect to the tax price is about -1.8.

The estimating models are specified in section 4.2. Section 4.3 describes the data. Section 4.4 discusses the econometric issues and presents the results. Section 4.5 concludes with a summary.

4.2 The Model

4.2.1. Preliminaries

Analysis of the effects of deductibility on community decision making is complicated by the fact that it leads to different voters having different effective prices for local public spending. For a nonitemizer, the effective price of a dollar of local spending is just a dollar. For an itemizer, the effective price is one minus the marginal tax rate, and among itemizers, marginal tax rates differ across people. Which tax price is relevant for understanding community decisions?

One possible approach is to appeal to the median voter model, and argue that the median of the community's tax prices is the relevant figure. However, the person with the median tax price is not necessarily the person with the median demand for public goods. More fundamentally, the median voter model has a number of well-known deficiencies—it ignores such potentially important effects on fiscal decisions as logrolling, coalition formation, and bureaucratic power. (See Inman forthcoming.)

In the absence of a generally accepted model of community decision making to serve as a framework for our analysis, some sensible and convenient ad hoc formulation is required. We follow Feldstein and Metcalf and assume that the community's decision depends upon its average tax price. That is, if the average marginal federal tax rate for itemizers is τ and the proportion of itemizers is m, then we assume that the price that is relevant for community decision making is $(1 - m)1 + m(1 - \tau)$.[4]

4.2.2 Estimating Equations

The Basic Model

Our goal is to estimate the impact of the tax price on a community's deductible taxes per capita (T_D), nondeductible own sources of revenue per capita (T_N), and expenditures per capita, (E). Earlier empirical work suggests that each of these variables will depend upon the community's tax price (P), family income (Y), and other economic and demographic variables that might affect the community's budget constraint and/or preferences (a k-dimensional vector $\mathbf{X}$). Employing the convenient constant elasticity specification, the estimating equation for (say) T_D is

$$(1) \quad \ln T_{Dit} = \alpha_0 + \alpha_1 \ln P_{it} + \alpha_2 \ln Y_{it} + \sum_{j=1}^{k} \alpha_{2+j} \mathbf{X}_{jit} + f_i + \mu_{it},$$

where i indexes communities, t indexes years, the α's are parameters, μ_{it} is a random error term, and f_i is an "individual effect" for community i—a composite of those characteristics of the community that affect its fiscal decisions and do not change over time. (Examples might be "political make-up," climate, etc.)[5] Importantly, it is quite likely that f_i is correlated with the right-hand-side variables, with the result that an *OLS* regression leads to inconsistent estimates of the parameters. The equations for $\ln T_{Nit}$ and $\ln E_{it}$ take the same form.

In order to estimate equation (4.1), take first differences in order to eliminate f_i:

$$(2) \qquad \ln T_{Dit} - \ln T_{Dit-1} = \alpha_1(\ln P_{it} - \ln P_{it-1})$$

$$+ \alpha_2(\ln Y_{it} - \ln Y_{it-1}) + \sum_{j=1}^{k} \alpha_{2+j}(\mathbf{X}_{jit} - \mathbf{X}_{jit-1})$$

$$+ (\mu_{it} - \mu_{it-1}).$$

Again, the equations for $(\ln T_{Nit} - \ln T_{Nit-1})$ and $(\ln E_{it} - \ln E_{it-1})$ take the same form.

The first problem one faces in implementing this framework is construction of the average tax price. It would clearly be desirable to compute P separately for each community on the basis of its taxable income. However, data limitations make it difficult to do this in a convincing way.[6] Instead, we form P using data for the state in which the community is located. Specifically, denote by P_{it}^s the statewide average tax price of the state in which community i is located. Suppose that the discrepancy between P_{it}^s and P_{it} depends on the differences between the community's values of certain variables and their statewide counterparts. For example, if a community's income exceeds state income, we expect that its tax price will be lower, *ceteris paribus*. Similarly, a community with a homeownership rate higher than the state average will have a lower tax price, *ceteris paribus*. Suppose that we denote all variables that affect the tax price in this way by an *n*-dimensional vector $\mathbf{z}$. Then we can write

$$(3) \qquad \ln P_{it} = \ln P_{it}^s + \sum_{j=i}^{n} \gamma j \, (\mathbf{z}_{jit} - \mathbf{z}_{jit}^s) + g_i,$$

where the superscript s indicates a statewide value, and g_i is an individual effect.

Recall now that our basic estimating equation is in first differences. Therefore, when $(\mathbf{z}_{jit} - \mathbf{z}_{jit}^s)$ does not change much over time, its effect on the tax price can be ignored. This is likely to be true of most candidates for inclusion in the $\mathbf{z}$ vector. For example, one does not expect the difference between a community's proportion of homeowners and the statewide average to change much from year to year. We assume that income is the only variable in the $\mathbf{z}$ vector for which the difference between state and community values might change substantially over time. Under this condition, taking first differences of equation (3) yields

(4) $\ln P_{it} - \ln P_{it-1} = (\ln P_{it}^s - \ln P_{it-1}^s)$

$+ \gamma_1 \times [\ln Y_{it} - \ln Y_{it}^s) - (\ln Y_{it-1} - \ln Y_{it-1}^s)],$

where Y_{it}^s is per capita income in community i's state during year t. Provided that the tax price goes down as income goes up, we expect $\gamma_1 < 0$. Substituting into equation (2) gives us

(5) $\ln T_{Dit} - \ln T_{Dit-1} = \alpha_1(\ln P_{it}^s - \ln P_{it-1}^s) + (\alpha_2 + \alpha_1\gamma_1)$

$\times (\ln Y_{it} - \ln Y_{it-1}) + \sum_{j=1}^{k} \alpha_{2+j}(\mathbf{X}_{jit} - \mathbf{X}_{jit-1})$

$- \alpha_1\gamma_1(\ln Y_{it}^s - \ln Y_{it-1}^s) + (\mu_{it} - \mu_{it-1}).$

The same logic can be applied to the estimating equations for ($\ln T_{Nit} - \ln T_{Nit-1}$) and ($\ln E_t - \ln E_{t-1}$).

In short, our use of the state tax price to "proxy" for the community tax price requires that we include state income on the right side of each equation. In doing so, notice that each of the three equations—$\ln T_D$, $\ln T_N$, $\ln E$—incorporates equation (4). As a result, the system of equations is subject to a nonlinear constraint: the ratio of the coefficient on (the change in) state income to the coefficient on (the change in) the tax price is identical in all three equations. In the empirical work below, we test this constraint as a check on our specification of the estimating equations.

Another issue related to P_{it} is its possible endogeneity. Imagine that community i has an unexpectedly high preference for using deductible sources of revenue, i.e., a positive μ_{it}. This positive μ_{it} will be associated with a relatively high propensity to itemize in community i, and, conditional on itemizing, with a relatively low federal marginal tax rate. Both of these tendencies will affect the value of P_{it}. Hence, there is probably some correlation between P_{it} and μ_{it}. When estimating the parameters from a single cross section of data, this may be quite a serious problem. However, its severity is likely to be attenuated in an individual-effects model. This is because the presence of f_i in (1) better controls for the unobserved preferences determining the left-hand-side variables. Still, some correlation between the price variable and the error term may remain, so we employ an instrumental variables estimation technique, as described below.

We now turn to the variables in the **X**-vector. These include:

SHARE = state government spending as a percentage of the state and local total for that state

GRANTS = sum of federal and state grants, per capita

ASSETS = per capita market value at the beginning of the fiscal year of holdings of federal securities, mortgages, bonds, cash, sinking funds, bond funds, etc.

DEBTS = market value of outstanding long and short-term debt per capita

POP = population

The inclusion of most of these variables is routine, but a few require some comment. The presence of the *SHARE* variable is in response to the fact that states differ in the division of taxing and expenditure decisions between states and communities. *SHARE* is a simple way, suggested by Oates (1975), of controlling for such institutional differences. The *ASSETS* and *DEBTS* variables are present to allow for intertemporal aspects of community decision making. Communities can finance current expenditures by drawing down their assets or by borrowing, even though these activities are sometimes subject to institutional constraints.

Alternative Specifications.

We also consider a number of departures from the basic model. The purposes of analyzing these variants are to assess the robustness of our results, and to facilitate comparisons with earlier work.

First, we estimated a group of regressions leaving out the *ASSETS, GRANTS,* and *DEBTS* variables from the right-hand side. Feldstein and Metcalf excluded these variables from their models. Doing likewise can help us determine whether discrepancies between our substantive results and theirs depends on this difference in specification.

A second set of variations is suggested by the fact that most of the earlier work on the impact of deductibility on local public finance has used single cross sections rather than panel data. Our individual effects model analyzes the *changes* in budget structure in response to *changes* in the tax price. This corresponds more closely to the proposed policy intervention than cross-community variation. Nevertheless, it is interesting to compare the results when the same data are used to estimate both an individual effects model and a series of cross-sectional models. Of course, in cross-sectional models one must include slow changing factors that are differenced out of the individual effects specification. Accordingly, we augment the **X** vector with a number of such variables:

PUPILS = individuals aged 3 and older enrolled in school, per capita
POOR = individuals below the poverty line, per capita
OLD = individuals aged 65 and above, per capita
OWN = proportion of occupied housing units that are owner occupied
NONWHITE = proportion of population that is not white
PCT810, PCT1015, PCT1525, PCT25 = proportion of families with incomes in the ranges $8,000–$9,999; $10,000–$14,999; $15,000–$24,999; and above $25,000, respectively

4.2.3   Localities vs. States as Observations

In all the models we estimate, the observations are individual localities. In contrast, Feldstein and Metcalf employ state and local totals by state.[7] Thus, while one of our observations is Bridgeport, Connecticut, they would use the sum of all communities in Connecticut plus the state government itself. Feldstein and Metcalf argue emphatically that analyzing community budgets is not a good way to learn about the effects of deductibility. They note that the division of taxing and spending responsibilities between state and local governments varies enormously among the states. Moreover, some communities are under institutional constraints with respect to the kind of tax instruments they can employ. Finally, they observe that it is virtually impossible to get good tax price data on a community level.

It seems to us that Feldstein and Metcalf overstate their case. To be sure, some communities may be legally constrained in their choice of tax instruments, but within these constraints, there may be scope for choice between deductible and nondeductible revenue sources. In any case, to the extent that these constraints can be viewed as individual effects, our econometric procedure controls for them. Similarly, we can control at least crudely for across state differences in the state-local division of responsibilities by including our *SHARE* variable, the share of state expenditures in the state and local total.

As noted above, we agree with Feldstein and Metcalf that the inability to compute a tax price for each community is a major problem. However, their procedure does not really solve this problem; in effect they circumvent it by assuming that the state and all localities make their decisions on the basis of the statewide average tax price. This does not seem too much different from our procedure of approximating the community tax price as the state tax price plus a correction factor.

Lest this all sound too defensive, we should emphasize that there are several real advantages to using local data. First, communities and states do not act in concert to set state and local totals; rather, the totals are the aggregate of each jurisdiction's decisions. What one gets by lumping all communities together and then combining them with the state government is unclear. In short, the underlying model purports to describe the behavior of decision-making units; these units are the jurisdictions themselves. A second advantage of using local data is that there are a lot of communities, and they differ substantially in their fiscal practices. As an econometric matter, greater sample size and variation are aids to obtaining precise parameter estimates.

We conclude that neither type of data is obviously superior. They both have advantages and disadvantages. We view analyses of the two types of data as complementary—each can shed light on the problem.

4.3 Data

Our budgetary data[8] are drawn from the *Census of Governments* for 1977 and the *Annual Survey of Governments* for 1976 and 1978–1980. A random sample of municipal governments was selected from the data tape for 1979 (the year with the least coverage), and these same governments were selected for the remaining years when possible.[9] There was usable information on 172 municipal governments.

In each year the record for each government contains information on revenues, expenditures, assets, debts, and grant receipts. Par values of all outstanding debt and holdings of financial assets are converted to market values using the indices provided by Eisner and Pieper (1984). Finally, budgetary variables are converted to real dollars using a region-specific CPI and then deflated to per capita terms.

We divide real per capita revenues into deductible taxes and non-deductible revenues. The former is composed of (with means in parentheses) property taxes ($281.76), sales taxes ($12.62), and income taxes ($3.69). Clearly the property tax is dominant. Indeed, of the 172 governments in the sample, only 39 used a general sales tax, 37 used a selective sales tax, and only 3 had an income tax.[10] Unfortunately, the census data do not allow us to distinguish between property taxes from residential and nonresidential sources; the implications of this problem are discussed in section 4.4 below.

Nondeductible revenues are simply the difference between total revenues from own sources and deductible taxes. These revenues display considerable diversity in the sample, but all communities rely heavily on taxes and charges for water supply, utilities, and sewerage and sanitation. The mean per capita value of nondeductible revenue sources was $187.28.

As noted above, each community's tax price is assumed to be a function of the tax price of its state. The latter is calculated in the following fashion. For each state in every year under consideration, the average taxable income per itemized return is computed from the IRS's *Statistics of Income* and the corresponding marginal federal income tax rate (τ) determined. In addition, the proportion (m) of itemized returns for each state is calculated. The state's tax price, P^s, is then $P^s = (1 - m) + m(1 - \tau)$. [11]

Population characteristics such as the proportion of homeowners, proportion below the poverty line, etc., are taken from the *County and City Data Book* for 1983, which contains data for 1980. Because these variables change relatively slowly, we use the 1980 values in the cross-sectional regressions for 1978 and 1979 as well. In some cases, data for a municipality were not available from the *County and City Data*

Book. In these cases, data for the county in which the municipality is located are used.

The final data issue is the measurement of income. Yearly observations, needed to complete the panel data set, are not available from census sources. Instead, we use median family "effective buying income" taken from *Sales Management* magazine as published in the annual *Survey of Buying Power*. In effect, this variable is the predicted value of a hedonic disposable income equation based on the characteristics of the area. Data on the income distribution within each community are taken from the same source. Because "effective buying income" is a disposable income concept, it does not conform exactly to the census measure of income used by Feldstein and Metcalf. Nonetheless, it is quite similar. For 1980 (when both are available), the simple correlation between this measure and census median family income is 0.828; the correlation with census per capita income is 0.772.

Table 4.1 lists the means of each variable for 1980. The figures indicate that our communities relied more on deductible than nondeductible forms of revenue; the difference between the means of $\ln T_D$

Table 4.1   Means of Variables in 1980

ln T_D	5.443 (0.609)	*OLD*	0.128 (0.0247)
ln T_N	4.936 (1.147)	*OWN*	0.561 (0.147)
ln E	6.564 (0.382)	*PCT810*	5.221 (1.455)
ln P^s	−0.110 (0.0287)	*PCT1015*	14.312 (3.216)
ln *GRANTS*	5.345 (0.543)	*PCT1525*	29.58 (3.522)
ln Y	9.542 (0.218)	*PCT25*	30.58 (11.33)
ln *ASSETS*	4.811 (1.003)	*POOR*	0.126 (0.0512)
ln *DEBT*	5.930 (0.591)	ln *POP*	10.58 (1.15)
ln *PUPILS*	−1.319 (0.134)		
SHARE	45.59 (6.315)		
NONWHITE	0.139 (0.164)		

Note: Standard deviations of each variable are in parentheses.

and $\ln T_N$ was 0.507. The other general feature worth noting is the large amount of across community variation. The standard deviations of the logarithms imply large variations in the levels.

Table 4.2 shows the means of the first differences of the variables during 1978–1980. During this period, in real terms collections of deductible taxes per capita fell by about 4.7 percent annually, while nondeductible revenue sources increased by about 1.7 percent a year. Real expenditures per capita fell about 1.8 percent annually. Note, however, the relatively large standard deviations. As in the case of the figures reported in Table 4.1, there is substantial variability across jurisdictions, so one must be cautious in thinking about the mean values as being "typical."

Table 4.2   **Means of the First Differences, 1978—1980[a]**

$\ln T_{Dt} - \ln T_{Dt-1}$	-0.0473
	(0.130)
$\ln T_{Nt} - \ln T_{Nt-1}$	0.0165
	(0.281)
$\ln E_t - \ln E_{t-1}$	-0.0181
	(0.164)
$\ln P_i^s - \ln P_i^s{}_{-1}$	-0.0119
	(0.0184)
$\ln GRANTS_t - \ln GRANTS_{t-1}$	-0.0286
	(0.327)
$\ln Y_t - \ln Y_{t-1}$	-0.0156
	(0.0393)
$\ln ASSETS_t - \ln ASSETS_{t-1}$	-0.0710
	(0.585)
$\ln DEBT_t - \ln DEBT_{t-1}$	-0.105
	(0.280)
$SHARE_t - SHARE_{t-1}$	1.131
	(1.792)
$\ln POP_t - \ln POP_{t-1}$	0.00068
	(0.04229)

[a]Standard deviations of each variable are in parentheses.

4.4   Estimating the Model

4.4.1   Econometric Issues

There are several general issues in estimation. First is the potential endogeneity of the tax price. As noted above, there are good reasons to believe that in a cross-sectional regression the tax price will be correlated with the error term. Similarly, it has long been recognized that grant receipts are endogenously determined. In the individual effects model, the correlation between the tax price term and the error is likely to be less pronounced because one controls for the potential presence of unobserved taste differences. Still, such a correlation remains a possibility, and we therefore use lagged values of the changes in the tax price and grants as instrumental variables. Note that although we start out with five years of data, one is used up because of differencing, and another because lagged variables are used as instrumental variables. Hence, our estimates are based on three years, or equivalently, two first differences.

A second econometric issue is that the error terms may be heteroskedastic. To check this, in each case we compute White's (1980) heteroskedasticity test. In no case is there even weak evidence of heteroskedasticity. As pointed out in White (1982), this test is biased toward rejection of homoskedasticity in the instrumental variables context, so the failure to reject is even more striking.

A final issue is a measurement problem associated with the dependent variable in the deductible taxes equation. Only *residential* property taxes are deductible on personal tax returns, and, hence, belong in T_D. As noted above, the census data used do not permit us to identify residential versus nonresidential property taxes. To gauge the impact of this, notice that the log of residential property taxes (T_R) is related to the log of total property taxes (T_P) by the identity: $\ln T_{Rit} = \ln \psi_{it} + \ln T_{Pit}$, where ψ_{it} is the ratio of residential to total property taxes. Viewed in this way, and ignoring income and sales taxes,[12] the error term in our equation for T_{Dit} contains the component $\ln \psi_{it}$.

If ψ_{it} is time invariant, no problem arises. However, ψ_{it} may fall as the tax price rises. This will induce a positive correlation between the tax price and the error term. Other things equal, this will bias upward (toward zero) the estimated coefficient on the tax price.[13] Moreover, the standard errors of our coefficients will be larger than they would have been in the absence of this measurement problem. In short, our coefficient will understate the importance of the tax price, both quantitatively and from the point of view of statistical significance. In the same way, the coefficient on the tax price in the equation for nondeductible revenues will be biased downward toward zero.

4.4.2 Results

The estimates of the basic model, equation (1.5), are in Table 4.3. From the coefficient of $(\ln P_i^s - \ln P_{i-1}^s)$ in column (1), the elasticity of deductible taxes with respect to the tax price is about -1.55. This elasticity is quite precisely estimated; the coefficient exceeds its standard error by a factor of about 3.1. In this context it is important to emphasize that the first differences specification provides a very stringent test of the importance of deductibility because it focuses on the effect of *changes* in the tax price on *changes* in deductible taxes. The

Douglas Holtz-Eakin and Harvey S. Rosen

Table 4.3 **Individual Effects Model: Basic Results[a]**

	(1) $\ln T_{Dt} - \ln T_{Dt-1}$	(2) $\ln T_{Nt} - \ln T_{Nt-1}$	(3) $\ln E_t - \ln E_{t-1}$
Intercept	−0.0940 (0.0125)	−0.0324 (0.0330)	−0.0522 (0.0171)
$\ln P_t^s - \ln P_{t-1}^s$	−1.553 (0.490)	−0.787 (1.291)	−1.833 (0.669)
$\ln Y_t - \ln Y_{t-1}$	0.00142 (0.233)	−0.495 (0.613)	0.154 (0.318)
$\ln GRANTS_t - \ln GRANTS_{t-1}$	−0.0185 (0.0613)	0.0646 (0.161)	0.0889 (0.0837)
$\ln ASSETS_t - \ln ASSETS_{t-1}$	−0.00787 (0.0118)	0.000794 (0.0310)	−0.00234 (0.0161)
$\ln DEBT_t - \ln DEBT_{t-1}$	−0.00362 (0.0284)	0.0274 (0.0747)	−0.0890 (0.0388)
$SHARE_t - SHARE_{t-1}$	−0.00345 (0.00483)	0.00820 (0.0127)	−0.00659 (0.00659)
$\ln POP_t - \ln POP_{t-1}$	−0.759 (0.155)	−0.808 (0.407)	−0.988 (0.211)
$\ln Y_t^s - \ln Y_{t-1}^s$	−1.26 (0.410)	−1.16 (1.080)	−1.649 (0.560)

[a]Estimation is by instrumental variables. Numbers in parentheses are standard errors.

fact that the coefficient from the first differences specification is significant at conventional levels seems strong evidence that an effect really is present.

From the second column in Table 4.3, the elasticity of nondeductible revenues with respect to the tax price is −0.787, but it is imprecisely estimated. This is similar to Feldstein and Metcalf's finding that one cannot reject the hypothesis that the tax price has no effect on the use of nondeductible revenue sources.

The coefficient on the tax price variable in the third column of the table suggests that the impact of deductibility on local expenditures is substantial. The elasticity with respect to the tax price is −1.83, and the coefficient exceeds its standard error by a factor of 2.7. This figure is considerably larger than most estimates of individual price elasticities of demand for public goods and services. However, as Feldstein and Metcalf emphasize, it is quite possible that the aggregate response to a change in the tax price will exceed the individual response. This follows directly from the fact that any given percentage change in an itemizer's tax price produces a much smaller percentage change in the community tax price. For any observed variation in expenditure, the elasticity computed with respect to the community tax price will exceed that computed with respect to the itemizer's tax price.

Most of the other coefficients in the table are imprecisely estimated. One interesting finding is that increases in population are associated with statistically significant decreases in per capita expenditures and per capita collections of both deductible and nondeductible revenue sources. One possible explanation is the existence of scale economies in the provision of public goods and services. Another possibility is that this effect is due to sluggish adjustment to population changes. That is, when population increases, communities are slow to change their behavior, so per capita magnitudes fall. To examine the second possibility, we estimated a simple stock adjustment version of equation (1.5). This amounts to including the lagged dependent variable (DEP_{t-1}) in each of the equations in Table 4.3. These results, which are reported in Table 4.4, suggest that one cannot reject the hypothesis that the coefficient on the lagged dependent variable is zero. Thus, slow adjustment does not appear to be a major factor in our data. Moreover, in each equation inclusion of the lagged dependent variable leaves the other coefficients basically unchanged. While we do not interpret these results as "proof" that past decisions have no effect on current tax and expenditure patterns, they do indicate that allowing for dynamics,

Table 4.4   **Individual Effects Model With Slow Adjustment**[a]

	$\ln T_{Dt} - \ln T_{Dt-1}$	$\ln T_{Nt} - \ln T_{Nt-1}$	$\ln E_t - \ln E_{t-1}$
Intercept	−0.0916	−0.0420	−0.0521
	(0.0137)	(0.0571)	(0.0174)
$\ln P_t^s - \ln P_{t-1}^s$	−1.575	−0.442	−1.843
	(0.504)	(2.230)	(0.685)
$\ln Y_t - \ln Y_{t-1}$	0.00703	−0.441	0.154
	(0.239)	(1.052)	(0.324)
$\ln GRANTS_t - \ln GRANTS_{t-1}$	−0.0233	0.117	0.0882
	(0.0635)	(0.280)	(0.0854)
$\ln ASSETS_t - \ln ASSETS_{t-1}$	−0.00731	−0.000256	−0.00246
	(0.0121)	(0.0532)	(0.0164)
$\ln DEBT_t - \ln DEBT_{t-1}$	−0.00278	0.0220	−0.0889
	(0.0291)	(0.128)	(0.0395)
$SHARE_t - SHARE_{t-1}$	−0.00350	0.00695	−0.00654
	(0.00494)	(0.0218)	(0.00671)
$\ln POP_t - \ln POP_{t-1}$	−0.763	−0.791	−0.988
	(0.159)	(0.699)	(0.215)
$\ln Y_t^s - \ln Y_{t-1}^s$	−1.261	−1.231	−1.649
	(0.420)	(1.852)	(0.570)
DEP_{t-1}	0.0862	1.207	0.0349
	(0.173)	(0.954)	(0.247)

[a]Estimation is by instrumental variables. Numbers in parentheses are standard errors. DEP_{t-1} is treated as endogenous and DEP_{t-2} is included as an instrumental variable.

at least in a simple way, appears to have no impact on our results about the effects of deductibility.[14]

As noted above, the use of equation (1.4) imposes a constraint across equations of our model; namely, that the ratio of the coefficient on the state income variable to the coefficient on the tax price variable should be identical in each of the equations. This ratio is our estimate of $-\gamma_1$. Imposing this constraint on the estimated coefficients does not alter any of the qualitative results of the model. A test of the null hypothesis that the data satisfy the constraint yields a statistic of 0.158 which is distributed as a chi square with 2 degrees of freedom. The null hypothesis is not rejected at conventional levels of significance.[15] Further, the estimated value of γ_1 is $-.972$ (with a standard error of .286). Thus, as expected, the community tax price falls relative to the state tax price as community income rises relative to state income.[16]

In our next set of experiments, we deleted *ASSETS, DEBTS,* and *GRANTS* from the set of right-hand-side variables. As mentioned earlier, although we think that a good case can be made for including these variables, they were omitted from Feldstein and Metcalf's specification, hence, it is interesting to see whether their omission induces any substantive changes. Note that because grants are excluded from consideration, it makes sense for the dependent variable in the "expenditures" equation to be expenditures from own sources only. In terms of our notation, the appropriate variable is $\ln(T_D + T_N)$ rather than $\ln E$.

The results are reported in Table 4.5. A comparison with Table 4.3 indicates that all of the substantive results are basically unchanged. Thus, while we prefer the specification in Table 4.3 on theoretical grounds, use of the Feldstein-Metcalf set-up does not affect our con-

Table 4.5   **Omitting *GRANTS, ASSETS* and *DEBTS* from the *X*-Vector[a]**

	$\ln T_{Dt} - \ln T_{Dt-1}$	$\ln T_{Nt} - \ln T_{Nt-1}$	$[\ln (T_{Dt} + T_{Nt}) - \ln (T_{Dt-1} + T_{Nt-1})]$
Intercept	-0.0922	-0.0380	-0.0912
	(0.0107)	(0.0283)	(0.0140)
$\ln P_t - \ln P_{t-1}$	-1.525	-0.869	-1.724
	(0.457)	(1.210)	(0.598)
$\ln Y_t - \ln Y_{t-1}$	-0.0328	-0.548	-0.706
	(0.224)	(0.592)	(0.292)
$SHARE_t - SHARE_{t-1}$	-0.00298	0.00740	0.00384
	(0.00469)	(0.0124)	(0.00614)
$POP_t - POP_{t-1}$	-0.746	-0.785	-0.916
	(0.151)	(0.401)	(0.198)
$Y_t^s - Y_{t-1}^s$	-1.218	-1.142	-0.583
	(0.401)	(1.062)	(0.524)

[a]Estimation is by instrumental variables. Numbers in parentheses are standard errors.

clusions. In particular, we still find no evidence that a higher tax price leads to greater reliance on nondeductible sources of revenue.

Our last set of results consists of the basic specification estimated for individual cross sections. As emphasized above, we think the individual effects model is more suitable. It is therefore of some interest to see how the results would have differed if we had used a cross section instead.

The cross-sectional results for 1980 are reported in Table 4.6. From the first column, we see that contrary to what one would expect, increases in the tax price *increase* the reliance on deductible sources of revenue. However, this coefficient is imprecisely estimated. Moreover, from the second column, increases in the tax price decrease reliance on nondeductible revenue sources by a huge amount (the elasticity is minus 15), and this coefficient is more than twice its standard error.

What accounts for these peculiar results? One possibility is that the year 1980 was atypical for the communities in our sample. We therefore estimated the cross-sectional equations for the years 1978 and 1979 as well. The results are reported in the top portion of Table 4.7. (To conserve space, we report only the coefficients on the tax price and income coefficients.) A glance at the figures in Tables 4.6 and 4.7 suggests that the point estimates vary considerably from year to year. Indeed, the elasticities of E with respect to P^s flip signs from year to year.

Thus, we cannot "blame" the implausible results of Table 4.6 on the choice of year. An alternative possibility is that the cross-sectional equations are estimated with inappropriate instruments. The estimates presented so far use lagged tax price as an instrument. If: (a) the primary source of endogeneity in the cross section arises from the fact that unobserved tastes for spending induce correlation between P_{it} and the error term, and (b) these unobserved taste differences persist over time; then lagged price will do little to purge the correlation between P_{it} and the error term.

Fortunately, for the year 1980 we have available an alternative set of instrumental variables suggested by Feldstein and Metcalf. These are (1) the proportion of taxpayers in the state who would be expected to itemize if each taxpayer's probability of itemizing were equal to the national average for his or her adjusted gross income class; (2) the marginal tax rate on the *first* dollar of state and local tax deductions; and (3) the average tax rate on state and local tax deductions. These variables are expected to be correlated with the state tax price, but uncorrelated with the error term in the regression. (See Feldstein and Metcalf [1986] for further details.) The estimates that are obtained with this alternative set of instrumental variables are reported at the bottom of Table 4.7. A comparison of those elasticities with those reported in

Table 4.6   **Cross-Sectional Results for 1980[a]**

	(1) $\ln T_D$	(2) $\ln T_N$	(3) $\ln E$
Intercept	−14.88 (10.68)	65.06 (21.50)	26.16 (7.329)
$\ln P^s$	0.451 (3.786)	−15.16 (7.62)	0.451 (2.598)
$\ln Y$	1.631 (1.294)	−6.011 (2.604)	−2.314 (0.888)
$\ln GRANTS$	0.0487 (0.0880)	−0.0141 (0.177)	0.317 (0.0604)
$\ln ASSETS$	−0.0420 (0.0342)	0.303 (0.0689)	0.0895 (0.0235)
$\ln DEBT$	0.0974 (0.0582)	0.419 (0.117)	0.164 (0.0400)
$\ln PUPILS$	0.199 (0.279)	0.286 (0.562)	0.0942 (0.192)
$SHARE$	0.0164 (0.00623)	−0.0391 (0.0125)	−0.0150 (0.00427)
$NONWHITE$	0.114 (0.309)	−0.477 (0.622)	−0.289 (0.212)
$POOR$	−5.586 (1.314)	5.778 (2.646)	1.101 (0.902)
OLD	3.932 (1.610)	0.615 (3.242)	0.966 (1.105)
OWN	−1.316 (0.317)	0.841 (0.638)	0.0338 (0.217)
$PCT810$	0.0336 (0.0806)	−0.212 (0.162)	−0.0372 (0.0553)
$PCT1015$	0.0479 (0.0348)	0.0678 (0.0701)	0.00855 (0.0239)
$PCT1525$	−0.0228 (0.0225)	0.0322 (0.0452)	0.0107 (0.0154)
$PCT25$	−0.0112 (0.0300)	0.112 (0.0605)	0.0477 (0.0206)
$\ln POP$	0.114 (0.0382)	−0.126 (0.0770)	−0.0556 (0.0262)
$\ln Y^s$	1.948 (0.638)	−5.002 (1.284)	−0.518 (0.438)

[a]Estimation is by instrumental variables. Numbers in parentheses are standard errors.

Table 4.6 indicates that the "wrong" signs are still present. We conclude that the use of single cross sections to estimate the fiscal response of communities to changes in their economic environments can produce quite misleading results.

Nevertheless, we think that cross-sectional data may help shed some light on a measurement problem that was discussed above. Namely,

Table 4.7   **Additional Cross-Sectional Results**

	(1) ln T_D	(2) ln T_N	(3) ln E
1978			
lnP^x	−11.76	−0.0334	−4.138
	(4.452)	(7.817)	2.655
ln Y	2.172	−5.707	0.198
	(1.851)	(3.251)	(0.104)
1979			
lnP^x	3.053	−21.90	−4.393
	(3.660)	(7.530)	(2.678)
ln Y	1.491	−5.550	−1.105
	(1.541)	(3.172)	(1.128)
1980[a]			
lnP^x	7.898	−8.750	3.289
	(3.356)	(6.217)	(2.140)
ln Y	1.192	−6.764	−2.691
	(1.361)	(2.520)	(0.867)

Note: Estimation is by instrumental variables. Numbers in parentheses are standard errors.
[a]Feldstein and Metcalf's instruments.

our property tax data include payments from both residential and non-residential sources, which in theory can bias toward zero the tax price coefficients in the T_D and T_N equations. For a subset of our communities, we obtained 1980 data on the proportion of the property tax base that was residential. (Such data were not available for other years). Assuming that residents paid property taxes in proportion to their share in the tax base, we were able to estimate residential and nonresidential property taxes paid. For this subsample, the cross-sectional equations for T_N and T_D were then estimated both with and without nonresidential property taxes included in the respective left-hand-side variables. The results with and without the adjustment were essentially the same for both the T_D and T_N equations. This suggests that in our sample, the share of nonresidential property taxes is sufficiently small that only an inconsequential bias is induced by lumping residential and nonresidential property taxes together. Of course, we recognize the tenuous nature of this exercise. It is no substitute for an analysis of longitudinal data with information on the mix of property tax receipts.

4.5   Conclusion

We have examined fiscal data on 172 communities over the period 1978 to 1980 in order to estimate the effects of deductibility on local taxing and spending behavior. From a methodological point of view, our first main result is that local data provide a fruitful source of information on the impact of deductibility on fiscal decisions. Difficulties in defining tax prices and accounting for differences in institutional structures across states do not seem to prevent us from obtaining sensible and useful results. The second methodological result is that parameters estimated from a single cross section of fiscal data must be interpreted with care. Such parameters may depend upon the particular year chosen, and may be inconsistent because of the failure to account for individual effects.

Our main substantive findings are:

1. Deductibility does affect the choice of revenue sources. The elasticity of deductible taxes with respect to the tax price is in the range -1.2 to -1.6. In our sample, the mean value of the logarithm of the tax price in 1980 was -0.110. Thus, if deductibility were removed, i.e., if $\ln P$ became zero, then collections of deductible taxes would fall by more than 13 percent.

2. However, we have not been able to find any evidence that removing deductibility would increase reliance on nondeductible sources of finance. Indeed, the point estimates of these elasticities are negative, although they are imprecisely estimated. Thus, there is no reason to think that tax substitutions at the local level would mitigate against increased federal tax revenues if deductibility were removed.

3. Local spending is quite responsive to changes in the tax price, with an elasticity of about -1.8. Thus, removing deductibility could have major effects on local spending.

Notes

1. See U.S. Department of the Treasury (1984) and *President's Tax Proposals to the Congress for Fairness, Growth, and Simplicity* (1985).

2. There are also claims that removing deductibility would lead to an unfair increase in the tax burden on middle class taxpayers. The distributional implications of deductibility, both across states and across income classes, are discussed in Feenberg and Rosen (1986) and Kenyon (1986).

3. "What Happens if Washington Changes the Rules?" *New York Times,* 23 June 1985, E5.

4. As Fisher (1986) has noted, another factor that might affect the tax price is the fact that some state income taxes allow credits and deductions for local property tax payments. To examine this possibility, we computed the state income tax liability of a household that had the average taxable income on all itemized returns in its state. In every case, if this household paid the average property tax in its community, then the credit or deduction had no *marginal* effect on the tax price of local spending. This is because the credits and de-

ductions are capped at a sufficiently low level that the household with the average property tax is not affected on the margin.

5. Note that equation (1.1) ignores differences in the (quality-adjusted) resource cost of public sector inputs across communities. Implicitly, this assumes a national market for such inputs. Alternatively, input costs may vary across communities, but if they do not change over time, they are included in the individual effect. Holtz-Eakin (1986) tests for the presence of individual effects in these data and finds that they are present. In addition, this specification does not allow for year effects. In some preliminary experiments we included year effects, and found that they did not change any of the substantive results.

6. Inman (1985) provides an interesting attempt along these lines.

7. Hettich and Winer (1984) employ state data without including figures from localities in the totals.

8. A more complete description of the data set from which this sample is drawn is contained in Holtz-Eakin, Newey, and Rosen (1985).

9. To remain in the sample, communities had to report positive school expenditures.

10. The econometric results below are unchanged when income and sales taxes are excluded in the computation of deductible taxes.

11. This procedure differs substantially from that used by Feldstein and Metcalf, who took advantage of data from individual tax returns. Nevertheless, the two methods yield quite similar results. In 1980, Feldstein and Metcalf calculate the mean tax price as 0.92 with a standard deviation of 0.02; the range is from 0.87 to 0.96. In comparison, our statewide tax prices for 1980 have an average value of 0.90, a standard deviation of 0.03, a minimum of 0.86, and a maximum of 0.94.

12. Allowing for income and sales taxes would introduce some nonlinearity into the problem, but not change the qualitative results.

13. Of course, a general analysis of the bias requires consideration of the complete set of covariances among the right-side variables and the vector of covariances between each of these variables and ψ_{it}. We think that in this particular case, these other covariances are unlikely to change our conclusion.

14. Holtz-Eakin, Newey, and Rosen (1985) discuss dynamic aspects of local government taxing and spending behavior.

15. The test is computed by estimating the three equations as a system using three-stage least squares both with and without imposing the constraint. The covariance matrix from the unconstrained estimation is used in both cases. The test statistic is the difference between the constrained and unconstrained weighted sum of squared errors for the system.

16. With an estimate of γ_1, one can use equation (1.5) to work backward coefficients on $\ln(P_{it}^s - \ln P_{it-1}^s)$ and $(\ln Y_{it} - \ln Y_{it-1})$ to solve for α_2, the effect of community income on the left-hand-side variable. In the expenditures equation, this turns out to be negative, a result counter to a number of previous studies. However, the estimate is statistically insignificant. We conjecture that mismeasurement of the income variable may be the cause of this result.

References

Eisner, R., and J. Pieper. 1984. A new view of the federal debt and budget deficits. *American Economic Review* 74: unpublished appendix.

Executive Office of the President, Office of Management and Budget. 1986. *Special analyses, budget of the United States government fiscal year 1987.* Washington, D.C.: U.S. Government Printing Office.

Feenberg, Daniel R., and Harvey S. Rosen. 1986. The deductibility of state and local taxes: Impact effects on state and income class. *Growth and Change:* 11–31.

Feldstein, Martin, and Gilbert Metcalf. 1986. The effect of federal tax deductibility on state and local taxes and spending. Boston: Working Paper no. 1791, National Bureau of Economic Research.

Fisher, Ronald C. 1986. Intergovernmental tax incentives and local fiscal behavior. East Lansing: Michigan State University, mimeo.

Hettich, Walter, and Stanley Winer. 1984. A positive model of tax structure. *Journal of Public Economics* 24: 67–87.

Holtz-Eakin, D. 1986. Unobserved tastes and the determination of municipal services. *National Tax Journal V. 39:* 527–532.

Holtz-Eakin, D., W. Newey, and H. S. Rosen. 1985. Implementing causality tests with panel data, with an example from local public finance. Boston: National Bureau of Economic Research, Technical Working Paper no. 48.

Inman, Robert P. 1979. The fiscal performance of local governments: An interpretive review. In *Current Issues in Urban Economics,* ed. P. Mieszkowski and M. Straszheim, 270–321. Baltimore: Johns Hopkins University Press.

———. 1985. Does deductibility influence local taxation? University of Pennsylvania. Mimeo.

———. Forthcoming. Markets, government, and the "new" political economy. In *Handbook of Public Economics,* ed. Alan J. Auerbach and Martin Feldstein. Amsterdam: North-Holland Press.

Kenyon, Daphne A. Forthcoming. Implicit aid to state and local governments through federal tax deductibility. In *Intergovernmental Fiscal Relations in an Era of New Federalism,* ed. M. Bell. Greenwich, Conn.: JAI Press.

Noto, Nonna, and Dennis Zimmerman. 1984. Limiting state-local tax deductibility: Effects among the states. *National Tax Journal* 37: 539–50.

Oates, Wallace E. 1975. "Automatic" increases in tax revenues. The effect on the size of the public budget. In *Financing the New Federalism,* ed. Wallace E. Oates. Baltimore: Johns Hopkins University Press: 139–60.

President's Tax Proposals to the Congress for Fairness, Growth, and Simplicity. Office of the President 1985. Washington, D.C.: U.S. Government Printing Office.

Sales and Marketing Management Magazine. Survey of Buying Power. New York: Bill Publications. Various years.

U.S. Bureau of the Census. 1972. *Census of governments.* Washington, D.C.: U.S. Government Printing Office.

———. 1977. *Census of governments.* Washington, D.C.: U.S. Government Printing Office.

———. 1983. *County and city data book.* Washington, D.C.: U.S. Government Printing Office.

———. *Annual survey of governments.* Washington, D.C.: U.S. Government Printing Office. Various years.

U.S. Department of the Treasury. 1984. *Tax reform for fairness, simplicity, and economic growth.* Vol. 2.

White, H. 1980. A heteroskedasticity-consistent covariance matrix estimator and a direct test for heteroskedasticity. *Econometrica* 48: 817–38.

———. 1982. Instrumental variables regression with independent observations. *Econometrica* 50: 483–500.

Comment   Ronald C. Fisher

Although economists have carefully examined, during the past 25 years, the effects of intergovernmental grant incentives on state and local government fiscal behavior, the effects of intergovernmental tax incentives on both the amount of spending and the choice of the revenue structure were largely ignored until very recently. [Notable exceptions are Inman (1971) and McLure (1967).] In the past four years, however, a substantial number of both theoretical and empirical papers have appeared which explicitly consider the effect of tax incentives provided by the national and state governments on the expenditure and revenue decisions of all subnational governments. Indeed, this conference is evidence of that trend as four of the eight papers presented deal directly with the effects of intergovernmental tax incentives.

Although this change perhaps reflects an increased awareness of and interest in the economics of the subnational government sector, the fact remains that the primary motivating factor for the new interest in tax incentives was a national government policy issue, reform of the federal individual income tax and the appropriate treatment of the deduction for state and local taxes. Tax incentives are largely unimportant for national government taxes (although federal income taxes are deductible against state income taxes in 16 states), and the overwhelming dominance of income taxes at the national level effectively reduces interest in questions about the choice among alternative revenue instruments. Even the voluminous intergovernmental grant literature, while providing insight to the fiscal behavior of subnational governments, has often been focused on the appropriate structure of grants from the viewpoint of the national government.

Despite the origins of these new research interests, the inevitable result is likely to be increased attention to the fiscal policy of subnational governments for its own sake and not just as it relates to national economic policy decisions. This is an important change in direction for both practical and academic reasons. Subnational government expenditures from own-sources in the United States account for more than 10 percent of gross national product. And the substantial economic and fiscal diversity among subnational governments simply provides an opportunity for examining issues of economic behavior which cannot be considered by focusing on the national government (except through international comparisons, where the institutional and data problems are even more severe than in the world of state and local governments). For instance, the diversification of state and local government revenues

Ronald C. Fisher is professor of economics at Michigan State University.

among alternative sources is largely the factor that makes analysis of tax incentives both interesting and possible.

Recent Analyses of Tax Incentives

A common issue in the intergovernmental grant literature is the influence of grants, through income and price effects, on the level of recipient subnational government spending in the aggregate and for specific functions. In a few cases, consideration is also given to the influence of grants on the revenue structure of the recipient governments, such as the incentive in the U.S. general revenue-sharing formula for tax as opposed to user-charge financing, and for state income taxes in particular. Tax incentives, including federal income tax deductions for subnational taxes as well as state income tax deductions and credits for local government taxes, were first incorporated into the grant models as an additional factor affecting the tax price for subnational government services. The issue is whether tax incentives influence the level and type of government spending. But because these tax incentives are often not neutral among alternative revenue sources, the most recent research considers the effect of the incentives on the mix, as well as level, of subnational government taxes.

This recent research includes work by Hettich and Winer (1984), Kenyon (forthcoming), and Gade (1987) examining the revenue decisions of state governments; a paper by Feldstein and Metcalf (1986) which considers the revenue decisions of state and local governments combined; and work by Inman (1979 and 1985), Gramlich (1985), Bell and Bowman (1987) and Fisher (1986) about the influence of tax incentives on the fiscal decisions of individual local governments.

The paper by Holtz-Eakin and Rosen fits in this last group. They provide a careful examination of the effect of federal income tax deductibility on the amount of spending and the use of deductible as opposed to nondeductible revenue sources to finance that spending for a set of municipal governments. Holtz-Eakin and Rosen's conclusions—that deductible taxes and expenditures are increased by federal tax deductibility—are generally consistent with the results of the other studies of local fiscal decisions, particularly considering the degree of disaggregation of the revenue options. What particularly distinguishes the Holtz-Eakin and Rosen work, however, is the clever, and apparently important, advances in the method for estimating tax price elasticities.

There are at least two major innovations in this work by Holtz-Eakin and Rosen compared to these other papers. First, by using panel data for 172 municipal governments over the years 1975 to 1980, they estimate the effects of deductibility with difference equations, effectively comparing changes in revenue amounts to the change in tax prices caused by deductibility. This method corrects for unobservable community-specific factors that can influence these decisions and that apparently can be important, as Holtz-Eakin argues elsewhere (*National Tax Journal*, 1986). They also demonstrate that estimation using first-differences can give substantially different results than estimation from cross-sectional analysis using the same data.

Second, because tax prices net of federal deductions cannot be measured directly for these municipalities, Holtz-Eakin and Rosen estimate those local tax prices based on the weighted-average marginal tax price for the *state* in which the city is located adjusted for the difference between the per capita income in the locality and the state. The presumption is that as the income of a locality rises above that of the state, the tax price falls below that for the state. Taking first differences, this is represented by their equation (4).

$$\ln P_{it} - \ln P_{it-1} = (\ln P^s_{it} - \ln P^s_{it-1}) + \gamma_1 \times [(\ln Y_{it} - \ln Y^s_{it}) - (\ln Y_{it-1} - \ln Y^s_{it-1})],$$

where P is price, Y is per capita income, i represents the municipality, s represents municipality i's state, and t is year. If there are other variables which influence tax prices, the assumption is that the difference between the state and local values is stable over time (and thus eliminated by the differencing).

Holtz-Eakin and Rosen estimate first differences of constant elasticity equations for per capita deductible taxes (property, income, sales), nondeductible taxes, and expenditures as a function of tax price (measured as above), per capita family income, grants, the state government share of spending, per capita assets, per capita debt outstanding, and population. They report that per capita deductible taxes and expenditures of these municipalities are significantly negatively related to tax prices, but that there appears to be no substitutability between deductible and nondeductible taxes. These results are generally consistent with those in the other papers examining local governments, with the exception of Inman's 1985 paper.

Evaluation of the Holtz-Eakin and Rosen Approach

My comments about the approach taken by Holtz-Eakin and Rosen fall into two groups, those concerning the approximation of tax burden prices for localities based on the corresponding state tax price and those about the overall structure of the model.

Local Tax Burden Prices

Measuring Local Tax Burden Prices by State Tax Prices. Theoretically, Holtz-Eakin and Rosen's assertion that differences between the state and local tax prices net of deductibility depend on the differences between the community's values for a vector of variables and their state counterparts seems clear. But as implemented, the assumption is that changes in local tax prices over time relative to changes in the state prices can be reflected solely by changes in the difference between local and state per capita incomes. And that assumption is based on the notion that there is a significant relationship between the difference between state and local tax prices and the difference between state and local per capita incomes in any one year. The tax price net of deductibility depends both on taxpayers' federal marginal tax rates and on the fraction of taxpayers who itemize federal deductions. There is evidence suggesting that the correlation between income and itemizing at a given time is tenuous.

In a survey of research on tax incentives, Kenyon (forthcoming, 29) notes that among states with effectively identical per capita incomes, there can be wide differences in the percentage of taxpayers who itemize federal income tax deductions. The survey data reported and used by Gramlich (1985) suggest that even among localities in the same state, the probability of itemizing is not explained well by income alone. The average family income and percentage of voters who itemize for various sets of localities in Michigan in the Gramlich study are shown in table C4.1. Comparing both the city of Detroit to the city of Lansing and the Detroit suburbs to the Lansing suburbs, the percentage of itemizing *voters* is substantially greater for the Detroit area despite the fact that average family incomes are higher in the Lansing area. One likely explanation for the difference between those areas is that renting rather than owning housing is relatively more common in the Lansing area than in the Detroit area. The opposite pattern, the one hypothesized by Holtz-Eakin and Rosen, applies however for the "rural" and "other urban" counties.

Table C4.1   **Itemizing Behavior and Community Income in Michigan: Results From Gramlich, 1985**

Jurisdiction	Average Family Income	Percentage of Voters Who Itemize Deductions
Detroit	$12,556	39.6
Lansing	15,371	35.7
Rural counties	16,292	43.4
Other urban counties	17,221	50.8
Total sample	17,544	49.0
Detroit Suburbs	21,574	62.0
Lansing Suburbs	22,078	50.0

Source: Gramlich, 1985, Table 1, p. 454, and Table 4, p. 459.

But because Holtz-Eakin and Rosen use first differences, if the factors other than income which influence itemizing and tax prices (such as housing type) are relatively stable over time, then changes in local tax prices relative to the state may be captured entirely by changes in local income relative to the state. Holtz-Eakin and Rosen do assume that those other factors, the Z_{it}'s in their notation, are stable. But in estimating the tax and expenditure functions, the authors assume that there are economic and demographic variables affecting the budget constraint and/or preferences, the X_{it}'s, which are changing. There is something of an internal inconsistency here if one expects that some of the factors affecting the level of taxes and expenditures also influence the difference between state and local tax prices. In addition, the income data used are hedonic estimates based on changes in some characteristics of the community. Without changes in those characteristics over time, there can be no income changes over time.

How well their method works is an empirical question and a difficult one to test because of the absence of local tax prices to begin with. One possibility is to evaluate how well the method works for estimating *state* tax prices by using the national average tax price and changes in the difference between state and national per capita incomes. Because I did not have average marginal federal income tax rates by state available, I estimated Holtz-Eakin and Rosen's equation (4) using the percentage of taxpayers who itemize returns for 1983 and 1984 in each state and nationally as the measure of tax price. The result is shown below:

$$\ln I_{i84} - \ln I_{i83} = 1.3092 (\ln I_{N84} - \ln I_{N83}) +$$
$$(.4637)$$
$$- 1.0576 [(\ln Y_{i84} - \ln Y_{N84}) - (\ln Y_{i83} - \ln Y_{N83})]$$
$$(.4928)$$

$R^2 = .0875$, $F = 4.61$

where I_i = percentage of itemizers in state i or nationally,

Y_i = per capita income in state i or nationally.

This estimating equation for state tax prices based on the national average price behaves quite differently than Holtz-Eakin and Rosen hypothesize for local prices based on the state average. If the difference between state and national per capita income decreases over the period, itemizing in that state *decreases* (and thus the tax price increases); itemizing in a state apparently goes down as income goes up. Although this result suggests caution about Holtz-Eakin and Rosen's approach, there are at least two reasons why the results for the local estimates may be different from these results for state itemizing. First, the state results for *tax price* may differ from those for *itemizing;* it seems clear that marginal rates will rise (and tax prices fall) as income rises. Second, states are such large and diverse areas that the assumption of no change in other factors influencing tax prices over the period may be less accurate for states than localities.

State Property Tax Incentives. A second concern about the measurement of local tax prices arises for two related reasons. Holtz-Eakin and Rosen consider only the incentive created by federal deductibility, ignoring state tax incentives from deductions, credits, and grants, and as a result they lump together all the deductible taxes on property, income, and sales. My sense is that for many local governments the potential revenue tradeoff among these three taxes is both more significant and likely than a tradeoff between these taxes as a group and other revenues (nondeductible taxes and charges). But obviously, substitution between property taxes on the one hand and a local income or sales tax on the other cannot be considered in this framework. It does not seem surprising that Holtz-Eakin and Rosen find no effect of tax prices on use of nondeductible revenues, which are mostly user charges. Because of the administrative costs of establishing and operating a user fee system, marginal adjustments of user charge reliance are unlikely—either user charges are used to cover a substantial portion of costs or they are not.

The difficulty from grouping property taxes with income and sales taxes is intensified by the fact that specific state government incentives influencing property taxes are common. Taxpayers in 33 states are allowed an itemized deduction against state income tax for local property taxes, and state government credits for local property taxes are provided in 32 states, with both incentives used to some degree in 21 states. Both of these state tax incentives reduce the marginal price of local property taxes. In addition, Holtz-Eakin and Rosen apparently (see their footnote 8) restricted their sample to cities with responsibility for local education expenditures. In many states, the state aid formula for education includes either the property tax rate for education or per pupil property tax revenue. Such a grant formula also reduces the relative tax price for property taxes.

The available evidence from other studies suggests both that local governments do respond significantly to these state property tax incentives and that localities may respond to all tax incentives differently for property, income, and sales taxes. Property tax responses to state government property tax credits are examined by Bell and Bowman (1987) for Minnesota cities, and Fisher (1986) for Michigan local governments. Both report statistically significant increases in property taxes as a result of the credits, although the magnitude of the increase is somewhat smaller than the effect estimated by Holtz-Eakin and Rosen.

Inman's (1985) study of the revenue and expenditure choices of 41 large cities is perhaps most comparable to the work by Holtz-Eakin and Rosen. Inman tried to include influences of both federal deductibility and state incentives in the tax price measures, however, and estimated separate equations for the different taxes. And his results certainly showed differences in the price elasticities for the major taxes— the own-price elasticities for property and general sales taxes were statistically significant and *positive* while the price elasticity for income taxes took the usual negative sign. These counterintuitive results prompted an energetic, if not convincing, supply-side explanation. Inman also found different responses to different components of the tax prices for any given tax. These results (counterintuitive ones and all) certainly suggest that local government substitution among deductible taxes needs to be considered, and that the possibility of local governments responding differently to federal deductibility and state tax incentives might also warrant examination.

It seems to me that there are at least two possibilities for estimating separate burden prices for property taxes and other deductible taxes so that Holtz-Eakin and Rosen's method can be applied to these questions of allocation among deductible taxes. First, data about use of state tax incentives in various localities are sometimes available from the state governments, from which more detailed burden prices can be computed. Second, state income tax simulation models, such as those developed and used by Feenberg and Rosen (1985), may be able to be used to calculate the effects of state income tax deductions and credits on marginal property tax prices either for taxpayers at selected income levels or perhaps for all state taxpayers on average. Although Holtz-Eakin and Rosen note that these credits and deductions have no marginal effect for average income taxpayers with average property taxes in their sample, that is not parallel to how tax prices net of deductibility were computed. In the latter case, the price is the average of prices for itemizers and nonitemizers rather than the effect of deductibility for an average income taxpayer.

Modeling Local Government Fiscal Decision Making

Voter or Bureaucratic Choice? One important theoretical issue for all studies of government fiscal choice is whether that choice arises directly from voting or as a result of some bureaucratic decision. This distinction is common in the intergovernmental grant literature; using Inman's terminology, the usual choice is between the median voter and dominant party models. In the voting models, an individual voter with specific characteristics is decisive, and that voter's characteristics are used to estimate the demand function for the government. In the bureaucratic models, an official makes choices taking into account the preferences of the entire community, with an average of community characteristics usually used to estimate the expenditure or tax equations.

Among the recent studies of the effect of tax incentives on expenditure and tax structure choice, only Gramlich (1985) explicitly adopts the voting approach, specifically the median voter model. All of the others, including Holtz-Eakin and Rosen, implicitly or explicitly use bureaucratic models and, therefore, measure the tax prices as a weighted average of the marginal prices for individuals or groups of individuals in the community. But these average marginal burden prices suggest a smoothness in the tax price distribution that generally simply does not exist. Holtz-Eakin and Rosen note this issue briefly early in their paper, but they reject the median voter alternative as having even greater problems.

This issue deserves careful consideration. In the simple case where federal tax deductibility is the only tax incentive, taxpayers obviously fall into one of two groups, those who itemize and those who do not. If there is a state tax credit in addition to federal deductibility, there are four major groups of taxpayers—those who take the federal deduction only (and are not eligible for the credit); those who receive the state credit but do not itemize for federal taxes (perhaps because they have no mortgage interest to deduct or because they are renters); those taxpayers who itemize and receive the state credit; and those who can take advantage of neither option. The implication is that there may be significant discontinuities in the distribution of tax prices among taxpayers in a given community. Can such an environment be adequately represented by an average of those prices?

In a voting model, tax incentives will influence the community choice only if the decisive voter's tax price is reduced by the incentives or if the identity of the decisive voter is changed by the tax incentives. In many cities, a majority of taxpayers obviously do not itemize federal deductions; indeed, median income taxpayers do not itemize in many cities. These observations are at least part of the reason why Gramlich finds smaller effects on local government expenditures from changes in deductibility than in many other studies. Indeed, Gramlich finds no expenditure effect from changes in deductibility in the two large and relatively lower income central cities in his sample, Detroit and Lansing. This stands in contrast to the relatively large expenditure effects reported by Holtz-Eakin and Rosen [even after allowing for the difference in tax price elasticities measured for an individual as opposed to all individuals, as discussed by Feldstein and Metcalf (1986)].

Alternative Responses to Tax Incentives. Of course, changes in deductibility or other tax incentives may cause changes in tax structure even if there are no changes in desired or selected expenditures or in the mix of revenue sources used. By altering their tax structures, state or local governments may attempt to offset the distributional changes caused by the change in tax incentives.

As Gramlich and others have pointed out, the main effect of altering deductibility is to change the distribution of the tax burden toward those who gain most from deductibility. Because elimination of deductibility is expected to increase the progressivity of subnational government taxes, states and localities may respond not only by changing the level of spending or the mix of revenue sources, but also by changing the type of services provided or the distribution (progressivity) of their tax burden. The last response need not require changes in the mix of taxes which is used, but simply changes in tax structure. For instance, state governments might adopt a less graduated income tax rate structure or alter the sales tax base, while local governments might change assessment practices or adopt property tax credits or exemptions. I am a bit skeptical that an average tax price can adequately reflect those potential distributional effects. Median voter models may be no better, however, because the distributional changes occur even if the median voter's tax price is unaffected by deductibility.

References

Bell, Michael, and John Bowman. The effect of various intergovernmental aid types on local own-source revenues: The case of property taxes in Minnesota cities. *Public Finance Quarterly* 15, 3: 2–97.

Feenberg, Daniel R., and Harvey S. Rosen. 1985. State personal income and sales taxes: 1977–1983. Working Paper no. 1631. Cambridge, Mass.: National Bureau of Economic Research.

Feldstein, Martin, and Gilbert Metcalf. 1986. The effect of federal tax deductibility on state and local taxes and spending. Working Paper no. 1791. Cambridge, Mass.: National Bureau of Economic Research.

Fisher, Ronald C. 1986. Intergovernmental tax incentives and local fiscal behavior. Michigan State University. Mimeo.

Gade, Mary. 1987. Optimal state tax design. Oklahoma State University. Mimeo.

Gramlich, Edward M. 1985. The deductibility of state and local taxes. *National Tax Journal* 38, no. 4:447–65.

Hettich, Walter, and Stanley Winer. 1984. A positive model of tax structure. *Journal of Public Economics* 24, 67–87.

Holtz-Eakin, Douglas. 1986. Unobserved tastes and the determination of municipal services. *National Tax Journal* 39: 527–32.

Inman, Robert P. 1971. Towards an econometric model of local budgeting. In *Proceedings of the Sixty-Fourth Annual Conference on Taxation*, 699–719. National Tax Association. Columbus, Ohio.

———. 1979. Subsidies, regulations, and the taxation of property in large U.S. cities. *National Tax Journal*, Supplement, 32, no. 2: 159–68.

———. 1985. Does deductibility influence local taxation? Working Paper no. 85-6, Federal Reserve Bank of Philadelphia.

Kenyon, Daphne. (Forthcoming). Implicit aid to state and local governments through federal tax deductibility. In *Intergovernmental Fiscal Relations in an Era of New Federalism,* ed. M. Bell. JAI Press.

McLure, Charles E., Jr. 1967. The interstate exporting of state and local taxes. *National Tax Journal* 20, no. 1: 49–77.

U.S. Department of the Treasury. Internal Revenue Service. 1985. *Statistics of Income Bulletin.* Washington, D.C.: U.S. Government Printing Office.

———. 1986. *Statistics of Income Bulletin.* Washington, D.C.: U.S. Government Printing Office.

5 Federal Deductibility of State and Local Taxes: A Test of Public Choice by Representative Government

Lawrence B. Lindsey

5.1 Introduction

The recent tax reform debate focused attention on the continued deductibility of state and local taxes in the calculation of federal taxable income. The original tax reform proposal by the Department of Treasury, issued in November 1984, called for the complete elimination of deductibility of state and local taxes. Later proposals by the president, the House of Representatives, and the Senate, maintained deductibility of nearly all state and local taxes. The final product of the tax reform debate, the Tax Reform Act of 1986, maintained deductibility of all state and local taxes except for retail sales taxes.

The deductibility of state and local taxes is a significant feature of fiscal federalism. Had deductibility of personal state and local taxes—retail sales, personal income, and residential property taxes—been eliminated in 1983, federal income taxes would have been $30.4 billion higher. By contrast, total federal grants-in-aid to state and local governments were $86.2 billion that year.

Unlike the direct grants-in-aid, the income tax saving from deductibility does not accrue directly to state and local governments. Instead, it is received by individual taxpayers in the form of lower income tax liability. This is likely to affect state and local tax collections in two ways. First, local taxpayers have higher disposable income as a result of deductibility. If state and local public services are normal goods,

Lawrence B. Lindsey is assistant professor of economics at Harvard University and faculty research fellow at the National Bureau of Economic Research.

This paper was written as part of NBER's State and Local Taxation Program. The author is grateful to NBER for support of this research. Deep thanks are also in order for Andrew Mitrusi for outstanding computer assistance and to Gilbert Metcalf and other members of the Program for their thoughtful comments.

this higher disposable income will lead to greater demand for such spending. Second, federal deductibility lowers the net cost to itemizing taxpayers of incremental dollars of state and local tax collections. This lower price on incremental public spending may also increase the quantity of public services demanded.

Academic investigation of this issue has properly focused on the "price" effect. The entire tax saving from state and local tax deductibility amounted to 1.25 percent of disposable personal income in 1983. On the other hand, deductibility lowered the price of incremental taxation for itemizers to 69 cents per dollar collected. Given these results, even modest price elasticities and large income elasticities are likely to show that price effects are dominant. This paper therefore follows the existing academic literature in focusing on price effects.

Unlike ordinary price changes, changes in the price of local taxation do not translate directly through consumer optimization into changes in the equilibrium quantity of services demanded. The quantity and type of taxes and services are not determined by individual consumers but by collective decision-making apparatuses. The elasticity of demand for public services therefore depends on the mechanism by which price changes are translated into changes in public policy.

The dominant model of converting individual preferences into collective actions has been the median voter model, first proposed by Hotelling (1929) and formally developed by Bowen (1943). In this model, the collective decision reflects the preferences of the swing or median voter. Half of the remaining voters are assumed to want more of the given commodity, half less. A change in the price of local taxation for some voters will only affect the outcome if the price facing the median voter is changed, or if the ranking of voters is changed in a way so that the median voter becomes someone new.

The median voter model places enormous stress on the capacity of representative governments to reflect voter preferences accurately. Rules controlling the election process, the setting of the legislative agenda, and the process of coalition formation may well produce a different outcome than that preferred by a majority of the voters.

The present paper tests a number of different modes of public choice, focusing on the subject of state and local tax deductibility. Three issues are considered: the effect of deductibility on the level of state and local taxation, the effect of deductibility on the type of tax used at the state and local level, and the effect of proposed changes of federal tax rules regarding deductibility on congressional voting on tax reform. On each issue, a number of different methods for translating individual taxpayer preferences into collective decisions are tested.

Section 5.2 below describes the theoretical issues involved and reports on academic findings to date. Section 5.3 describes the data used in this analysis, and discusses its appropriateness to the issues at hand. The following section produces the results of the tests of various types of models of translating individual preferences into collective actions. The paper concludes with a brief summary of the findings.

5.2 Theoretical Issues and Academic Findings

Most academic investigations of the price elasticity of demand for locally provided public services have relied on the geographic variability of the cost of public good provision, and the variations in the demographic makeup of communities. There are two major explanations for this emphasis. The obvious reason is that the available data permit such a construct. The second reason is a theoretical one: the reliance on the median voter model of public choice.

Many communities rely on the sequential referendum method of budgeting for local public goods, particularly education. Such referenda generally begin with a high proposed level of spending and reduce the figure in subsequent referenda until the budget proposal passes. This voting procedure lends itself nicely both to empirical testing and to the theoretical attraction of the median voter model.

In practice, the median voter model requires a far more restrictive set of assumptions. The first is that there be a single public good in question so that logrolling and coalition formation do not dominate the voting procedure. This condition is arguably present in those referenda systems where the local public good in question is typically education. However, Bergstrom and Goodman (1973) lay out an extremely rigorous set of assumptions needed to establish the result of a referendum as representative of the preferences of the median voter in the community. These include restrictive assumptions on the income distribution in the community and the price and income elasticities of demand for housing—a necessary condition where local public spending is financed by taxation of residential real estate.

Even laying aside the theoretical problems of establishing median voter criteria, there are a number of practical problems with the model. The first is the problem of agenda setting. If sequential referenda are not guaranteed, or if the change in the amount of taxation in each referendum is substantial rather than marginal, it may be that the preferences of the median voter will not be realized. Romer and Rosenthal (1978) argued that the tendency for spending to revert to some substantially lower level if a referendum were defeated would lead voters who prefer a modestly lower amount of spending than that proposed to support the referendum. They argued that this procedure would produce a higher level of spending than that supported by the median voter.

The process of voting is also not free, especially given the time commitment necessary for the sequential referendum process. Work by Rubinfeld (1980) tested for differences between voters and nonvoters. An earlier paper by Rubinfeld (1977) found that renters were less likely to vote than were homeowners. A high price of voting puts constraints on the sequential referendum process, and will produce outcomes which are not consistent with the median voter hypothesis.

Ladd (1975) showed that the existence of a tax base other than residential real estate might produce a higher level of taxation. The existence of commercial and industrial property in the local tax base opens the possibility that the tax will be shifted forward in the form of higher prices, and not borne by the local residents.

Gramlich and Galper (1973) investigated the use of grants by higher levels of government to subsidize local public goods and services. This can be a substantial issue. For example, federal grants-in-aid to states and municipalities in 1983 exceeded collections from state personal income taxes that year. Gramlich concluded that many grants produce corner solutions and thus affect the income or wealth of the community but not the marginal price of public services.

These issues are of consequence in the present paper as well. The issues of differential voting patterns, shifting of business taxes, and grants-in-aid, are all dealt with explicitly. This paper also raises a further practical objection to the median voter model: that the functioning of representative governments is quite different from the sequential referendum procedure in determining the level of spending.

The representative system offers the potential for greater economic efficiency in determining the level of municipal spending than does the median voter model. One clear fault of the median voter model is that, if it works, it is unlikely to produce the efficient level of public services. Samuelson's condition that the sum of the marginal rates of substitution for the residents equal the marginal rate of transformation requires that the mean demand for public services, not the tastes of the median demander, be reflected in the outcome. Representative government offers the possibility that majoritarian outcomes may yield to more economically efficient outcomes such as those favored by the "omniscient" planner. This possibility is explicitly tested in the present paper.

This paper uses the federal tax deductibility of state and local taxes as the basis for empirical investigation. Studies designed to estimate the demand for state and local services based on tax deductibility have been fairly recent. Zimmerman (1983) uses an explicit median voter model to determine the demand for public goods. His analysis assumes that the median voter and the median income household in the state are synonymous. This is equivalent to assuming that all taxpayers have identical demands for local services, and all variation in quantity demanded is the result of price differences. The fact that a median income family is unlikely to itemize drives Zimmerman's conclusion that federal deductibility has no effect on state and local spending.

Hettich and Winer (1984) examined the share of state taxes derived from the personal income tax in the context of federal deductibility. Their results on the deductibility variable has the wrong sign, meaning that greater deductibility leads to a lower share of income taxes in total taxes. Their study has a number of statistical flaws. Furthermore, some of their findings on tax sources' own price and cross-price elasticities are counterintuitive. Nonetheless, their public choice model of maximization subject to political constraints may well be appropriate.

Inman (1985) examined 41 large cities over the period 1960 to 1980 using an estimate of the average federal tax price prevailing locally. Like Hettich and Winer, Inman reports counterintuitive signs for cross-price elasticities between property and income and sales taxes. Again, an implicit median voter model was used to calculate tax prices. Incomes at the 25th, 50th, and 75th percentiles of local incomes were applied to the national probability of itemizing at those incomes to obtain a federal tax price.

Feldstein and Metcalf (1987) substantially remedied the problems with estimating federal tax price. They used the National Bureau of Economic Research TAXSIM model to calculate the probability of itemizing and the tax rates faced by itemizers in each state. The highly disaggregated data provided by TAXSIM allowed the construction of instrumental variables to avoid the problems of statistical endogeneity between tax collections and tax price. They find very high elasticities of demand for deductible personal taxes with respect to after federal tax price. Feldstein and Metcalf's parameter estimates generally have very large standard errors, but the robustness of the results with respect to model specification lends support to their findings.

Feldstein and Metcalf experiment with three measures of deductibility: the average tax price facing itemizers and nonitemizers, the proportion of taxpayers itemizing, and the tax price facing itemizers. They find that the decomposition of the weighted average tax price into its two components, the proportion of taxpayers itemizing and the itemizers' price, has no substantial effect on their conclusions.

The present paper takes Feldstein and Metcalf as a starting point for analysis, but has a different methodological emphasis. While Feldstein and Metcalf sought a quantitative estimate of the elasticity of state and local spending with respect to tax price, this paper focuses on the mechanism by which the tax price facing individuals is translated into a collective decision, although the present text also quantifies the effect of federal deductibility on state and local tax collections. Several different models of state and local legislative behavior are considered.

First, this paper considers the appropriateness of modeling the expenditure process as representing the wishes of the electorate. This requires a departure from the Feldstein-Metcalf approach, to use the voter, rather than the taxpayer, as the unit of analysis. There are two key differences between voters and taxpayers. First, taxpayers may be family units consisting of more than one voter. Married taxpayers who file a joint return are counted as a single taxpayer by the IRS and on the TAXSIM file. On the other hand, such taxpaying units are likely to have two qualified voters in them. Second, survey evidence suggests that voting is positively correlated with income. Data from exit polls following the 1984 election[1] was used to estimate the likelihood of each tax return producing a voter.

For examination of voter-based models, this analysis adopts, with some modification, two of the Feldstein and Metcalf indicators of tax price: average tax price for all taxpayers and proportion of taxpayers itemizing. The first indicator assumes that the price facing each voter is weighted equally in the legislative process. In the standard version of this model, the price facing nonitemizing voters is unity while the price facing itemizing voters is unity less the value of their tax deduction. The sum of the prices facing all voters is divided by the number of voters to obtain the average price. This measure of price will be termed the "average price facing voters" (APFV) model. This is a more complex version of the median voter model. In that model, all voters are ranked by price and the median voter selected as representative. This model weights the price facing all voters equally, including the prices facing inframarginal voters.

The second voter-based model is the naive deductibility model, or naive write-off (NWO) model. This model assumes that taxpayers only care about whether they can write something off, without regard to the value of the income tax deduction. Although seemingly irrational to public finance economists, this model is in keeping with survey data suggesting that the great majority of the public do not know the marginal tax rate they face. This model is essentially identical to the proportion-itemizing model of Feldstein and Metcalf.

The final Feldstein and Metcalf model—average price facing itemizers—is not considered here. Such a model would be appropriate to a dominant party arrangement where itemizers were the dominant party, selected their median price in a primary election in which only itemizers could vote, and then carried that choice to victory in an election decided strictly by itemizer status.

Unlike Feldstein and Metcalf, the present paper also considers a planner model of public decision making. In this model, the legislative process is viewed as a collective decision based on maximizing collective well being. Here, the price of taxation is the weighted average price of taxes. To compute this weighted average price, the tax saving due to deductibility of a tax is divided by the total revenue collected from that tax. This fraction is then subtracted from unity to obtain the weighted average price to the state of collecting a particular tax.

Unconstrained, the planner model would levy taxes on the taxpayer with the lowest postfederal tax price first, until that taxpayer was pushed to a higher tax price. Then all taxpayers at the higher tax price would be taxed until they were pushed to the next higher tax price. Such a model would maximize the federal share of the total cost of the revenue collected. States might be constrained in adopting extreme versions of this approach because of the mobility of high federal income tax rate voters.

The adoption of this model required consideration of the Feldstein-Metcalf arguments regarding endogenously determined prices. A specification of the effect of prices on taxes is given by equation (1):

$$(1) \qquad T_i = a_0 + a_1 Y_i + a_2 P_i + a_3 \mathbf{Z}_i + u_i.$$

In this model, T is per capita tax collections, Y, per capita income, $\mathbf{Z}$, a vector of demographic attributes of the state, and P, some measure of prices facing voters.

Ordinary least squares will produce unbiased parameter estimates only if values of u_i are independent of price and income. There are two reasons to suspect such independence. First, higher levels of taxation will increase the likelihood that taxpayers will itemize, thus depressing the price variable. Second, among itemizers, as taxes are increased, the taxpayer is pushed into lower tax brackets, thus increasing the value of the price variable.

Feldstein and Metcalf choose three instrumental variables to avoid this problem. The first is the "first-dollar price" which is computed by excluding state and local tax deductions from the itemizer calculus. A marginal tax rate is then assigned to each return from the tax table as is the probability of itemizing based on the national proportion of taxpayers itemizing at the taxpayer's income level. The second instrument is constructed in the same manner as the first, except that the national average amount of state and local tax deductions for the taxpayer's income class replaces the taxpayer's actual deduction before the marginal tax rate is computed. The third instrument is the proportion of taxpayers in the state who would be expected to itemize if each taxpayer's probability of itemizing was equal to the national average for his adjusted gross income class.

The case for such an instrumental variables approach relies on the assumption that an exogenous positive taste for state taxes reduces the federal tax price and induces a negative correlation between the price variable and the stochastic disturbance. Such a situation would overstate the magnitude of a negative price elasticity.

This paper adopts two of these instruments, with some modification, and omits the third. The first-dollar price is computed for each of the three measures of price by eliminating the state and local tax deduction before computing the taxpayer's itemizer status or tax rate. This first-dollar price is then used as the first instrumental measure of the actual price.

Feldstein and Metcalf's second measure is to substitute the average state and local deduction in each taxpayer's income class for the actual deduction claimed by that taxpayer. This instrument seems appropriate for some classes of taxpayers, but not for others. On the one hand, this measure is appropriate for taxpayers who will itemize regardless of their level of state and local taxes. Substitution of the national average level of state and local tax deduction for the actual level eliminates the simultaneity between tax rate and the level of deductions for taxpayers whose itemizer status is not dependent on their level of state and local deductions.

On the other hand, for taxpayers whose itemizer status depends on their level of deductions, the Feldstein-Metcalf method of calculating the instrument may be inappropriate. The key issue is whether or not the taxpayer's deductions are above or below the national average for his or her income class. In the case of taxpayers who have above average levels of state and local deductions, no problem exists. Substituting the average level of such deductions for the actual level implies lowering the level of deductions claimed by that taxpayer. Some of these taxpayers may become nonitemizers as a result. For these taxpayers, with above average state and local deductions, the average level of deductions properly instruments their itemizer status.

But, this instrument is not symmetric for taxpayers with below average state and local deductions. For these taxpayers, substituting the average level of such deductions for the taxpayer's actual level implies raising the total deductions claimed by the taxpayer. Some of these taxpayers should switch from being nonitemizers to being itemizers as a result. But, because no data exist on their deductions, simply adding the average level of deductions to their existing deduction level of zero will not properly instrument their itemizer status. The result is an underestimate of the number of itemizers in states with below average levels of taxes. This underestimate produces a measure of price which is too high in states with low levels of taxes. As a result, it is likely to underestimate the sensitivity of taxes to tax price.

The present study mitigates this problem by determining an estimate of non–state and local tax deductions for these taxpayers. This is accomplished by creating a distribution of non–state and local taxes paid deductions for taxpayers in each income group who would not itemize in the absence of the state and local tax deduction. These taxpayers are assigned a level of non–state and local tax deductions based on this distribution using a Monte Carlo procedure. The average level of state and local tax deductions is then added to the synthetic level of non–state and local deductions to determine the taxpayer's itemizer status and tax rate.

The third instrument used by Feldstein and Metcalf, determining the tax price based solely on the state's income distribution, is not used. This instrument, by substituting a national average measure of price for the actual state price, may be omitting a factor which is uncorrelated with the tastes for spending, but is correlated with the actual price in the state. For example, the state of Utah has the highest proportion of itemizers of any state in the union. The probable reason for this is that the dominant religious group in the state, the Latter Day Saints, practices tithing with regard to their charitable contributions. Substituting a nationally determined instrument for itemizing behavior will overstate the price of taxes in Utah, even though tastes for state spending and for Mormonism are uncorrelated.

Thus, for the voter model, two instruments were selected for each of the two measures of price. For the planner model of behavior, the same kind of instruments were computed for the weighted average price of each tax. Federal taxes were calculated for taxpayers in each state with the deduction for the particular tax in question removed. This zero deduction level of federal taxes was compared with the regular level of federal taxes to calculate the saving from the deductibility of the particular type of taxes. The saving was divided by the total state tax collection from the tax, from itemizers and nonitemizers alike, and the resulting ratio subtracted from unity to obtain a price.

In the case of the first-dollar price instrument, only the deductions of taxpayers who would itemize in the absence of the state and local tax deductions were considered in computing the saving. In the case of the second instrument, only the deductions for taxpayers who were considered itemizers were considered in computing the saving. In both cases, the denominator of the measure of price, total state tax collections, was unaffected.

The price thus obtained was the average price of collecting revenue from the tax. Except in the case of taxpayers who switched tax brackets as a result of the deduction, this is the same as the marginal price of collecting the tax. This measure of price differs from the others considered in that it weights the marginal price faced by each taxpayer by the amount of the tax that taxpayer paid.

The contrast between the voter models and the planner model is based on a choice of perception of the political process as derivative of voter preferences or as exhibiting maximizing behavior on its own.

In the case of the state and local legislative process, the dependent variables in the exercise are the level and composition of state taxes. A similar contrast of models can be made at the federal level. The voting of congressional delegations on the tax reform bill is modeled as functions of both a direct voting procedure by taxpayers and by the impact of the tax reform on the state overall.

The direct voting measure of support for the tax reform bill was computed using the NBER TAXSIM program to conduct a "referendum" among voters. Voters who saw their taxes reduced by at least 0.2 percent of income were assumed to vote yes, while those who saw their taxes increased by at least 0.2 percent of income were assumed to vote no. The voting results were calculated by state for comparison with the vote of the state's congressional delegation.

The planner model of congressional behavior is based on the effect of the tax reform bill on the total federal taxes paid by the state. In this case, congressmen may be assumed to ignore the will of the majority in the referendum if the impact on the state was adverse. The ratio of new to old federal taxes paid by the state was used as the independent variable.

Both models of congressional behavior also provide a means to check on the importance of federal deductibility of state and local taxes in the delegation's set of preferences. State and local elected officials, together with municipal employee organizations, are known to be a potent and organized political force. If the rise in the price of state and local revenue collections is indeed a serious matter, congressional voting on the tax reform bill should reflect that fact. The various measures of the cost of state and local revenue before and after tax reform are therefore entered as independent variables in the congressional voting equations.

Three sets of tests of the importance of federal deductibility of state and local taxes emerge. First, how does the deductibility affect the level of state and local tax collections? Second, how does deductibility affect the mix of taxes used to collect revenues? Finally, was the rise in the price of state and local tax collections (no matter how measured) of sufficient importance to affect congressional voting on the tax reform bill? The next section considers the issues involved in generating the data to examine these questions.

5.3   Sources and Construction of the Data Base

The data used in this study come from two primary sources, *Facts and Figures on Government Finance,* prepared by the Tax Foundation, and simulations performed using the National Bureau of Economic Research TAXSIM model. The former source provided data on the aggregate levels of tax collection, by source, for each state. The latter source was used to calculate the level of itemized deductions and the price of revenue for each revenue source, by state. Data for 1983 were used both for revenue collection and for tax simulation purposes.

5.3.1   Deductibility of Nonpersonal Taxes

In 1983, state and local governments collected $487 billion, or $2,080 per capita. Of this, $385 per capita, or about 18 percent, represented transfer payments from the federal government. An additional $480 per capita represented various charges and miscellaneous sources of revenue, while $1,216 was collected in direct taxes for each person. This latter figure includes personal taxes such as personal income, retail sales, and residential real estate taxes, as well as direct taxes on businesses such as corporate profits taxes and taxes on commercial and industrial real estate. These direct forms of taxation constituted only about 60 percent of all state and local revenue.

Personal taxes made up about three-fifths of these direct taxes, so that typically, only 36 percent of state revenues came from direct personal taxes. Map 5.1 shows the importance of personal taxes in each state. Personal taxes are most important in the industrial states of the Northeast and Midwest, plus California. On the other hand, personal taxes are least important in the resource extraction states. Severance taxes are particularly significant in Alaska, Texas, and Louisiana, and the surface coal mining states of Montana, Wyoming, and the Dakotas.

The net cost to state residents of these various types of revenue is an issue subject to a substantial amount of interpretation. For example, aid from the federal government was treated as exogenous to the price of raising state and local taxes for the purposes of this study. However, a significant amount of federal aid is in the form of matching grants which requires some spending by the state or locality. This matching may alter the effect of differences in the cost of raising revenue. However, the benefits of matching are separable from the benefits of subsidized tax revenue since matching is done based on the gross expenditures of the municipality and not on the net-of-federal-tax cost of raising the money for those expenditures. The assumption of exogeneity of federal aid programs is therefore appropriate. In this conclusion we are largely following the findings of Gramlich (1977).

The various charges levied by the states and municipalities are also subject to interpretation regarding the appropriate measure of their cost. Fees which are levied on the basis of use, rather than wealth or income, are not deductible from the federal personal income tax. Water bills and highway tolls fit into this category. However, the bulk of these charges are borne, at the level of first incidence, by business. These fees include utilities taxes, airport use fees, highway use charges, and

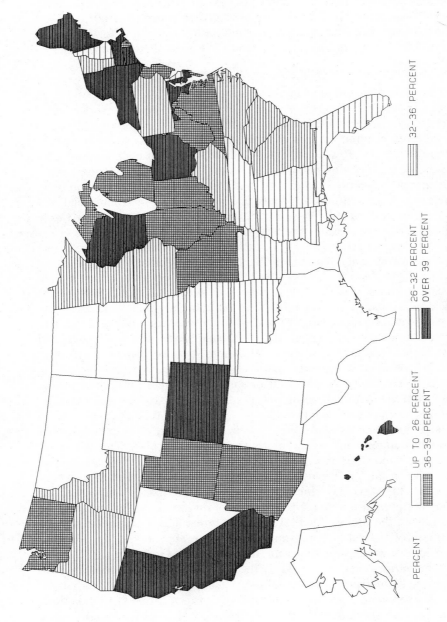

Map 5.1   Personal taxes as a share of revenue. (Map by Andy Mitrusi)

severance taxes. To the extent that these taxes are passed along in product prices, the effect on business profits, and on the net cost of raising the revenue, is nil. This fact makes a case for assuming no federal offset in the cost of raising these taxes.

However, the final consumers who bear the incidence of these taxes may be found in a diffuse national market. Such a conclusion would represent a case for a municipality to view the levying of such taxes as a "free" good since nonresidents would pay the tax. Ladd (1975) investigates this hypothesis.

The possibility that firms may be mobile produces a Tiebout model of location at the firm level. A municipality which is small relative to the national market might therefore view increments to business taxes as falling on land rents. To the extent that these taxes are levied by all municipalities, there will be no diminution of local land rents, since there is no change in relative location values. This study therefore models these taxes in a two-step procedure. First, a base amount equal to the state's revenue from these other sources up to 80 percent of the 50-state average is viewed as passed through to final consumers and therefore nondeductible at the federal level. The excess over this amount is viewed as deductible at the federal corporate rate.

Taxes paid by corporations to states and localities are deductible against the federal corporation income tax. This reduces the net cost of the state tax payment if the corporation has positive profits. If the corporation does not have positive profits, the effect of the state taxes paid is to increase the loss carryforward of the corporation. When the corporation returns to profitability these losses will then be used to offset profits and tax liability. It is not clear from the available data how much state and local taxes are paid by taxable corporations and how much by corporations not subject to tax. This study assumes that state corporate income taxes are fully deductible, since profitability at the state level implies profitability at the federal level. The *Statistics of Income* shows that roughly 80 percent of total sales were made by taxable corporations in 1983. This study therefore assumes that 80 percent of business taxes are deductible.

The available data does not specify the source of property tax revenue. However, the *Census of Governments* provides data on the gross assessed value of locally assessed taxable real property in each state. This study apportioned total property tax collections in proportion to assessed values. Residential real estate was assumed to be taxed to individuals while commercial and industrial real estate plus vacant land was assumed to be taxed to corporations. This neglects the fact that some residential real estate is owned by corporations and that some commercial and industrial real estate is owned by proprietorships and partnerships.

5.3.2   Personal Taxes

The three major sources of personal tax revenues are personal income taxes, sales taxes, and property taxes. As mentioned above, residential property was assumed to be owned by individuals and real estate taxes on such property deducted at the individual level. Individual income and sales taxes required no such apportionment.

Map 5.2 shows which of these taxes is the primary source of personal tax revenue in each of the states. As the map clearly shows, the largest source of personal taxes is the retail sales tax, being the dominant tax in 25 states. Property taxes dominate in 10 states while personal income taxes are the dominant form of personal taxation in 15 states. The regional variation is quite marked. Sales taxes are the most popular in the South and West. Income taxes dominate in the East, except for New England where residential property taxes generate the most revenue.

The deductibility of these personal taxes depends on the itemizer status of the taxpayer, and the value of the deduction depends on the taxpayer's marginal tax rate. In order to compute these values, the National Bureau of Economic Research TAXSIM model was used. This computerized model, like similar models at the Department of Treasury and the Joint Committee on Taxation relies on a large data base of actual tax returns. For this study, the 1983 Individual Tax Model File Public Use Sample was used. This data base contains a stratified random sample of roughly 120,000 individual tax returns for 1983. Because of cost considerations, a one in four random sample of the data was used.

The TAXSIM routine calculates the itemizer status, tax liability, and marginal tax rate of each taxpayer by simulating the effect of the tax law on the data contained on the taxpayer's tax return. Values for 1983 were computed based on the tax law and tax rates prevailing in that year.

In order to simulate the effect of the new tax law, the Tax Reform Act of 1986, the 1988 version of that law was selected. The dollar values contained in that version were deflated to 1983 levels using the estimated change in the consumer price index between those years. Thus, the tax brackets, standard deduction, and personal exemptions all reflected the real value of their actual 1988 levels evaluated in 1983. The effect of the new law was then simulated in the same manner as the old law, with a new itemizer status, tax liability, and marginal tax rate for each taxpayer.

The Individual Tax Model File contains state identifiers for all taxpayers with incomes under $200,000. State identifiers are withheld from the top bracket taxpayers in order to protect confidentiality. These taxpayers constituted only 0.2 percent of the total number of tax returns

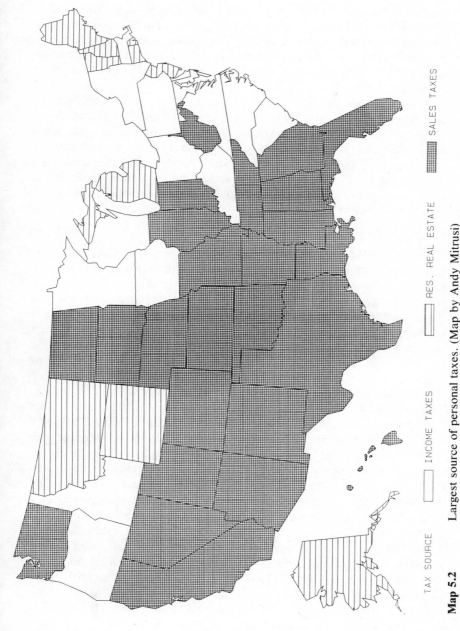

TAX SOURCE   ☐ INCOME TAXES   ☐ RES. REAL ESTATE   ▦ SALES TAXES

Map 5.2   Largest source of personal taxes. (Map by Andy Mitrusi)

filed in 1983. Thus, for measures which weighted all taxpayers equally, such as those used by Feldstein and Metcalf, neglect of the top bracket taxpayers was of little consequence. However, these taxpayers pay state and local taxes, particularly income taxes, out of proportion to their numbers. Thus, a weighted average measure of the price of raising state and local revenue must include the effect of deductibility on these taxpayers.

To accomplish this, the distribution among the states of income for taxpayers earning over $200,000 was computed from the 1981 *Statistics of Income*. (This was the last *SOI* to include a state-by-state breakdown by income class.) The national aggregate values for the income and tax data from the 1983 Individual Tax Model File were apportioned among the states using this data. This high-income data was then added to the data for taxpayers with incomes under $200,000 to obtain a state-by-state total level of taxes, deductions, and income.

5.3.3 Other Measures

The TAXSIM program automatically converts the number of taxpayer files it studies into a representative number of actual taxpayers by using a sample weight from the taxpayer file. The analysis done in this paper was not done by tax return, however, but by voter. Given the objective of measuring the importance of public sentiment, this is a key transformation. TAXSIM assigned a number of voters to each tax return using the income and marital status of the household filing the return based on data drawn from exit polls following the 1984 election.

The probability of voting varies most significantly with income class. The data showed that 29 percent of eligible persons with incomes under $5,000 vote, as do 40 percent with incomes between $5,000 and $10,000, 45 percent with incomes between $10,000 and $20,000, 66 percent with incomes between $20,000 and $30,000, 74 percent with incomes between $30,000 and $40,000 and 85 percent with incomes over $40,000. The adjusted gross income of elderly taxpayers was augmented by $6,000 for single returns and $10,000 for joint returns with two elderly exemptions in order to calculate the likelihood of taxpayers on those returns voting. Tax returns filed using single taxpayer, head of household, and married filing separately filing status were assumed to represent a single potential voter. Tax returns filed by married taxpayers filing jointly were assumed to have two potential voters. The probability of voting given the income class of the taxpayer was multiplied by the number of potential voters in the household to assign an actual number of voters to each tax return.

The calculations done on deductibility and price used these new sample weights to determine statewide levels. A tax return was calculated as itemizing if the total deductions claimed on the return exceeded the standard deduction for the tax law being simulated. Households which itemize face lower prices than those which do not. These taxpayers are therefore more likely to favor state and local public spending than are other households.

Map 5.3 shows the proportion of voters itemizing in each state. The earlier study by Feldstein and Metcalf found that nonitemizers filed a majority of the tax returns in each state. As married couples are more likely to itemize than nonmarried individuals and as higher income taxpayers are more likely both to itemize and to vote, their finding is reversed with the use of this measure. Nonitemizers are a majority of voters in 22 states while itemizers dominate in 28. Higher-income states clearly tend to have more itemizers than do lower-income states.

Separate calculations were done to find the average price facing itemizers and the cost of all state and local tax deductions. For these variables, the values for all state and local taxes were set to zero and taxes recomputed. The price of state and local taxation facing each itemizer was the difference between his taxes with and without his tax deduction divided by the amount of state and local taxes claimed. The total change in taxes for all itemizers was divided by total personal taxes collected to obtain a weighted average price of collecting personal taxes.

The average price of revenue facing voters, the APFV measure of price, was computed by averaging the prices faced by itemizers, multiplying this figure by the proportion of the state's voters who itemized, and adding the proportion of the state's voters who did not itemize. Map 5.4 shows this average price measure in the various states. Again, poorer states have higher prices of revenue than do richer states. The lowest prices are found in the industrial parts of the Northeast and Midwest while the highest prices are found in the South.

The average price of revenue differs from the average price facing voters in that it weights each taxpayer's price by the amount of taxes that taxpayer paid. The average price of revenue is generally lower than the average price facing voters because higher-income taxpayers, with lower prices, are likely to pay an above average portion of the state's taxes. The average price of revenue, known as the weighted average price (WAP), is shown in map 5.5. The same basic regional pattern emerges for this measure of price as for the earlier measures of price.

5.4   Econometric Results

The objective of this research was to test the mechanism by which state and local tax deductibility affects decision making by elected

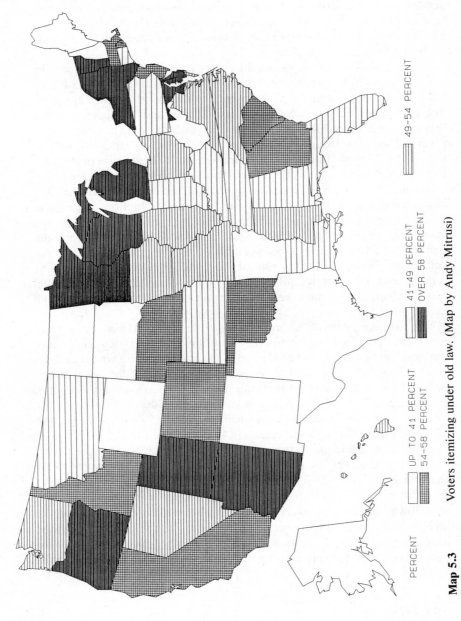

PERCENT

UP TO 41 PERCENT   41-49 PERCENT   49-54 PERCENT

54-58 PERCENT   OVER 58 PERCENT

Map 5.3   Voters itemizing under old law. (Map by Andy Mitrusi)

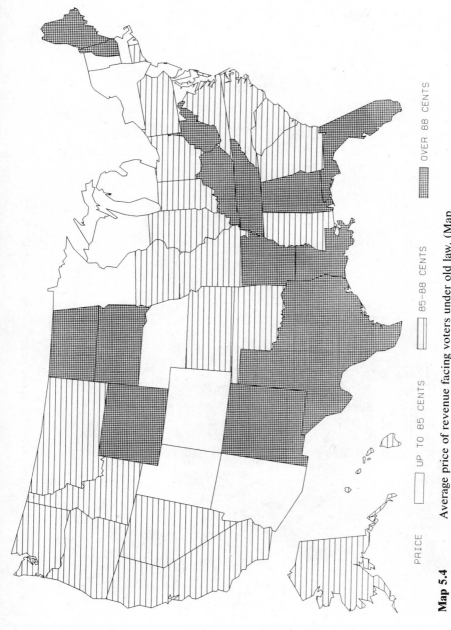

PRICE   UP TO 85 CENTS   85-88 CENTS   OVER 88 CENTS

Map 5.4   Average price of revenue facing voters under old law. (Map by Andy Mitrusi)

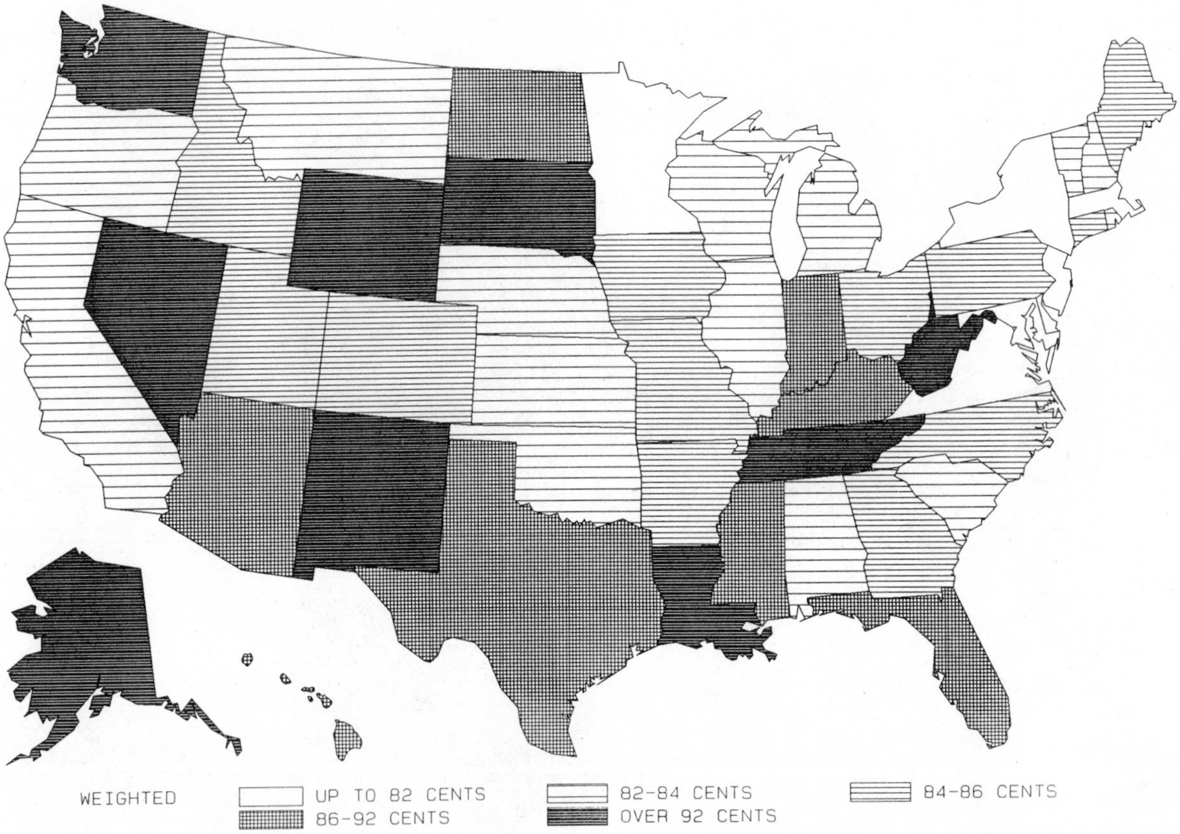

Map 5.5 Average price of revenue under old law. (Map by Andy Mitrusi)

WEIGHTED

UP TO 82 CENTS
82–84 CENTS
84–86 CENTS
86–92 CENTS
OVER 92 CENTS

representatives. Three sets of tests are considered. First, how much, and by what mechanism, are state and local decision makers influenced by deductibility in setting the level of taxes. Second, how much, and by what mechanism, are state and local decision makers influenced by deductibility in setting the type of taxes levied? Third, did state congressional delegations take account of the effect of the Tax Reform Act of 1986 on the cost of raising state and local revenue? Each question is considered in turn.

5.4.1 Deductibility and the Level of Taxes

To test the relationship between deductibility and the level of taxes, a reduced form equation was specified with the per capita level of taxes as the dependent variable. Independent variables included personal income per capita, price, and other forms of revenue. Since no single specification is structurally related to the decision making process, a variety of definitions of the variables were tried. The general form of the specification is given by equation (2):

$$(2) \qquad T_i = b_0 + b_1 Y_i + b_2 P_i + b_3 R_i + b_4 \mathbf{D}_i + e_i.$$

In this case T represents the per capita level of taxes collected in the state, Y, the per capita level of personal income, P, the price of revenue, R, the level of per capita revenue from exogenous sources, and $\mathbf{D}$ is a vector of demographic characteristics of the state designed to capture tastes for public expenditure.

Absent the demographic variables, the expected results would include positive values for the income coefficient, b_1. In linear form, the income coefficient tells the fraction of each additional dollar of personal income which would be taken in taxes. The demographic variables used to control for tastes are often correlated with income. Absent these taste considerations, which also to some extent reflect the costs of public service provision, there is no particular reason to expect higher state and local taxes in higher income states.

The coefficient on the price term, b_2, describes how federal deductibility influences the level of taxes collected. Greater deductibility lowers the price of raising revenue. If b_2 is negative, as expected, this will imply greater state and local revenue collections as a result of deductibility. Three measures of price are tried. The first is the proportion of taxpayers who are not itemizers. This is the naive write-off model of deductibility since it implies that itemizers only consider the fact that state and local taxes are deductible, not the amount of tax saving such deductibility entails. The second price measure is the average price facing voters. This measure assigns a price of unity to nonitemizers and unity minus the taxpayer's marginal tax rate to itemizers. All voters are counted equally in computing the average price. The final measure is the weighted average price of taxes which weights the prices facing each voter by the amount of personal taxes each pays. This measure is designed to test the planner model of representative behavior. No individual voter should care about the amount of taxes paid by other voters, and hence the weighted average price. But, decision makers who evaluate the net cost of revenue to the state as whole, and not to individual voters, should use the weighted average measure. In some specifications, a weighted average price of revenue, including business taxes, was also tried. As discussed in the previous section, two instrumental variables were used for each of these measures of price: one representing the first-dollar price and the second representing the tax price if the average level of state and local taxes is assigned.

The existence of other revenue sources should influence the level of taxation in the state. For example, states which levy severance taxes on natural resource extraction, or which run very successful state lotteries, might be expected to use this revenue to reduce taxes on the residents. Grants-in-aid from the federal government should substitute for locally raised revenue. As a result, the expected sign on the other revenue coefficient, b_3, is negative. A number of definitions of other revenue are tried to see if some forms of revenue affect state and local tax collections differently from other sources of revenue.

In order to control for the role of tastes in determining the level of state and local taxation, a series of demographic variables were used. In the tables which follow, *PUPILS* represents the ratio of students in school to the state's total population, *ROAD* indicates road mileage per capita, *NONWHITE* is the proportion of the state's population which was nonwhite in the 1980 census, *URBAN* is the proportion of the state's population living in urban areas in 1980, *POVERTY* is the percentage of the state's population below the poverty line, and *ELDERLY* is the percentage of the state's population over age 65. Finally, *HOMEOWN* represents the percentage of the state's population living in a home they own.

Two independent variables are tried, personal taxes per capita and personal plus business taxes per capita. A comparison of the regressions done on just personal taxes with those done on personal plus business taxes shows the amount of substitutability between these taxes.

The results of these regressions are presented in tables 5.1 and 5.2. Table 5.1 shows the regression results when personal taxes per capita is the dependent variable while table 5.2 presents the results when the dependent variable is personal and business taxes per capita. The first set of regressions ignored the effect of other sources of revenue on tax collections, while the second set of regressions included federal aid and interest receipts per capita, and the third set of regressions included

Table 5.1   **Regression Results for Personal Taxes per Capita Using Various Measures of Price**

Variable	Measure of Price					
	NWO1	NWO2	APFV1	APFV2	WAP1	WAP2
Intercept	2089*	2702*	3054	6069*	1982	2444*
INCOME P.C.	−0.02	−0.02	−0.02	−0.05*	−0.02	−0.02
PRICE	−126	−1180*	−1073	−4079*	−12	−484
PUPILS	11	14	13	8	8	10
ROAD	−0.31	−0.36	−0.29	−0.24	−0.32	−0.29
NONWHITE	2.34	2.33	2.23	1.31	2.25	2.07
URBAN	1.58	−1.57	0.99	0.05	2.25	2.00
POVERTY	−34*	−28*	−35*	−31*	−34*	−32*
ELDERLY	20	32	32	27	17	16
HOMEOWN	−18*	−21*	−19*	−21*	−17*	−18*
R^2	0.542	0.634	0.549	0.623	0.540	0.549
Intercept	1984	2579*	2930	6118*	1687	2324
INCOME P.C.	−0.01	−0.01	−0.01	−0.03	−0.01	−0.02
FED&INT P.C.	−0.05	−0.06	−0.05	−0.08	−0.06	−0.03
PRICE	−120	−1202*	−1046	−4302*	−179	−417
PUPILS	15	21	18	16	13	13
ROAD	−0.36	−0.42	−0.34	−0.31	−0.37	−0.32
NONWHITE	2.08	1.98	1.99	0.82	2.01	1.95
URBAN	1.20	−2.20	0.62	−0.77	1.85	1.79
POVERTY	−32*	−26*	−33*	−27*	−31*	−31*
ELDERLY	17	28	21	23	13	14
HOMEOWN	−18*	−22*	−20*	−23*	−17*	−18*
R^2	0.546	0.641	0.552	0.635	0.545	0.550
Intercept	1851	2441*	2785	6034*	1410	2104
INCOME P.C.	−0.00	0.00	−0.01	−0.02	−0.00	−0.01
FED,INT, & OTH	−0.02	−0.02	−0.02	−0.03	−0.02	−0.02
PRICE	−123	−1210*	−1034	−4376*	296	−320
PUPILS	18	23	20	18	16	16
ROAD	−0.36	−0.42	−0.34	−0.31	−0.38	−0.34
NONWHITE	1.97	1.89	1.87	0.72	1.92	1.84
URBAN	0.85	−2.56	0.30	−1.16	1.53	1.48
POVERTY	−30*	−24*	−31*	−25*	−30*	−30*
ELDERLY	15	26	19	21	11	12
HOMEOWN	−18*	−22*	−20*	−22*	−17*	−18*
R^2	0.553	0.650	0.560	0.623	0.554	0.555

Note: An (*) indicates significance at the 95 percent confidence interval.

Table 5.2   **Regression Results for Personal and Business Taxes per Capita Using Various Measures of Price**

Variable	NWO1	NWO2	APFV1	APFV2	WAP1	WAP2
			Measure of Price			
Intercept	1336	2076	1982	6203*	582	1339
INCOME P.C.	0.05	0.05*	0.05	0.02	0.05	0.05
PRICE	−22	−1259*	−669	−4888*	709	−20
PUPILA	45	51	48	44	42	45
ROAD	0.06	0.02	0.08	0.16	0.05	0.07
NONWHITE	0.58	0.65	0.56	−0.56	0.81	0.56
URBAN	−1.93	−5.88	−2.59	−4.43	−1.38	−1.83
POVERTY	−33*	−27*	−33*	−29*	−33*	−33*
ELDERLY	21	36	25	33	20	20
HOMEOWN	−23*	−8*	−24*	−28*	−21*	−23*
R²	0.609	0.671	0.611	0.678	0.617	0.609
Intercept	1736	2388*	2468	6115*	1463	2248
INCOME P.C.	0.01	0.03	0.01	−0.01	0.01	0.00
FED & INT P.C.	0.18	0.16	0.18	0.14	0.17	0.21*
PRICE	−45	−1202*	−773	−4492*	209	−527
PUPILS	28	35	31	30	28	27
ROAD	0.24	0.17	0.25	0.28	0.22	0.29
NONWHITE	1.55	1.51	1.51	0.29	1.53	1.46
URBAN	−0.50	−4.28	−1.14	−2.97	−0.22	−0.29
POVERTY	−40*	−34*	−41*	−35*	−40*	−40*
ELDERLY	31	44	36	40	30	31
HOMEOWN	−22*	−26*	−23*	−26*	−21*	−22*
R²	0.642	0.698	0.644	0.699	0.642	0.647
Intercept	1796	2461*	2516	6240*	1443	2303
INCOME P.C.	0.01	0.02	0.01	−0.01	0.01	0.00
FED, INT, & OTH	0.04	0.04	0.04	0.03	0.04	0.05
PRICE	−28	−1214*	−745	−4569*	283	−487
PUPILS	31	38	34	33	31	30
ROAD	0.16	0.11	0.18	0.23	0.15	0.20
NONWHITE	1.29	1.29	1.27	0.07	1.31	1.21
URBAN	−0.52	−4.42	−1.22	−3.13	−0.32	−0.36
POVERTY	−40*	−34*	−40*	−35*	−39*	−39*
ELDERLY	30	44	34	39	29	30
HOMEOWN	−23*	−27*	−24*	−28*	−22*	−23*
R²	0.634	0.691	0.636	0.693	0.635	0.638

Note: An (*) indicates significance at the 95 percent confidence interval.

federal aid, interest, and other nontax revenue per capita as a dependent variable.

Six different price measures were used, representing two different instruments for each of three different prices. The naive write-off model is indicated by NWO, the average price facing voters by APFV, and the weighted average price by WAP. For each price, the first measure uses the first-dollar method of instrumenting the variable while the second measure uses the imputed national average technique. Both techniques are described in the previous section.

The results strongly suggest that the first-dollar measure of price is inferior to the imputed national average measure, particularly in the two voter-based models—NWO and APFV. In all of the regressions using these measures of price, R^2 was substantially lower using the first-dollar price than when the imputed national average technique was used. In addition, the price variable was consistently statistically significant using the second instrument but never significant using the first instrument.

A likely reason for this is that the first-dollar technique ignores the effect of the state and local tax deduction on the probability of itemizing. Actual decisions regarding the level of state and local spending are likely to be marginal, with little likelihood of affecting a voter's price or itemizing status. The first-dollar instrument calculates price on the extreme assumption that the taxpayer has no state and local tax deduction. While roughly half the voters actually itemize their deductions, the first-dollar method estimates that less than one-third do. The relationship between the proportion itemizing under the first-dollar method and the proportion actually itemizing may be monotonic, but it is likely to be quite complex and certainly not linear. The first-dollar measure therefore is a poor instrument.

The data also show that the voter-based models, NWO and APFV, are much better at estimating the level of personal taxes than is the planner model using the WAP measure of price. The R^2 measure of explanatory power shows that the WAP measure is no better than the first-dollar price measure in the voter-based models. Furthermore, no statistically significant relationship between price and the level of taxation is found using the WAP measure of price.

This evidence strongly supports the conclusion that deductibility of state and local taxes affects the level of state and local spending in a rather egalitarian manner. It seems that the number of voters affected by deductibility is the primary determinant of support for higher state and local spending. Legislatures seem to take very little account of the actual aggregate cost to the state of raising additional revenue, except as it affects the cost faced by typical voters.

Under the NWO model, a switch from having all voters itemize to that in which no voters may itemize would lower personal taxes per capita by about $1,200. Stated in a more realistic context, a decrease in the fraction of voters itemizing of one percentage point would lower personal taxes per capita by $12. This is a very dramatic result. Personal taxes per capita averaged less than $1,000 in 1983, with roughly half of all voters itemizing. An extension of this parameter to the extreme worlds of universal deductibility and no deductibility suggest that tax collections would vary from $400 with no deductibility to $1,600 with universal deductibility.

Three important caveats should be placed on this interpretation. First, it is always dangerous to extrapolate parameters estimated from relatively small cross-sectional differences to extreme situations. Second, such extrapolation is particularly inappropriate if majoritarian decision processes are involved. Given the current state of between 40 percent and 60 percent of voters itemizing, each one percentage point change in the number of itemizers is likely to have a major impact on the outcome of an election. Such an impact would necessarily be diminished in situations where less than 30 or more than 70 percent of the voters itemized. Third, it is important to keep in mind that a reduction in personal taxes does not necessarily mean an equal reduction in spending. Revenue sources such as user charges would become both more economically rational and more politically popular when federal deductibility of other revenue sources is eliminated.

The results from the APFV model reinforce the findings from the NWO regressions. In these regressions, a rise in the APFV measure of price by one percentage point reduces personal taxes by about $4,200. More realistically, this measure says that a one percentage point rise in the average price of taxation for the typical voter reduces personal taxes by $42. It is important to consider the determinants of the APFV measure. First, if the proportion of itemizers falls by one percentage point, the APFV measure of price rises only by the itemizers' marginal tax rate. Thus, a change in the proportion of itemizers moves this measure of price by only about 28 percent as much as it moves the NWO measure of price. Given this interpretation, the $4,200 parameter in the APFV model has almost exactly the same meaning as the $1,200 parameter in the NWO model.

Second, the APFV measure of price rises as itemizers' marginal tax rates fall, but a one percentage point fall in tax rates moves the price only by the percentage of voters itemizing, or about 0.5 percentage points. Thus, a one percentage point fall in the average marginal tax rate faced by itemizers would lower the level of personal taxes by about $21. As a rule of thumb, it would take a 5 percentage point rise in tax rates, equivalent to nearly a 20 percent income tax surcharge, to raise state and local personal taxes per capita by $100. The same change could be accomplished by an 8 percentage point change in the share of voters who itemize.

Table 5.2 presents the same set of regressions as table 1 except that personal and business taxes together form the dependent variable. Once again, the voter-based models determine the level of taxes better than the planner model. The R^2 terms are higher on the NWO and APFV regressions than on the WAP regressions. Also, the first-dollar measure of price again is inferior to the imputed national average instrument.

The results in table 5.2 also mirror those in table 5.1 regarding the relative sizes of the NWO and APFV parameter values. This is somewhat surprising as it implies that increases in the price of personal taxes will not significantly alter the level of business taxes. In other words, the expected drop in personal taxes when the price of such taxes rises, will not be offset by increases in business taxes. Since only direct business taxes are measured here, it does not mean that indirect taxes such as user charges will not be substituted for lower personal tax revenue.

A comparison of tables 5.1 and 5.2 also produces an interesting conclusion about the use of business taxes as a revenue source. Although the parameter value is rarely significant, all 18 regressions of personal taxes per capita have a negative sign for the per capita income parameter. This suggests that, other things equal, personal taxes are lower in higher-income states than in lower-income states. By contrast, the per capita income parameter has a positive sign in 16 of the 18 regressions in which business and personal taxes form the dependent variable. Taken together, it seems that upper-income states clearly rely more on business taxes than do lower-income states.

This calls for a reinterpretation of the Tiebout model with regard to firms. One possibility is that firms are unable to move easily, and can therefore be heavily taxed. A second possibility is that low-income states deliberately maintain low business taxes in order to attract new firms while high-income states need not be as aggressive in attracting new sources of employment.

The existence of nonpersonal, nonbusiness sources of revenue does little to change the basic relationships among tax revenue, income, and price. However, the addition of these variables to the regressions produces the surprising result of very little substitution of these other forms of revenue for personal and business taxes. For example, the regressions show that each dollar of federal aid and interest received lowers personal taxes by between 3 cents and 8 cents, while the sum of personal and business taxes actually rises by between 14 and 21 cents with each dollar of federal aid and interest received! The addition of other own-source revenue implies that personal plus business taxes rise only about 4 or 5 cents per dollar received while personal taxes fall by between 2 and 3 cents per dollar received.

This data suggests that, at the margin, other own-source revenue largely substitutes for business taxes. As these other forms of tax are roughly as large as federal aid and interest, the coefficients mean that other revenue reduces direct business taxes by about 10 cents on the dollar. Still, all of these results are strikingly low. The frequent claim that a new excise is being introduced to "hold the line" on other taxes is given a new interpretation: the new excise will mean that personal taxes will be just as high as they otherwise would have been.

5.4.2   Deductibility and the Type of Taxes

The preceding section showed that higher costs for raising personal taxes lower the level of personal taxes raised, other things equal. This section examines the effect of tax deductibility on the choice of which type of personal tax is used. While most states raise personal taxes from each of the three major sources of taxation—income, retail sales, and real estate—the mix of taxes used varies substantially among the states.

Per capita levels of sales, income, and residential property tax revenues were regressed against the same variables as were personal and personal plus business taxes in tables 5.1 and 5.2. Weighted average price measures were dropped because of the endogeneity of the weights with the type of tax used. In each case, the sum of federal aid plus interest received was used to control for other revenue sources. The results are summarized in table 5.3.

The data show radically different explanations for the three types of taxes analyzed: sales, income, and residential real estate. The models are not very good at predicting the level of sales or income taxes, but the R^2 value is quite good in the case of residential real estate taxes. In the case of sales taxes, the R^2 values show that only about one quarter of the variation in the data is explained by the model. None of the estimated parameters is statistically significant. This suggests that the sales tax may be a "default" tax, only collected if there is no attractive alternative.

Income tax collections are negatively correlated with the price of taxation in a statistically significant manner. An increase of one percentage point in the fraction of taxpayers itemizing produces an $8 increase in the amount of income taxes collected per capita. By contrast, a cut in the APFV measure of price produces about $27 more in income taxes.

As in the case of the NWO and APFV parameters in the total tax regressions, these $8 and $27 figures are essentially equivalent. A one percentage point increase in the proportion of voters itemizing would raise the NWO measure by one point, but the APFV measure by only the itemizers' marginal tax rate. As this rate is approximately 28 percent, the net change in income taxes is about $8 by either measure. By contrast, a one percentage point increase in the itemizers' marginal tax rate would lower the APFV measure by the fraction of voters itemizing, or roughly one-half of 1 percent. In turn, this would imply an increase in income tax revenue of about $13 per capita.

Table 5.3   **Regression Results for Type of Personal Tax Levied Using Various Measures of Price**

Variable	NWO1	NWO2	APFV1	APFV2
		Measure of Price		

Dependent Variable: Sales Taxes per Capita

Variable	NWO1	NWO2	APFV1	APFV2
Intercept	-94	27	-1063	-184
INCOME P.C.	-0.01	-0.01	-0.01	-0.01
FED & INT P.C.	-0.07	-0.06	-0.07	-0.06
PRICE	114	-44	1051	179
PUPILS	17	19	15	19
ROAD	-0.04	-0.04	-0.06	-0.04
NONWHITE	2.54	2.64	2.60	2.67
URBAN	2.97	2.27	3.56	2.49
POVERTY	-0.13	-0.48	1	-1
ELDERLY	-1.07	2.72	-5	2
HOMEOWN	-2.53	-3.60	-1	-3
R^2	0.264	0.261	0.282	0.262

Dependent Variable: Income Taxes per Capita

Variable	NWO1	NWO2	APFV1	APFV2
Intercept	1551	1752	3817*	3934*
INCOME P.C.	0.01	-0.00	-0.01	-0.02
FED & INT P.C.	-0.13*	-0.12	-0.13*	-0.13*
PRICE	-449	-805*	-2604*	-2714
PUPILS	-6	-11	-3	-14
ROAD	0.05	0.01	0.10	0.09
NONWHITE	0.66	0.49	0.36	-0.27
URBAN	-4.29	-4.42	-4.90*	-3.39
POVERTY	-10	-6	-12	-7
ELDERLY	1	0	6	-4
HOMEOWN	-10	-9	-12	-9
R^2	0.310	0.354	0.365	0.342

Dependent Variable: Residential Real Estate Taxes per Capita

Variable	NWO1	NWO2	APFV1	APFV2
Intercept	-344	-18	-984	1137
INCOME P.C.	0.03*	0.04*	0.04*	0.03
FED & INT P.C.	-0.03	-0.02	-0.03	-0.02
PRICE	267	-161	847	-1254
PUPILS	19	24	20	23
ROAD	-0.46	-0.46	-0.48	-0.43
NONWHITE	-2.61	-2.35	-2.42	-2.65
URBAN	0.73	-1.10	0.31	-1.26
POVERTY	-6	-7	-6	-7
ELDERLY	2	11	4	13
HOMEOWN	-4	-7	-4	-7*
R^2	0.659	0.642	0.653	0.661

Note: An (*) indicates significance at 95% confidence interval.

Income taxes are the most efficient revenue source to pass on to the federal government since the amount collected from each taxpayer rises with the taxpayer's federal tax rate. Progressive tax systems may be imposed at the state level with actual burdens which may be quite close to proportional.

In spite of the advantages of progressivity within a state, there is no evidence that the income tax is distributed in a progressive fashion among the states. In fact, the high positive intercept term (significant in the APFV model) and negative, if insignificant, per capita income coefficient ensure that income tax collections take a smaller share of personal income in high-income states than in low-income states. In general, the level of income within a state is a poor explanator of the level of the state's income tax collections.

By contrast, residential real estate taxes are quite closely tied to the level of income in the state. The low and insignificant intercept terms in these regressions coupled with the statistically significant income coefficients suggests that residential real estate collections are roughly proportional to income across the states. The price effect is not significant and is of indeterminant sign.

5.4.3 Voting Behavior of State Congressional Delegations

The Tax Reform Act of 1986 greatly reduced the federal subsidy of state and local tax collections, and eroded the political base for state and local spending. This reduction in federal tax subsidies occurred in three ways. First, the deductibility of state and local sales taxes was eliminated. As map 5.2 indicated, sales taxes are the largest source of personal tax revenue in 25 states. Second, the tax reform act substantially reduced the proportion of voters who will itemize their tax returns. This is due to the elimination of some deductions and to the increase in the standard deduction, the threshold level of deductions needed to become an itemizer. Third, the tax reform act reduced tax rates, thereby cutting the effective federal subsidy for those taxpayers who itemize.

The effect of this on the cost of state and local tax deductions is illustrated by a series of maps. Map 5.6 shows the change in the fraction of voters itemizing in each state. The map indicates that this change is substantial everywhere, with one voter in six switching from itemizer status to nonitemizer. The preceding results showed that the proportion of voters itemizing was a statistically significant indicator of the level of state and local taxes collected.

Map 5.7 evaluates the proportionate reduction in the federal subsidy of state and local tax collections. The map shows that roughly half of the subsidy which existed under old law is eliminated. Generally states in the North with progressive income tax systems fare the best, while

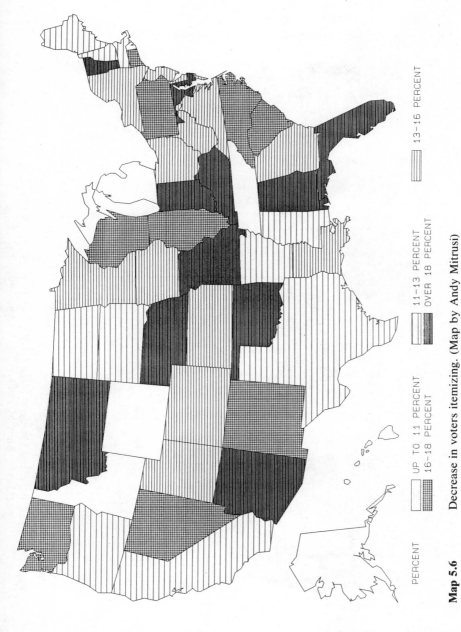

PERCENT

UP TO 11 PERCENT   11-13 PERCENT   13-16 PERCENT

16-18 PERCENT   OVER 18 PERCENT

Map 5.6   Decrease in voters itemizing. (Map by Andy Mitrusi)

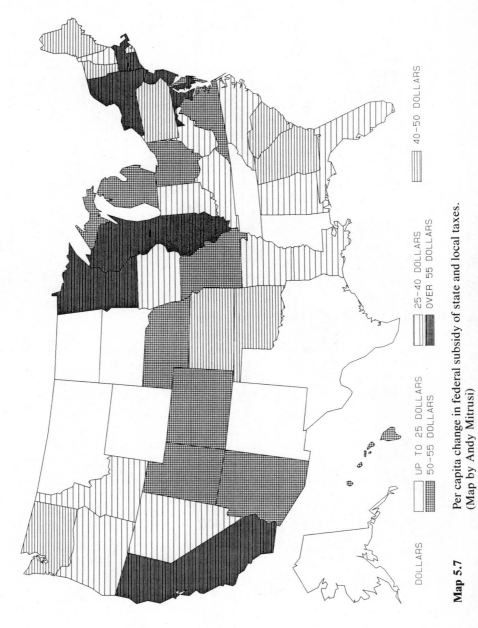

Map 5.7   Per capita change in federal subsidy of state and local taxes.
(Map by Andy Mitrusi)

DOLLARS

UP TO 25 DOLLARS   25–40 DOLLARS   40–50 DOLLARS

50–55 DOLLARS   OVER 55 DOLLARS

states which rely on sales taxes for their revenue fare the worst. The results in map 5.7 may be viewed as overly dramatic. In terms of the weighted average price of revenue, a decline in the federal subsidy of 50 percent typically means a rise in the price from 85 cents to 92.5 cents. Thus, even the dramatic reductions in the federal subsidy should be interpreted as price increases on the order of 10 percent.

Map 5.8 shows the effect of the tax changes on the per capita level of federal subsidy of personal taxes. Here the effect of the tax reform is shown as much more modest. The roughly $11 billion reduction in the federal subsidy is spread among some 230 million people, producing an average per capita change of about $50. This amounts to about 3 percent of state and local personal tax revenue.

Map 5.9 shows the per capita decrease in federal income taxes in the various states. As the map shows, some states will show net tax increases. This is because the bill is revenue neutral overall. Personal taxes are cut while corporate taxes are increased. In this study, the difference between personal taxes under the old law and personal taxes under the new law was taken as the amount of corporate tax increase. This increase was apportioned among taxpayers according to the amount of dividends they received. The corporate tax increase was therefore allocated among the states in proportion to the dividends received by taxpayers in each state. Fully 23 states will see a rise in their federal taxes under this bill.

Clearly the effect of the Tax Reform Act varied substantially among the states. Several indicators of this differential effect were considered. The primary motivation for congressmen was assumed to be the impact on their states overall. The impact of the tax reform bill on the cost of raising revenue for state and local spending was viewed as a secondary, "special interest" concern. A two-stage modeling procedure was therefore undertaken, first to obtain the primary motivations for congressional voting, and then to add the effect of state and local tax deductibility.

First, we constructed a voter model of the tax reform bill. The NBER TAXSIM model was used to compute each taxpayer's taxes under the old law and under the new law. If a taxpayer's taxes declined by at least 0.2 percent of income, the votes assigned to that taxpayer were counted as voting yes on the tax reform bill. If the taxpayer's taxes increased by at least 0.2 percent of income, the votes assigned to that taxpayer were counted as voting no on the tax reform bill. Other voters were assumed to abstain. The votes were tabulated on a state-by-state basis for comparison with the votes of the congressional delegation.

The second model of the impact of the tax bill was the ratio of new tax revenue to old tax revenue. For this purpose two measures were devised: the change in personal taxes only, and the change in personal taxes when the added corporate tax was imputed to individuals.

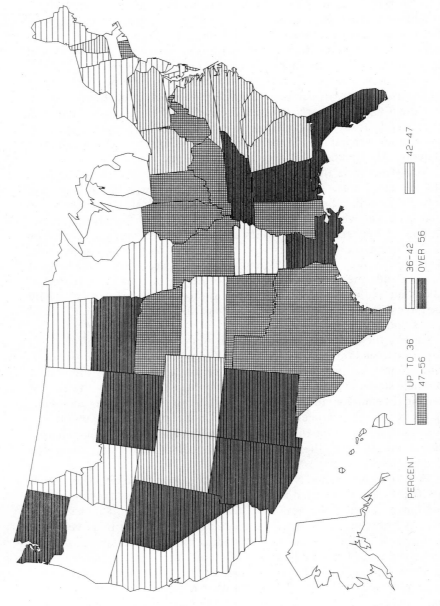

Map 5.8   Decline in federal subsidy of state and local taxes. (Map by Andy Mitrusi)

PERCENT   □ UP TO 36   ▦ 36–42   ▥ 42–47

▩ 47–56   ▤ OVER 56

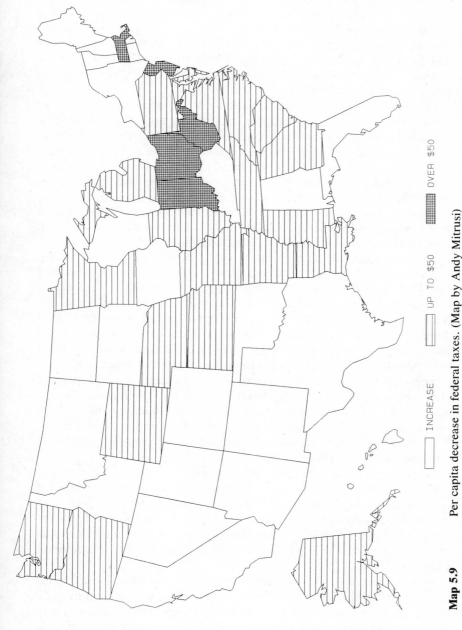

Map 5.9   Per capita decrease in federal taxes. (Map by Andy Mitrusi)

INCREASE   UP TO $50   OVER $50

Congressional delegations were divided along party lines. The dependent variable was the fraction of the congressional delegation voting against the tax reform bill. This fraction was regressed on various combinations of the variables described above. As the tax reform bill was largely a committee compromise bill, the members of the tax-writing committees were not counted in measuring the fraction of the delegation voting on the bill.

The voting of Republican congressional delegations was not explained in a statistically significant manner by any of the variables, either separately, or in combination. In view of the distributional effects of the tax bill, constituent pressure would be likely to incline Republican voters to oppose the tax bill. In addition, Republicans were generally excluded from the tax-writing process under the majoritarian rules of the House of Representatives. On the other hand, Republicans were under pressure from the president to support the bill. Republican voting was therefore determined more by conflicting political pressure than by the economic variables considered here.

The voting of Democratic congressional delegations was explained by the economic impact variables, although the results were not clear-cut. Democrats' opposition to the tax bill was positively correlated with the rise in taxes in their state. Generally, a 1 percent rise in the ratio of new taxes to old taxes increased opposition in the congressional delegation by about 3 percent. Democrats were more sensitive to the change in personal taxes alone, than the change in taxes which included the "pass-through" of the corporate tax increase. A 1 percent increase in personal taxes reduced support by 3.2 percent, but a 1 percent increase in total taxes reduced support by only 2.8 percent. At the margin, the corporate tax increase pass-through had very little effect on Democrats' voting behavior. This may reflect either a belief in the "corporate veil" or an economic expectation that the pass-through was not paid by the constituents that Democrats represent.

Surprisingly, the voter referendum variable was negatively correlated with the vote of the congressional delegation. Generally, a 1 percent increase in the opposition to the tax reform among the voters decreased opposition among the Democratic congressional delegation by about 1.6 percent. The standard errors on these coefficients were marginal to insignificant, however, ranging from 50 to 70 percent of the parameter estimate.

Three explanations for this phenomenon are possible. First, majorities supported the tax reform bill in the TAXSIM referendum in all 50 states. Thus, a median voter model would suggest that an increase in marginal opposition would have no effect on the outcome. Second, given the distributional considerations of the tax reform bill, opposition was likely to be concentrated among constituents supporting the other party. Finally, voter surveys at the time indicated that most voters thought their taxes would go up, in contrast to the findings of TAXSIM. This would indicate that the TAXSIM referendum procedure did not reflect the underlying views of constituents, regardless of whether it was TAXSIM or the constituents who were in error.

Those models which produced statistically significant variables for explaining the behavior of Democratic congressional delegations were used to see if changes in the state and local tax situation had any effect. Changes in the likelihood of itemizing, in the average price facing voters, and in the weighted average prices of personal and total taxes were tried. None produced statistically significant results. Generally the standard errors were five to ten times the parameter estimates. Nor was any consistent sign discernible on the results. It is reasonable to conclude therefore, that the effect of the tax reform bill on state and local taxes had very little impact on congressional voting. This is particularly true about the effect of the tax reform bill on the price of raising state and local revenue. This is a surprising result in light of the intense lobbying on this matter by state and local public officials and public employee unions.

5.5   Conclusion

The results presented here provide a number of conclusions regarding the effects of state and local tax deductibility and the mechanism by which this is transformed by representative governments:

- The level of state and local spending is significantly affected by deductibility.
- The effect of deductibility is stronger on voter-based measures than on aggregate measures of cost.
- Income tax collections per capita were quite sensitive to the price of raising revenue. Low prices were associated with increased use of income taxes.
- Property taxes were insensitive to price, but were closely related to personal income.
- Sales taxes were not easily explained by economic variables and appear to be a residual form of revenue.
- Congressional voting seems more influenced by aggregate effects than by voter-based measures, unlike state and local spending.

Given the substantial changes in the value of federal deductibility of state and local taxes, future researchers have the prospect of sufficient variability in time-series data to test a number of hypotheses suggested by the cross-sectional data presented here.

Note

1. Turnout by income group was computed using exit poll information published in *Public Opinion* (December 1984–January 1985) and compared with the distribution of income on tax returns using TAXSIM.

References

Bergstrom, T. and R. Goodman. 1973. Private demand for public goods. *American Economic Review* 63 (June):286–96.
Bergstrom, T. C. 1979. When does majority rule supply public goods efficiently? *Scandinavian Journal of Economics* 81:216–26.
Bergstrom, T. C., D. L. Rubinfeld, and P. Shapiro. Micro-based estimates of demand functions for local school expenditures. *Econometrica* 50:1183–1205.
Bloom, H. S., H. F. Ladd, and J. Yinger. 1983. Are property taxes capitalized into house values? In *Local Provision of Public Services,* ed. G. R. Zodrow, 145–64.
Borcherding, T. E., and R. T. Deacon. 1962. The demand for the services of nonfederal governments. *American Economic Review* 52:891–901.
Bowen, H. R. 1943. The interpretation of voting in the allocation of economic resources. *Quarterly Journal of Economics* 58:27–48.
Bridges, Benjamin, Jr. 1966. Deductibility of state and local nonbusiness taxes under the federal individual income tax. *National Tax Journal* 14 (March):1.
Buchanan, J., and D. R. Lee. 1982. Tax rates and tax revenues in political equilibrium: some simple analytics. *Economic Inquiry,* 20 (July):344–54.
Feldstein, M., and G. Metcalf. 1987. The effect of federal tax deductibility on state and local taxes and spending. *Journal of Political Economy.* 95, no. 4 (August):710–36.
Gramlich, E., and H. Galper. 1973. State and local fiscal behavior and federal grant policy. *Brookings Papers on Economic Activity* 1:15–58.
Gramlich, E., D. Rubinfeld, and D. Swift. 1981. Why voters turn out for tax limitation votes. *National Tax Journal,* 34:115–24.
Hettich, W., and S. Winer. 1984. A positive model of tax structure. *Journal of Public Economics* 24:67–87.
Hotelling, Harold. 1929. Stability in competition. *Economic Journal* 39 (January):41–57.
Inman, Robert P. 1979. The fiscal performance of local governments: An interpretive review. In *Current Issues in Urban Economics,* ed. P. Mieszkowski and M. Streasizheim, 270–321. Baltimore: Johns Hopkins University Press.
———. 1979. Subsidies, regulations, and the taxation of property in large U.S. cities, *National Tax Journal,* 32 (June):159–68.
———. 1985. Does deductibility influence local taxation? NBER Working Paper No. 1714. Cambridge, Mass.: National Bureau of Econ. Research.
———. 1987. Markets, governments, and the "new" political economy. In *Handbook of Public Economics,* vol. 2, ed. A. Auerbach and M. Feldstein. Amsterdam: North Holland.
Ladd, Helen F. 1975. Local education expenditures, fiscal capacity, and the composition of the property tax base. *National Tax Journal* 28:145–58.

————. 1984. Federal aid to state and local governments. In *Federal Budget Policy in the 1980s,* ed. G. B. Mills and J. L. Palmer. Washington, D.C.: Urban Institute.

Noto, N. A. and D. Zimmerman. 1983. Limiting state-local tax deductibility in exchange for increased general revenue sharing: An analysis of the economic effects. Senate Print 98-77, Washington, D.C.: U.S. Government Printing Office.

————. 1984. Limiting state-local tax deductibility: Effects among the states. *National Tax Journal* 37:539.

Public Opinion, December 1984–January 1985. Opinion roundup, 23–43.

Romer, T. and H. Rosenthal. Political resource allocation, controlled agendas, and the status quo. *Public Choice,* 33:27–43.

————. 1979. Bureaucrats vs. voters: On the political economy of resource allocation by direct democracy. *Quarterly Journal of Economics* 93:563–87.

————. 1979. The elusive median voter. *Journal of Public Economics* 12:143–70.

————. (December, 1980). An institutional theory of the effect of intergovernmental grants. *National Tax Journal* 33:451–58.

Rubinfeld, D. 1977. Voting in a local school election: A micro analysis. *Review of Economics and Statistics* 59:30–42.

————. 1980. On the economics of voter turnout in local school elections. *Public Choice* 35:315–31.

————. 1987. The economics of the local public sector. In *Handbook of Public Economics,* vol. 2, ed. A. Auerbach and M. Feldstein. Amsterdam: North Holland Press.

Tax Foundation, Inc. 1983. *Facts and figures on government finance.* Washington, D.C.: Tax Foundation.

U.S. Bureau of the Census. 1982. *Property taxation, census of governments.* Washington, D.C.: U.S. Government Printing Office.

Zimmerman, Dennis. 1983. Resource misallocation from interstate tax exportation: Estimates of excess spending and welfare loss in a median voter framework. *National Tax Journal* 36:183–202.

Comment   Daniel Feenberg

Because the publication version of this paper answers the more significant points raised in the original discussion these comments are limited to a few minor points.

First, in the regressions of state and local tax revenues on their after federal tax price Lindsey adopts improved instruments for the obviously endogenous tax price terms. These improvements take into account the potentially deductible expenses of the nonitemizer and provide an increase in efficiency over simpler instruments used by Feldstein and Metcalf. The statistically significant results are certainly

Daniel Feenberg is a research associate at the National Bureau of Economic Research.

welcome but the new instruments are not required for unbiased coefficient estimates. While the instruments used by Feldstein and Metcalf are certainly biased estimates of actual tax prices, this would not, in and of itself, lead to biased coefficients in the second stage of the regression, as the paper implies.

Given the relatively few degrees of freedom available and the plausibility (to me) of the results presented in table 5.1, I hesitate to suggest additional explanatory variables, yet the religious composition of states is readily available and might be an important determinant of the taste for public spending.

The regression predicting the voting behavior of Democratic congressmen on the Tax Reform Act of 1986 (TRA) is easily the most surprising (and interesting) result in the paper. In the regressions each state is an observation and the dependent variable is the proportion of Democratic representatives voting for the act. Lindsey calculates the number of voters in each state whose taxes will be raised or lowered significantly by the TRA and holds a mock referendum. The referendum result however has no explanatory power. Nor does the effect of the TRA on the after federal tax price of state and local revenues seem to have any effect on congressmen. The only effect seems to come from the TRA's effect on per capita federal tax liabilities. The obvious conclusion is that the congressmen were responding to regional interests while ignoring class interests normally thought to be very powerful. This result can be questioned on a number of grounds, including omitted variables, the presence of strategic voting and logrolling, the use of an inappropriate linear probability model, and the absence of formal hypothesis testing, but it remains a thought-provoking result.

6 Eliminating State and Local Tax Deductibility: A General Equilibrium Model of Revenue Effects

George R. Zodrow

6.1 Introduction

Much attention has been focused recently on the effects of eliminating or reducing federal deductibility of state and local taxes. Early congressional reform proposals recommended the elimination of deductibility for various state and local taxes, and the November 1984 Treasury proposal, as well as the May 1985 administration reform package recommended complete elimination. The Tax Reform Act of 1986 eliminates deductibility for general sales taxes, and further curtailment is frequently suggested as a means of reducing currently projected budget deficits.

Eliminating deductibility raises a host of troublesome issues, including a wide variety of allocational and distributional questions, which have been examined in the literature (see Kenyon 1986 and Advisory Commission on Intergovernmental Relations 1985a). This paper focuses primarily on the revenue issues raised in a recent paper by Feldstein and Metcalf (1987), who argue that changes in the revenue mix utilized by state and local governments will result in dramatic reductions in the federal revenue gained from eliminating deductibility, relative to revenue estimates that ignore such adjustments. Specifically, they argue that the elimination of deductibility of state and local personal taxes (income, property, and general sales taxes) will induce state and local governments to switch to business taxes which remain fully

George R. Zodrow is associate professor of economics at Rice University.

Research support from the National Bureau of Economic Research Project in State and Local Government is gratefully acknowledged. I would like to thank Dan Feenberg and Harvey Rosen for granting me access to their state tax data base, Andrew Mitrusi for computer programming assistance, and John Thornburgh and Oscar Hendrick for research assistance.

deductible against federal taxes under all the reform proposals. Since only the portion of personal taxes which are claimed by itemizers are deducted from the federal tax base while virtually all business taxes are deducted and at generally higher tax rates, this change in the state and local revenue mix potentially could have dramatic consequences for federal revenue. Indeed, Feldstein and Metcalf estimate that the change in the state and local revenue mix induced by eliminating deductibility would eliminate between one-half and all of the revenue gain predicted by "static" revenue estimating techniques which ignore such revenue mix effects.[1]

The impact of such a response on the extent to which marginal tax rates could be reduced within the context of a revenue-neutral tax reform is obviously significant. For example, Feldstein and Metcalf note that, by 1990, elimination of deductibility in the administration reform package would account for more than 85 percent of the revenue obtained from individual base-broadening items; the much more limited repeal of deductibility for only general sales taxes is predicted to raise approximately $4 billion by 1990.

There is a lack of consensus in the literature regarding the revenue effects of eliminating deductibility. The Feldstein and Metcalf results are in marked contrast to earlier studies by Zimmerman (1983), Hettich and Winer (1984), Noto and Zimmerman (1983), and Inman (1986), who find that the state and local revenue mix is not responsive (or responsive in the wrong direction) to changes in the effective cost of using various revenue instruments when the benefits of federal tax deductibility are taken into account; Feldstein and Metcalf provide a critique of these earlier studies. Other studies suggest that only certain taxes are responsive to changes in their effective costs due to changes in deductibility. For example, Kenyon (1986) finds that state use of income taxes is highly sensitive to changes in deductibility while state use of sales taxes is not, while Gade (1986) finds instead that state use of sales taxes is more responsive to changes in deductibility than is state use of income taxes; Holtz-Eakin and Rosen (in this volume) suggest that municipal use of deductible personal taxes is responsive to changes in federal deductibility, but the use of sources of finance that are not deductible at the personal level is not. Additional uncertainty is created by the fact that the estimated coefficients used by Feldstein and Metcalf to generate their revenue predictions are characterized by relatively large standard errors. Finally, the appropriate model of state and local government tax and expenditure determination is far from clear.

One frequently used candidate is the median voter model (e.g., see Gramlich 1985 and Zimmerman 1983); the median voter framework is utilized in this paper. However, several alternatives are equally plausible, including the "average voter" model (see Craig and Inman 1985) which accounts for the political influence of nonmedian voters on tax and expenditure policies, as well as various migration models (e.g., see Herzog and Schlottmann 1986) and "Leviathan" models of government behavior (e.g., see Romer and Rosenthal 1983). Since all these approaches have their proponents and detractors, any study based on a particular model is more likely to be viewed as simply providing another candidate for explaining the effects of eliminating deductibility rather than providing the definitive answer. For all of these reasons, it would seem fair to say that there is still some uncertainty regarding the effects of eliminating deductibility on the state and local revenue mix and on federal tax revenues.

In this paper, I construct a two-sector general equilibrium model which, although obviously not a substitute for the type of detailed revenue estimation performed by the Treasury, is designed to focus on these effects and to provide additional information relevant to the question of the directions and magnitudes of the revenue effects of eliminating deductibility. Three aspects of this approach differentiate it from previous analyses. First, the two-sector approach permits the modeling of two very different responses to the elimination of deductibility. In general it is clear that, within a framework where the government is acting to maximize the welfare of the median voter, the response will depend quite dramatically on whether the median voter is an itemizer. If this is the case, the median voter will experience a significant change in the effective price of government services—to a price of one from a price of one minus the individual marginal tax rate in the simplest case—while if the median voter is not an itemizer, eliminating deductibility will not directly affect the effective tax price for government services. The model is constructed to emphasize how the responses of jurisdictions where the median voter is an itemizer differ from the responses of jurisdictions where that is not the case, with the aggregate effects depending on the relative sizes of the itemizer and nonitemizer sectors.

Second, a general equilibrium approach permits an analysis of a number of endogenous responses to the elimination of deductibility, including the reallocation of capital which will occur in response to changes in state and local capital taxes and the associated changes in the net return to capital, wages, and income. These in turn permit an explicit calculation of the effects on both personal and corporate federal tax revenues, as well as a calculation of the reduction in tax rates made possible by eliminating deductibility when revenue mix and general equilibrium effects are taken into account. In addition, a general equilibrium analysis permits explicit calculation of the effects of the reduction in marginal tax rates on the endogenous variables in the model. As noted by Kenyon (1985), the effects of eliminating deductibility depend on views about incidence; the analysis in this paper provides an explicit calculation of these effects within the context of a Harberger-type general equilibrium model.

Third, in light of the uncertainty described above regarding the revenue effects of eliminating deductibility, the model may be useful in that it provides results that suggest what state and local governments "should" do in response to the elimination of deductibility if they are in fact following the median voter paradigm. The model makes explicit behavioral assumptions about governmental behavior, including the choice of revenue instruments, and then calculates the implications of those assumptions when deductibility is eliminated. To the extent the model and its behavioral assumptions are believable, some insight as to the optimal long-run response to eliminating deductibility may be obtained. In this sense, the paper is similar in spirit to the earlier work of Zodrow and Mieszkowski (1986), in which a general equilibrium framework is used to analyze the national effects of both tax and expenditure policies that are determined endogenously at the local level.

Before proceeding, it may be useful to comment briefly on the difficulties of using a Harberger-type model to analyze the effects of eliminating deductibility—in addition to the problem of determining which model of state and local tax and expenditure determination to employ. An obvious problem characteristic of such analytical models is that a very high level of aggregation is required; in the model analyzed, the economy is simply divided into two groups of states with each group assumed to act as a single sector with a government that is acting to maximize the welfare of a single median voter. Second, the initial equilibrium is necessarily characterized by existing taxes, expenditure levels, and policies regarding deductibility. As a result, the analytically convenient trick of assuming zero initial taxes and expenditures cannot be used; as is well known, this complicates the differential incidence analysis considerably. Third, in addition to the usual mix of prices and quantities in a general equilibrium model, state and local government behavior must be modeled endogenously. To examine the revenue mix question, a minimum of two tax variables in each sector is required; again, this complicates the differential incidence results. Moreover, an optimal tax problem must be formulated to determine how governments choose between taxes—in particular, an explanation must be found for why state and local governments use nonbenefit taxes on capital when, at least under certain circumstances, optimizing governments would avoid such taxes entirely if capital is perfectly mobile in the long run (see Zodrow and Mieszkowski 1983); one possibility is offered in the analysis below.

The paper is organized as follows. The assumptions and structure of the model are specified in the following section. Differential incidence results are presented in section 6.3, and numerical simulation results are presented in section 6.4. A brief concluding section summarizes the results and suggests directions for future research.

6.2   The Model

The analytical framework utilized in the paper is a two-sector general equilibrium model where expenditure and tax policies in each sector are selected to maximize the welfare of the median voter in that sector. The model is a highly aggregated one where the first sector represents a group of states where the median voter itemizes deductions for federal tax purposes, and the second sector represents the remaining group of states where the median voter is assumed to be a nonitemizer. The model is designed to analyze the effects of eliminating (or reducing) state and local tax deductibility on the mix and levels of state and local revenues and on federal tax revenue, with an emphasis on the differing responses of the two sectors and a variety of general equilibrium effects.

The model is constructed as follows. The fifty states and the District of Columbia are ranked in order of percentage of itemizers, with joint returns double-weighted to reflect the presence of two voters per return. The states are divided into two sectors indexed by j, with N^* states with a percentage of itemizers greater than some cut-off percentage (F^*) forming a sector $(j = 1)$ where the median voter is assumed to be an itemizer, and the remaining $51 - N^*$ states forming a sector $(j = 2)$ where the median voter is a nonitemizer.[2] The appropriate value of F^* and thus N^* is not entirely clear; however it is quite likely to be less than 50 percent if high-income individuals are more likely to vote or exert more influence in the political process (see Feldstein and Metcalf for a discussion of the role of the median voter in expenditure determination). Indeed, the new results presented by Lindsey (in this volume) are the first to provide an estimate of N^* (29) that reflects the fact that high-income individuals are much more likely to vote than are relatively low-income individuals.[3] In the simulations, results are presented for $N^* = 19$, 29, and 39; the results for $N^* = 19$ and $N^* = 39$ should bound the "true" value, with $N^* = 29$ providing the best point estimate.

Within each of the two sectors (hereafter, the "itemizer" and "nonitemizer" sectors), tax and expenditure policies are assumed to be set to maximize the welfare of a single representative median voter. The responses of each sector to changes in the federal deductibility of state and local taxes are thus determined by the effects of the policy change on each sector's median voter, subject to a sectoral government budget constraint. Such an approach should be viewed as suggestive since it is obviously subject to all the criticisms made of the median voter model (to even a greater extent since the level of aggregation is so great). Nevertheless, this application of the median voter framework makes the general equilibrium model analytically tractable, and focuses on how state and local government responses to the elimination of deductibility depend on whether the median voter is an itemizer.

The details of the model are as follows. The population is assumed to be fixed. Since most studies suggest that eliminating state and local deductibility is unlikely to result in much migration even within metropolitan areas (see Gramlich 1985, Herzog and Schlottmann 1986, and Chernick and Reschovsky 1987), an assumption of no interstate migration, which in turn implies no migration within the two-sector context analyzed here, seems plausible.

Production is modeled is as simply as possible. There is a single production good which is the numeraire. This single production good is produced with a Cobb-Douglas production function using a fixed factor (a composite of land and labor in each sector, hereafter referred to as labor and denoted as L_{Tj}) and capital (K_{Tj}), with the capital share parameter denoted as a. (In general, total quantities in a sector will be denoted with a T subscript, while median voter quantities will be denoted simply by the appropriate j subscript; for example, L_j refers to the amount of labor supplied by the median voter in sector j). Constructing a restricted profit function in each sector—$\pi_j(r_j, L_{Tj})$—implies that capital demands (K_{Tj}) and wages (w_j) are

(1) $$K_{Tj} = -\pi_{jr}(r_j, L_{Tj})$$

(2) $$w_j = \pi_{jL}(r_j, L_{Tj}),$$

where the subscripts following the j subscript denote differentiation with respect to the arguments of the restricted profit function in sector j.[4] The price elasticity of demand for capital is constant for the Cobb-Douglas production function and is denoted by μ_K,

$$\mu_K = (r_j/K_{Tj})(\partial K_{Tj}/\partial r_j) = -r_j\pi_{jrr}/\pi_{jr} = 1/(1 - a) > 0.$$

Public services are modeled as publicly provided private goods—government purchases of the single production good which are shared equally within a sector (see Hamilton 1983 for a justification). Total public services are denoted as G_{Tj} and the median voter in sector j receives $G_j = G_{Tj}/N_j$, where N_j is the number of households in sector j. Thus, the model ignores any benefit spillovers or utility interdependencies associated with state and local public goods, as well as any cost differences across jurisdictions in producing such goods.

Capital is perfectly mobile across sectors and earns a net return r. The total supply of capital in the economy (K) is fixed. The fixed factor (L_{Tj}) in each sector earns a net return specific to that sector (w_j). Note that the model thus has the hybrid long-intermediate-run characteristics typical of Harberger-type models; in this case, labor and the aggregate capital stock are fixed as would be expected in an intermediate-run model, but the allocation of capital and the tax and expenditure policies of the state and local governments are free to vary as would be expected in a long-run model. The fixed factors in each sector are assumed to be locally owned, and capital ownership is assigned independently of jurisdiction of residence.

The median voter in each sector has a standard utility function defined over consumption of private and public goods—$U_j(C_j, G_j)$. The model assumes that the tax and expenditure policies of each sector are set by a single government which acts to maximize the utility of the median voter in that sector. Each government has two tax instruments. The first is a personal general sales or proportional income tax rate t_j (hereafter, all deductible personal taxes are referred to as "sales" taxes). There is no saving in the model and all goods are assumed to be purchased locally with no transportation costs for intersectoral sales; thus, sales and proportional income taxes are equivalent in the model. Since there is no housing in the single-good model, residential property taxes are not treated explicitly.[5] (One interpretation is that housing capital is fixed and residential property taxes should be included in deductible sales tax revenues; this is the approach followed in the simulations.) In the initial equilibrium, sales taxes are fully deductible against federal taxes for itemizers.[6]

The second tax instrument is the business capital income tax rate k_j, which reflects nonbenefit taxation of mobile capital in the form of corporate income taxes or nonresidential property taxes (hereafter, the "capital" tax). Capital taxes are fully deductible against federal corporate taxes, and all firms are assumed to be corporations. The only other source of revenue is federal grants; debt, user charges, severance taxes, selective sales taxes, and any other taxes are ignored.

The response expected by each government to a change in its capital tax rate is a critical element of the model. Capital income is assumed to be subject to a fixed federal corporate tax rate (κ), with state and local capital taxes fully deductible against federal taxes.[7] Thus, the relationship between the net return to capital (r) and the gross price of capital in each jurisdiction (r_j) is

(3) $$r = r_j (1 - \kappa)(1 - k_j) .$$

In setting its capital tax rate k_j, each sectoral government perceives that an increase in k_j will be shifted to some extent. However, the expected extent of shifting is not constrained to be that which would correspond to a perfectly elastic supply of capital to that sector; instead the expected extent of shifting is determined (in a way that will be described below) from the revenue mix in the initial equilibrium. This modeling approach allows the two sectoral governments (and thus implicitly the individual jurisdictional governments which make up the two sectors) to differ in the extent to which they expect capital taxes to be shifted. This in turn allows the model to be consistent with the results presented by Lindsey (in this volume) which indicate that high-income states raise a higher amount of tax revenue per dollar of personal income (relative to low-income states) but that the extra revenue comes from relatively high business taxes rather than high personal taxes; one explanation for this phenomenon offered by Lindsey is that the high-income states expect that business firms are relatively immobile and that capital can be taxed relatively heavily. Within the context of the model in this paper, this interpretation would imply that the expected extent of shifting of capital taxes in the relatively high income itemizer sector would be greater than that in the relatively low income nonitemizer sector; this is indeed the pattern observed in the numerical simulation results reported below.

This expected or perceived extent of shifting of taxes on capital is modeled as a "gross" shifting parameter (μ_{Gj}) which equals the expected percentage change in the gross price of capital in response to a change in k_j—taking into account any expected reactions by other governments—or

$$\mu_{Gj} = (\partial r_j/\partial k_j)/r_j .$$

This definition implies the associated "net" shifting parameter (μ_{Nj})

$$\mu_{Nj} = (\partial r/\partial k_j)/r = \mu_{Gj} - 1/(1 - k_j) .$$

An expectation of full shifting by capital implies $\mu_{Nj} = 0$ or $\mu_{Gj} = 1/(1 - k_j)$, while an expectation of no shifting implies $\mu_{Gj} = 0$ or $\mu_{Nj} = -1/(1 - k_j)$. Thus, the expected ranges for these perception parameters are

$$0 \leq \mu_{Gj} \leq 1/(1 - k_j)$$

$$-1/(1 - k_j) \leq \mu_{Nj} \leq 0 .$$

As is shown in section 6.4, the initial values of these shifting parameters can be inferred from the mix of sales and capital taxes observed in the initial equilibrium. To calculate the new equilibrium, some assumption must be made regarding the behavior of these perception parameters. I assume that each government expects the degree of shifting, as measured by the negative effect of its capital taxes on the net return to capital, to be constant—that is, μ_{Nj} is assumed to be constant. This in turn implies that the government expects a larger impact on the gross return to capital (a larger μ_{Gj}) as the extent of capital taxation increases ($\partial \mu_{Gj}/\partial k_j = 1/(1 - k_j)^2 > 0$).

Thus, each sectoral government's optimization problem is to select k_j and t_j to maximize $U_j(C_j, G_j)$ subject to the constraint that total revenues cover own-expenditures on public services. Values of μ_{Nj} calculated in the initial equilibrium are used to calculate the equilibrium values of the endogenous capital tax rates when the extent of deductibility is altered by the federal government (as described in the following paragraph).

The federal government collects revenue from corporate and personal income taxes. Corporate taxes are assessed on capital income at a constant rate κ, and all state and local capital taxes paid are fully deductible. Personal income taxes have progressive marginal rates, with a fraction ϕ of state and local sales taxes deductible for itemizers; $\phi = 1$ in the initial equilibrium. The personal tax system is modeled as a multibracket structure where a constant marginal tax rate is assessed on income above an exemption amount in each bracket. For example, for the median voter in sector j, total personal income tax payments (T_j) are

$$(4) \qquad T_j = \theta \tau_j [Y_j - Z_j - \phi (t_j C_j)] \,,$$

where Y_j is gross income, Z_j is the exemption amount, and $\theta \tau_j$ is the marginal tax rate with $\theta = 1$ in the initial equilibrium. The reform proposal analyzed is the reduction of deductibility of sales taxes (a lowering of ϕ), coupled with an equal percentage reduction in marginal rates (a lowering of θ), subject to a fixed federal revenue constraint; the case where ϕ is reduced to zero corresponds to complete elimination of deductibility of personal sales taxes.

To simplify considerably the analysis of the government's optimization problem as well as the differential incidence results, I assume that the median voter's income (Y_j) is derived purely from labor income ($Y_j = w_j L_j$);[8] since median voter income in the simulations is always $20,000 or less, this assumption is not too unreasonable.[9] Gross expenditures on consumption for the median voter $(1 + t_j)C_j$ is equal to $Y_j - T_j$ which implies consumption of

$$(5) \qquad C_j = [(1 - \theta \tau_j)Y_j + \theta \tau_j Z_j]/[1 + (1 - \phi \theta \tau_j)t_j] \,.$$

Total sales tax revenues (R_{Cj}) are

$$(6) \qquad R_{Cj} = t_j C_{Tj} = t_j N_j C_j / \beta_j \,,$$

where C_{Tj} is total consumption and β_j is the ratio of median voter consumption to consumption per household ($\beta_j = C_j/(C_{Tj}/N_j)$), while total capital tax revenues (R_{Kj}) are

$$(7) \qquad R_{Kj} = k_j r_j K_{Tj} \,.$$

Denoting lump-sum grants by S_j and assuming a matching rate of m_j for matching grants implies total government services of

$$(8) \qquad G_{Tj} = (R_{Cj} + R_{Kj} + S_j)/(1 - m_j) \, ,$$

with government services provided to the median voter (G_j) equal to G_{Tj}/N_j.[10] Note that equations (4) and (8) can be combined to yield

$$(9) \quad C_j + [(1 - \phi\theta\tau_j)\beta_j(1 - m_j)]G_j$$
$$= [(1 - \phi\tau_j)Y_j + \theta\tau_j Z_j] + (1 - \phi\theta\tau_j)\beta_j(S_j + k_j r_j K_{Tj})/N_j$$

or

$$(10) \qquad\qquad C_j + P_{Gj}G_j = Y_{Fj} \, ,$$

where P_{Gj} is the effective price of government services faced by the median voter in sector j and, following Craig and Inman (1985), Y_{Fj} is that individual's "full fiscal income," which includes the value of his share of capital tax revenue and federal revenue sharing.

Given these assumptions, the two-sector general equilibrium model is described by a system of six equations as follows. The first two equations are the first-order conditions for the sales tax rates t_j. The government assumes that β_j is constant.[11] Substituting from (5) and (8) into $U_j(C_j, G_j)$, differentiating with respect to t_j, and setting the result equal to zero yields the expected result that the marginal rate of substitution of the median voter equals the effective price ratio of government services to private consumption goods.

$$(11) \qquad U_{jG}/U_{jC} = (1 - \phi\theta\tau_j)(1 - m_j)\beta_j, \qquad j = 1, 2 \, .$$

Note that since $\phi = 0$ for the median voter in the nonitemizer sector, the relative price of government services reduces to

$$(12) \qquad\qquad P_{G2} = (1 - m_2)\beta_2 \, .$$

The next two equations are the first-order conditions for the capital tax rates k_j. Differentiating $U_j(C_j, G_j)$ with respect to k_j, setting the result equal to zero, substituting from (11), and using the definition of the shifting perception parameter μ_{Gj} yields

$$(13) \quad \partial U_j/\partial k_j = -\alpha_j(1 - \theta\tau_j)\mu_{Gj} + (1 - \phi\theta\tau_j)\beta_j$$
$$[1 - k_j\mu_{Gj}\mu_K + k_j\mu_{Gj}] = 0 \, ,$$

where $\alpha_j = L_j/(L_{Tj}/N_j)$ is the ratio of labor supply of the median voter to per capita labor supply in the sector. This expression indicates that raising the capital tax rate has two primary effects on the welfare of the median voter. The first term reflects the loss from reduced wage income as capital leaves the sector and lowers the marginal productivity of the fixed factor, thus lowering both private consumption and government services (because of lower sales tax receipts). The second term reflects the net effect of raising capital tax rates on capital tax revenues R_{Kj}, and has three components as reflected by the three terms in the brackets. The first is the positive revenue effect of the higher tax rate, the second is the negative effect of the loss of capital, and the third is the positive effect of an increase in the gross price of capital; since $(\mu_K - 1) = a/(1 - a) > 0$, the second effect dominates the third and the tax base declines unambiguously. Increasing k_j thus involves balancing the gains from greater expropriation of capital income with a higher tax rate against the losses from (1) a reduction in the capital income tax base, and (2) the associated reduction in consumption and sales tax revenues due to the lower wages caused by capital emigration. Thus, the revenue mix chosen by the government can be viewed as a two-step process, where the capital tax rate is chosen to expropriate the income of capital owners to the optimal extent, and then the sales tax rate is chosen to allocate optimally the sector's resources across public and private uses.

Rearranging equation (13) and noting that $\phi = 0$ for $j = 2$ yields the expressions for the capital tax rates in the two sectors

$$(14) \quad k_1 = (\mu_K - 1)^{-1} (\alpha_1/\beta_1) \{ (\beta_1/\alpha_2 - \mu_{G1})/\mu_{G1}$$
$$+ [(1 - \phi)\theta\tau_1/(1 - \phi\theta\tau_1)]\}$$

$$(15) \quad k_2 = (\mu_K - 1)^{-1} (\alpha_2/\beta_2) [(\beta_2/\alpha_2 - \mu_{G2})/\mu_{G2} + \theta\tau_2] ;$$

note that the second term in (14) drops out in the initial equilibrium. These expressions indicate that the capital tax rates are inversely related to the perceived shifting parameters (μ_{Gj}). Moreover, the extent of deductibility (ϕ) plays a critical role. For sector one, a reduction in ϕ increases the capital tax rate; that is, as stressed by Feldstein and Metcalf, reducing the deductibility of personal sales taxes makes their use relatively less attractive and results in increased reliance on deductible business capital taxes. However, since personal sales taxes are not deductible in the initial equilibrium for the median voter in sector two, k_2 is initially high (relative to the case where the median voter is an itemizer) to reflect a preference for deductible capital taxes.

The fifth equation reflects the fixed national capital stock assumption

$$(16) \quad K - K_{T1} - K_{T2} = K + \pi_{1r} + \pi_{2r} = 0 .$$

Note that the shifting perception parameters are used only to determine the tax and expenditure policies of the sectoral governments; the capital market equilibrium equation reflects perfect capital mobility in the long run and a uniform net return (r) to capital in both sectors.

The final equation in the general equilibrium system is the federal government budget constraint. Assuming that federal revenue net of grants (R) is fixed yields

$$(17) \quad R = \sum_j [\gamma_{Yj}\theta\tau_j(Y_j - Z_j) - \gamma_{Cj}\phi t_j C_j$$

$$+ \kappa r_j(1 - k_j)K_{Tj} - m_j G_{Tj} - S_j],$$

where revenue sharing and the matching rates are assumed to be held constant, and γ_{Yj} and γ_{Cj} are multipliers which convert median voter personal income taxes (net of sales tax deductions) and sales tax deductions to the analogous quantities for the entire sector. The assumption of fixed federal revenue multipliers is made only to facilitate the differential incidence calculations, and is relaxed in the simulations where federal revenue effects are calculated explicitly. Note that in this formulation, federal matching grants are assumed to change when state and local revenues change although one could also assume that such grants are simply held constant; both approaches are analyzed in the simulations.

Thus, the model has a single exogenous variable ϕ (the extent of deductibility of state and local personal taxes), and six endogenous variables—t_1, t_2, k_1, k_2, r, and θ (which reflects the reduction in marginal tax rates made possible from the reduction or elimination of state and local tax deductibility).

6.3   Differential Incidence Results

The differential incidence results for the model are presented in a slightly unconventional format. Calculating expressions for the changes in the endogenous variables with respect to a change in the exogenous variable ϕ would be extremely cumbersome. Instead, the equations shown below separate the responses of various endogenous variables to changes in the two federal government instruments (ϕ and θ), and a final differential incidence equation calculates the endogenous response of θ (the reduction in marginal tax rates) to a change in ϕ (a reduction in the extent of state and local tax deductibility). Thus, the general form of the differential incidence expressions is

$$\hat{Z} = (\pm)\,\eta_{Z\phi}\,(-\hat{\phi}) + (\pm)\eta_{Z\theta}(-\hat{\theta})\,,$$

where the "^" denotes logarithmic differentiation, and the expressions for the elasticities $\eta_{Z\phi}$ and $\eta_{Z\theta}$ are defined so they are either unambiguously positive or positive for plausible parameter values. All expressions are evaluated at the initial equilibrium ($\phi = \theta = 1$). The explanation assumes that reducing deductibility ($d\phi < 0$) raises revenue, which in turn permits a reduction in marginal tax rates ($d\theta < 0$).

Differentiating (14) yields

(18) $\hat{k}_1 = \eta_{k1\phi} (-\hat{\phi}) > 0,$ $(\eta_{k1\theta} = 0)$,

where

$$\eta_{k1\phi} = \frac{[(1 - a)/a](\alpha_1/\beta_1) [\tau_1/(1 - \tau_1)]/k_1}{1 + [(1 - a)/a] [\mu_{G1}(1 - k_1)]^{-2}} > 0 .$$

Thus, reducing deductibility unambiguously increases the sector one capital tax rate, as the government substitutes away from now partially deductible sales taxes to fully deductible capital taxes. In contrast, differentiating (15) yields

(19) $\hat{k}_2 = -\eta_{k2\theta} (-\hat{\theta}) < 0,$ $(\eta_{k2\phi} = 0)$,

where

$$\eta_{k2\theta} = \frac{[(1 - a)/a] (\alpha_2/\beta_2) \tau_2/k_2}{1 + [(1 - a)/a] [\mu_{G2}(1 - k_2)]^{-2}} > 0 .$$

Thus, reducing deductibility unambiguously causes a decrease in the use of capital taxes in sector two. This occurs because the reduction in marginal tax rates which accompanies the reduction in deductibility increases the after-tax cost of reducing wages by driving out capital with high tax rates. In sector one, this cost increase is more than offset by the fact that reducing deductibility makes the use of non–sales taxes relatively more attractive to the median voter; this force does not operate in sector two where the median voter is a nonitemizer.

These two changes in capital tax rates have opposing effects on the net return to capital, as can be seen by differentiating equation (16) which yields

(20) $\hat{r} = -[\lambda_1 k_1/(1 - k_1)]\eta_{k1\phi} (-\hat{\phi}) + [\lambda_2 k_2/(1 - k_2)]\eta_{k2\theta} (-\hat{\theta})$,

where $\lambda_j = K_{Tj}/K$ is the fraction of the fixed capital stock initially in sector j. The net result depends on the relative magnitudes of the two effects, but generally one would expect the direct effect from the reduction in ϕ to outweigh the feedback effect from the reduction in θ; this implies a net increase in the average rate of taxation of capital in the economy which, in a Harberger-type fixed capital stock general equilibrium model, would be expected to be largely borne by capital.

Differentiating equation (3) yields the effects on the gross prices of capital

(21) $\hat{r}_1 = [\lambda_2 k_1/(1 - k_1)]\eta_{k1\phi} (-\hat{\phi}) + [\lambda_2 k_2/(1 - k_2)]\eta_{k2\theta} (-\hat{\theta}) > 0$

(22) $\hat{r}_2 = -[\lambda_1 k_1/(1 - k_1)]\eta_{k1\phi} (-\hat{\phi}) - [\lambda_1 k_2/(1 - k_2)]\eta_{k2\theta} (-\hat{\theta}) < 0$

which indicate that the gross price of capital unambiguously increases (decreases) in sector one (two) where the capital tax rate is rising (falling). As a result, the capital stock in sector one unambiguously declines while the capital stock in sector two unambiguously increases, as can be seen from differentiating (1) to yield

(23) $$\hat{K}_{T1} = -\mu_K \hat{r} < 0$$

(24) $$\hat{K}_{T2} = \mu_K \hat{r}_2 > 0 \ .$$

Calculation of the changes in the sales tax rates is somewhat more involved. Since by assumption median voter income is derived solely from returns to the fixed factor ($Y_j = wL_j$), calculation of the changes in median voter gross income follows straightforwardly from differentiating equation (2) and substituting into Y_j to yield

(25) $$\hat{Y}_1 = -\eta_{Y1\phi}(-\hat{\phi}) - \eta_{Y1\theta}(-\hat{\theta}) < 0 \ ,$$

where

$$\eta_{Y1\phi} = [a/(1-a)] \, [\lambda_2 k_1/(1-k_1)]\eta_{k1\phi} > 0$$

$$\eta_{Y1\theta} = [a/(1-a)] \, [\lambda_2 k_2/(1-k_2)]\eta_{k2\theta} > 0 \ .$$

Similarly,

(26) $$\hat{Y}_2 = \eta_{Y2\phi}(-\hat{\phi}) + \eta_{Y2\theta}(-\hat{\theta}) > 0 \ ,$$

where

$$\eta_{Y2\phi} = [a/(1-a)] \, [\lambda_1 k_1/(1-k_1)]\eta_{k1\phi} > 0$$

$$\eta_{Y2\theta} = [a/(1-a)] \, [\lambda_1 k_2/(1-k_2)]\eta_{k2\theta} > 0 \ .$$

Thus, median voter gross income unambiguously decreases in sector one, as wages fall in response to the outflow of capital induced by both the increase in the capital tax rate in sector one and the reduction in the capital tax rate in sector two; the opposing effects occur in sector two.

Differentiating equation (5), holding t_1 constant, and substituting from equation (25) yields the change in income net of federal taxes ($Y_{Nj} = (1 + t_j)C_j$)

(27) $$\hat{Y}_{N1} = -\epsilon_{YN1\phi}(-\hat{\phi}) + \epsilon_{YN1\theta}(-\hat{\theta}) \ ,$$

where the ϵ notation indicates a partial elasticity holding the sales tax rate constant and

$$\epsilon_{YN1\phi} = \eta_{Y1\phi}(1-\tau_1)Y_1/[(1-\tau_1)Y_1 + \tau_1 Z_1] + \tau_1 t_1/[1 + (1-\tau_1)t_1]$$

$$\epsilon_{YN1\theta} = [\tau_1(Y_1 - Z_1) - \eta_{Y1\theta}(1-\tau_1)Y_1]/[(1-\tau_1)Y_1 + \tau_1 Z_1] - \tau_1 t_1/$$
$$[1 + (1-\tau_1)t_1] \ .$$

The $\epsilon_{YN1\phi}$ expression reflects the reduction in net income due to lower wages and the reduction in sales tax deductions. The $\epsilon_{YN1\theta}$ expression reflects the increase in net income due to the reduction in marginal tax rates, which is offset by the reduction in wage income (due to capital outflow caused by the reduction in k_2) and the reduced values of the remaining sales tax deductions due to the reduction in θ.

Similarly, in sector two,

$$(28) \qquad \hat{Y}_{N2} = \epsilon_{YN2\phi}(-\hat{\phi}) + \epsilon_{YN2\theta}(-\hat{\theta}) ,$$

where

$$\epsilon_{YN2\phi} = \eta_{Y2\phi} (1 - \tau_2)Y_2/[1 - \tau_2)Y_2 + \tau_2 Z_2]$$
$$\epsilon_{YN2\theta} = [\eta_{Y2\theta}(1 - \tau_2)Y_2 + \tau_2(Y_2 - Z_2)]/[1 - \tau_2) Y_2 + \tau_2 Z_2] ,$$

with the terms in $\epsilon_{YN2\phi}$ and $\epsilon_{YN2\theta}$ reflecting increases in net income due to wage increases caused by the increase in k_1 and the reduction in k_2, and the increase in net income due to the reduction in θ. Substituting these expressions into the results of differentiating equation (5) yields the changes in consumption which are

$$(29) \quad \hat{C}_1 = -\epsilon_{C1\phi}(-\hat{\phi}) + \epsilon_{C1\theta}(-\hat{\theta}) - \{(1 - \tau_1)t_1/[1 + (1 - \tau_1)t_1]\}\hat{t}_1$$

$$(30) \qquad \hat{C}_2 = \epsilon_{YN2\phi}(-\hat{\phi}) + \epsilon_{YN2\theta}(-\hat{\theta}) - [t_2/(1 + t_2)]\hat{t}_2 .$$

Price changes follow directly from differentiating the P_{Gj} term in equation (9) which yields

$$(31) \qquad \hat{P}_{G1} = [\tau_1/(1 - \tau_1)](-\hat{\phi} - \hat{\theta}) = \eta_{PG1}(-\hat{\phi} - \hat{\theta}) > 0$$

$$(32) \qquad \hat{P}_{G2} = 0 ,$$

as the price of government services rises unambiguously for the median voter who itemizes, but is constant for the nonitemizing median voter.

The response of capital tax revenues must be obtained in order to calculate the change in government services provided to the median voter. Differentiating equation (7) yields

$$(33) \qquad \hat{R}_{K1} = \eta_{RK1\phi}(-\hat{\phi}) - \eta_{RK1\theta}(-\hat{\theta}) ,$$

where

$$\eta_{RK1\phi} = \{1 - [a/(1 - a)] [k_1/(1 - k_1)]\lambda_2\}\eta_{K1\phi} > 0$$

$$\eta_{RK1\theta} = [a/(1 - a)] [k_2/(1 - k_2)]\lambda_2\eta_{K2\theta} > 0 ,$$

indicating that capital tax revenues in sector one increase as a result of the increase in k_1 (for any reasonable parameter values—e.g., $a < 0.5$ and $k_1 < 0.5$ is a sufficient condition) but decrease because the reduction in k_2 causes an outflow of capital from sector one. Differentiating equation (8) and substituting from equations (27–29) yields

(34)
$$\hat{G}_1 = (-s_{C1}\epsilon_{C1\phi} + s_{K1}\eta_{RK1\phi})(-\hat{\phi})$$
$$+ (s_{C1}\epsilon_{C1\theta} - s_{K1}\eta_{RK1\theta})(-\hat{\theta})$$
$$+ \{s_{C1}/[1 + (1 - \tau_1)t_1]\}\hat{t}_1,$$

where s_{Cj} and s_{Kj} are the shares of sales and capital tax revenues in funds other than matching grants in sector j; that is, $s_{Cj} = t_j C_{Tj}/[(1 - m_j) G_{Tj}]$ and $s_{Kj} = k_j r_j K_{Tj}/[(1 - m_j) G_{Tj}]$.

Performing the analogous calculations in sector two yields

(35)
$$\hat{R}_{K2} = \eta_{RK2\phi}(-\hat{\phi}) - \eta_{RK2\theta}(-\hat{\theta}) ,$$

where
$$\eta_{RK2\phi} = [a/(1 - a)] [k_1/(1 - k_1)]\lambda_1\eta_{K1\phi} > 0$$
$$\eta_{RK2\theta} = \{1 - [a/(1 - a)] [k_2/(1 - k_2)]\lambda_1\}\eta_{K2\theta} > 0 ,$$

indicating that capital tax revenues fall in sector two because of the reduction in k_2 but rise because of the inflow of capital caused by the increase in k_1. Substituting into the result of differentiating (8) yields

(36)
$$\hat{G}_2 = (-s_{C2}\epsilon_{YN2\phi} + s_{K2}\eta_{RK2\phi})(-\hat{\phi}) + (s_{C2}\epsilon_{YN2\theta}$$
$$- s_{K2}\eta_{RK2\theta}) (-\hat{\theta}) + [s_{C2}/(1 + t_2)]\hat{t}_2 .$$

These results permit calculation of the change in the sales tax rates. Differentiating equation (11) and using the Slutsky equation as well as equation (32) yields the standard results

(37)
$$\mu_{GY1}\hat{C}_1 - \mu_{CY1}\hat{G}_1 - (\mu_{GPG1}/e_{C1})\hat{P}_{G1} = 0$$

(38)
$$\mu_{GY2}\hat{C}_2 - \mu_{CY2}\hat{G}_2 = 0 ,$$

where μ_{CYj} and μ_{GYj} are the income elasticities of demand (with respect to full fiscal income Y_{Fj}) for private and public services, μ_{GPG1} is the compensated price elasticity of demand for public services in sector one, and e_{Cj} is the share of full fiscal income spent on private consumption. Substituting from (29), (31), (34) and solving for the change in t_1 yields

(39)
$$\hat{t}_1 = -\eta_{t1\phi}(-\hat{\phi}) + \eta_{t1\theta}(-\hat{\theta}) ,$$

where
$$\eta_{t1\phi} = \{\epsilon_{YN1\phi} (\mu_{GY1} - \mu_{CY1}s_{C1}) + \mu_{CY1}s_{K1}\eta_{RK1\phi}$$
$$+ (\mu_{GPG1}/e_{C1}) [\tau_1/(1 - \tau_1)]\}/D_1$$
$$\eta_{t1\theta} = \{\epsilon_{YN1\theta} (\mu_{GY1} - \mu_{CY1}s_{C1})$$
$$+ \mu_{CY1}s_{K1}\eta_{RK1\theta} - (\mu_{GPG1}/e_{C1})[\tau_1/(1 - \tau_1)]\}/D_1$$
$$D_1 = [\mu_{GY1}(1 - \tau_1)t_1 + \mu_{CY1}s_{C1}]/[1 + (1 - \tau_1) t_1] > 0 .$$

These results are interpreted as follows. For $\eta_{t1\phi}$, the first term indicates that the sales tax rate t_1 (1) declines because of a negative "net income" effect which causes demand for government services to fall, with this effect tempered by the need to maintain the sales tax share of revenues in light of declining consumption; (2) declines because of a "revenue mix effect" which results in a shift to capital taxation; and (3) declines because the increase in the relative price of government services reduces demand. For $\eta_{t_1\theta}$, the sales tax rate t_1 (1) increases because the reduction in marginal tax rates causes net income to increase, (2) increases (mitigating the analogous revenue mix effect above) because the decrease in k_2 causes capital tax revenues to fall since capital leaves sector one, and (3) decreases since the reduction in θ also increases the relative price of government services in sector one and thus reduces demand. Although the net effect is ambiguous, it is likely that income effects of the reduction in ϕ, the revenue mix effect in sector one, and the price effects will dominate the negative effects so that the sales tax rate in sector one declines.

The analogous derivation in sector two yields

(40)
$$\hat{t}_2 = \eta_{t2\phi}(-\hat{\phi}) + \eta_{t2\theta}(-\hat{\theta}) ,$$

where

$$\eta_{t2\phi} = [\epsilon_{YN2\phi}(\mu_{GY2} - \mu_{CY2}s_{C2}) - \mu_{CY2}s_{K2}\eta_{RK2\phi}]/D_2$$
$$\eta_{t2\theta} = [\epsilon_{YN2\theta}(\mu_{GY2} - \mu_{CY2}s_{C2}) + \mu_{CY2}s_{K2}\eta_{RK2\theta}]/D_2$$
$$D_2 = (\mu_{GY2}t_2 + \mu_{CY2}s_{C2})/(1 + t_2) > 0 .$$

The interpretation of these results is analogous to that above; note that both net income effects are positive, the capital tax revenue effects imply an increase in t_2 due to the revenue mix effect in sector two (k_2 falls) but a reduction due to the increase in k_1 and the resulting increase in K_{T2}, and there are no price effects since the price of government services facing the nonitemizing median voter is unchanged.

Given the expressions for the changes in the four tax rate variables and the net return to capital, the changes in consumption and government service levels can be derived. Differentiating the definition of full fiscal income Y_{F1}, holding P_{G1} constant, yields

(41)
$$\hat{Y}_{F1} = -\epsilon_{YF1\phi}(-\hat{\phi}) + \epsilon_{YF1\theta}(-\hat{\theta}) ,$$

where

$$\epsilon_{YF1\phi} = \{\epsilon_{YN1\phi}s_{C1}[1 + (1 - \tau_1) t_1] - s_{K1}\eta_{RK1\phi}(1 - \tau_1)t_1\}/$$
$$\{[1 + (1 - \tau_1)t_1]D_1\}$$

$$\epsilon_{YF1\theta} = \{\epsilon_{YN1\theta}s_{C1}[1 + (1 - \tau_1) t_1] - s_{K1}\eta_{RK1\theta}(1 - \tau_1)t_1\}/$$
$$\{[1 + (1 - \tau_1)t_1]D_1\} .$$

Thus, there are four effects on full fiscal income in sector one. Reducing deductibility reduces Y_{F1} through a negative ϕ-net income effect because wages decline, but increases it through a positive ϕ-revenue mix effect because additional capital tax revenues are raised; the associated reduction in marginal tax rates directly increases Y_{F1} through a positive θ-net income effect but also reduces it through a negative θ-revenue mix effect due to the reduction in k_2 which causes an outflow of capital from sector one and thus reduces wages. The net effect is ambiguous, but is likely to be negative.

Similarly,

$$(42) \qquad \hat{Y}_{F2} = \eta_{YF2\phi}(-\hat{\phi}) + \eta_{YF2\theta}(-\hat{\theta}) \,,$$

where

$$\eta_{YF2\phi} = [\epsilon_{YN2\phi}s_{C2}(1 + t_2) + t_2 s_{K2}\eta_{RK2\phi}]/[(1 + t_2)D_2] > 0$$

$$\eta_{YF2\theta} = [\epsilon_{YN2\theta}s_{C2}(1 + t_2) - t_2 s_{K2}\eta_{RK2\theta}]/[(1 + t_2)D_2] \,.$$

Thus, both the ϕ-net income and θ-net income effects are positive on full fiscal income in sector two, while the ϕ-revenue mix effect is positive (the increase in k_1 drives capital to sector two and increases wages) and the θ-revenue mix effect is negative (the reduction in k_2 reduces full fiscal income).

Substituting into (29–30) from (39) and (40–42) yields the changes in consumption and government services broken down into the appropriate income and substitution effects:

$$(43) \quad \hat{C}_1 = \mu_{CY1}[-\epsilon_{YF1\phi}(-\hat{\phi}) + \epsilon_{YF1\theta}(-\hat{\theta})] + \mu_{CPG1}\eta_{PG1}(-\hat{\phi}-\hat{\theta})$$

$$(44) \quad \hat{G}_1 = \mu_{GY1}[-\epsilon_{YF1\phi}(-\hat{\phi}) + \epsilon_{YF1\theta}(-\hat{\theta})] - \mu_{GPG1}\eta_{PG1}(-\hat{\phi}-\hat{\theta})$$

$$(45) \qquad\qquad \hat{C}_2 = \mu_{CY2}[\epsilon_{YF2\phi}(-\hat{\phi}) + \epsilon_{YF2\theta}(-\hat{\theta})]$$

$$(46) \qquad\qquad \hat{G}_2 = \mu_{GY2}[\epsilon_{YF2\phi}(-\hat{\phi}) + \epsilon_{YF2\theta}(-\hat{\theta})] \,,$$

where μ_{CPG1} is the compensated cross-price elasticity of demand for consumption with respect to the price of government services for the median voter in sector one. Assuming that the first term in brackets in (43) outweighs the second, the net income effects operate to reduce (increase) public and private consumption in sector one (two), while the substitution effects in sector one increase the relative demand for private goods.

The changes in sales tax revenues are obtained by substituting equations (39–40), (43), and (45) into equation (6) which yields

$$(47) \qquad\qquad \hat{R}_{C1} = -\eta_{RC1\phi}(-\hat{\phi}) + \eta_{RC1\theta}(-\hat{\theta}) \,,$$

where

$$\eta_{RC1\phi} = \frac{\mu_{GY1}\,\epsilon_{YN1\phi}\,[1 + (1 - \tau_1)t_1] + \mu_{CY1}\,s_{K1}\,\eta_{RK1\phi} - (\mu_{GPG1}/e_{C1})\eta_{PG1}}{[1 + (1 - \tau_1)t_1]\,D_1}$$

$$\eta_{RC1\theta} = \frac{\mu_{GY1}\,\epsilon_{YN1\theta}\,[1 + (1 - \tau_1)t_1] + \mu_{CY1}\,s_{K1}\,\eta_{RK1\theta} + (\mu_{GPG1}/e_{C1})\eta_{PG1}}{[1 + (1 - \tau_1)t_1]\,D_1}$$

and

(48) $$\hat{R}_{C2} = \eta_{RC1\phi}(-\hat{\phi}) + \eta_{RC2\theta}(-\hat{\theta}),$$

where

$$\eta_{RC2\phi} = [\mu_{GY2}(1 + t_2)\,\epsilon_{YN2\phi} - \mu_{CY2}\,s_{K2}\,\eta_{RK2\phi}]/[(1 + t_2)D_2]$$

$$\eta_{RC2\theta} = [\mu_{GY2}(1 + t_2)\epsilon_{YN2\theta} + \mu_{CY2}s_{K2}\eta_{RK2\theta}]/[\theta(1 + t_2)D_2].$$

The interpretation of the income, revenue mix, and price effects on sales tax revenues is analogous to the description of effects on sales tax rates above.

Finally, differentiation of the federal government budget constraint yields the reduction in marginal tax rates (θ) in response to the reduction in deductibility. Differentiating equation (17) yields

(49) $$-f_{G1}\hat{G}_1 - f_{G2}\hat{G}_2 + f_{Y1}\hat{T}_{N1}$$
$$+ f_{Y2}\hat{T}_{N2} - f_{C1}[\hat{R}_{C1} - (-\hat{\phi})] - f_{C2}[\hat{R}_{C2}$$
$$- (-\hat{\phi})] + f_{K1}\,\hat{R}_{FK1} + f_{K2}\hat{R}_{FK2} = 0,$$

where $T_{Nj} = \theta\tau_j(Y_j - Z_j)$ is federal personal income taxes paid neglecting sales tax deductions in each sector, and $R_{FKj} = \kappa r_j(1 - k_j)K_{Tj}$ is federal corporate tax revenues paid in each sector. To solve for the changes in T_{Nj} differentiate the definition and substitute from equations (25–26) to yield

(50) $$\hat{T}_{N1} = -[Y_1/(Y_1 - Z_1)]\eta_{Y1\phi}(-\hat{\phi})$$
$$- \{1 + [Y_1/(Y_1 - Z_1)]\eta_{Y1\theta}\}(-\hat{\theta})$$

(51) $$\hat{T}_{N2} = -[Y_2/(Y_2 - Z_2)]\,\eta_{Y2\phi}(-\hat{\phi})$$
$$- \{1 - [Y_2/(Y_2 - Z_2)]\eta_{Y2\theta}\}(-\hat{\theta}).$$

Differentiating the definition of R_{FKj} and substituting from equations (18–24) yields

(52) $$\hat{R}_{FK1} = -\eta_{RFK1\phi}(-\hat{\phi}) - \eta_{RFK1\phi}(-\hat{\theta}) < 0$$

$$\eta_{RFK1\phi} = [1 + (\mu_K - 1)\lambda_2][k_1/(1 - k_1)]\eta_{K1\phi} > 0$$

$$\eta_{RFK1\theta} = (\mu_K - 1)\lambda_2\,[k_2/(1 - k_2)]\eta_{k2\theta} > 0$$

(53) $$\hat{R}_{FK2} = \eta_{RFK2\phi}(-\hat{\phi}) + \eta_{RFK2\theta}(-\hat{\theta})$$

$$\eta_{RFK2\phi} = (\mu_K - 1)\lambda_1[k_1/(1 - k_1)]\eta_{k1\phi} > 0$$

$$\eta_{RFK2\theta} = [1 + (\mu_K - 1)\lambda_1][k_2/(1 - k_2)]\eta_{k2\theta} > 0,$$

which indicates that federal corporate revenues decline because of the increased use of capital taxation in sector one, but increase because of the reduction in the use of capital taxation in sector two.

Substituting into equation (49) from equations (44), (46), and (50–53) yields

$$(54) \qquad (-\hat{\theta}) = \eta_\theta(-\hat{\phi}) = (\eta_{\theta n}/\eta_{\theta d})(-\hat{\phi}) ,$$

where

$$\eta_{\theta n} = [f_{G1}\mu_{GY1}\eta_{YT1\phi} - f_{G2}\mu_{GY2}\eta_{YT2\phi} + f_{G1}\mu_{GPG1}\eta_{PG1}]$$

$$- \{f_{Y1}[Y_1/(Y_1 - Z_1)]\eta_{Y1\phi} - f_{Y2}[Y_2/(Y_2 - Z_2)]\eta_{Y2\phi}\}$$

$$+ [f_{C1}\eta_{RC1\phi} - f_{C2}\eta_{RC2\phi}] - [f_{K1}\eta_{RFK1\phi} - f_{K2}\eta_{RFK2\phi}]$$

$$\eta_{\theta d} = f_{G1}\mu_{GY1}\eta_{YT1\theta} + f_{G2}\mu_{GY2}\eta_{YT2\theta} - f_{G1}\mu_{GPG1}\eta_{PG1}$$

$$+ f_{Y1}\{1 + [Y_1/(Y_1 - Z_1)]\eta_{Y1\theta}\} + f_{Y2}\{1 - [Y_2/(Y_2 - Z_2)]\eta_{Y2\theta}\}$$

$$+ f_{C1}\eta_{RC1\theta} + f_{C2}\eta_{RC2\theta} + f_{K1}\eta_{RFK1\theta} - f_{K2}\eta_{RFK2\theta} .$$

The terms in $\eta_{\theta n}$ indicate that, in each case, the effects on federal revenue due to changes in sector one are offset by analogous effects of opposite sign in sector two; the expression $\eta_{\theta d}$ is positive for any reasonable parameter values.

This general equilibrium multiplier for the reduction in marginal tax rates made possible by the elimination of deductibility can be compared to the analogous multiplier in the static case where revenue mix and general equilibrium effects are not considered. Although "static" could be defined in a variety of ways, suppose the static estimate simply ignores all changes in revenue mix, income, and consumption. In this case, the multiplier analogous to η_θ is

$$(55) \qquad \epsilon_\theta = (f_{C1} + f_{C2})/(f_{Y1} + f_{Y2}) .$$

A comparison of ϵ_θ and η_θ, assuming $\epsilon_\theta > \eta_\theta$, indicates the extent to which a static revenue estimate, in the specific sense defined above, overestimates the increase in federal revenues due to the elimination of state and local tax deductibility.

6.4 Simulation Results

Numerical simulation results with a version of the model described in section 6.2 are presented in this section. Since the model is fairly primitive and ignores a large number of features which would be included in a more complete representation of the U.S. economy, these results should be viewed as merely suggestive of the potential importance of the revenue and general equilibrium effects emphasized in the previous discussion.

The primary source of information was the data set on 1983 state personal income and sales taxes compiled by Daniel Feenberg and Harvey Rosen (1986) which the authors generously made available to me. Additional data was obtained primarily from various publications of the Advisory Commission on Intergovernmental Relations.

To determine the division of the fifty states and the District of Columbia into the itemizer and nonitemizer sectors, the states were ranked in decreasing order of percentage of itemizers, with joint returns double-weighted to reflect the presence of two voters; the percentage of itemizers varied from a high of 55.2 percent in Utah to a low of 19.9 percent in South Dakota. As discussed above, results are reported for $N^* = 19$, 29, and 39; the results presented by Lindsey (in this volume) suggest that $N^* = 29$ should be viewed as the best point estimate.[12] For a given N^*, states 1 through N^* were aggregated to form sector one (the itemizer sector), and states $N^* + 1$ through 51 were aggregated to form sector two (the nonitemizer sector).

The Feenberg-Rosen state and local data were divided into five adjusted gross income (AGI) brackets ($0–$10,000; $10,000–$15,000; $15,000–$20,000; $20,000–$30,000; and > $30,000) indexed by b. As indicated in equation (4), data on marginal and average tax rates were used to construct marginal tax rates (τ_{jb}) and exemption/deduction totals, net of sales tax deductions, for each bracket in the two sectors (Z_{jb}). Individuals are assumed to stay in the same income brackets, so that all changes in the personal tax structure are captured by changes in the θ variable. The value of the total nonresidential nonfarm capital stock in 1983 was determined from data on tangible asset holdings reported in Board of Governors of the Federal Reserve System (1986). Capital owners were assumed to receive a current net return of $r = 0.04$, and capital was allocated across states in proportion to the shares of nonresidential nonfarm property tax base reported in Advisory Commission on Intergovermental Relations (1986)—hereafter, ACIR (1986). Returns to capital were assumed to accrue entirely to individuals in the top two income brackets, with 81 percent of capital income assumed to be earned by individuals in the $30,000 and above class.[13] The remainder of AGI was attributed to earnings of the fixed factor (labor).

The determination of the sectoral tax rates in the initial equilibrium required a division of total property tax revenues into nonresidential and residential components. Feldstein, Dicks-Mireaux, and Poterba (1983) note that the correct way to perform this division is uncertain and argue that calculations which assume that the effective tax rate on nonresidential property ranges from one-third to three times the effective rate on residential property should bound the true value. Since I wish to emphasize the role of state and local capital taxation, and since Netzer's (1985) comments suggest that a value in the upper portion of this range would be realistic, I simply assume that the effective tax rate on nonresidential property is the upper bound of the range suggested by Feldstein, Dicks-Mireaux, and Poterba—three times that on residential property. The land component of these taxes is eliminated, assuming that it is proportional to the total land value reported in the Federal Reserve Board publication cited above. Data on tax bases and property taxes paid are from ACIR (1986).

Given this allocation of the property taxes paid, residential property taxes are included with general sales and personal income taxes and treated as deductible personal taxes, referred to in the text simply as sales taxes. State and local taxes are assumed to be proportional, so the sales tax rate in each sector (t_j) is calculated simply as an average tax rate; note however that the calculated rates are high in that no attempt is made to impute rents on owner-occupied housing and include them in gross income, even though residential property taxes paid are included in "sales" taxes.

The sectoral capital tax rates are also calculated assuming a proportional tax structure, where total "capital" taxes paid are the sum of nonresidential property taxes (excluding the land component), corporate income taxes, and corporate licenses, where data on the last two items are also obtained from ACIR (1986). Given the assumption regarding the split between residential and nonresidential property taxes described above, these tax rates are relatively high; however, note that no attempt was made to include the business capital share of selective excises, user charges, severance taxes, etc.

The calculations of the gross prices of capital, as specified in equation (3), and the value of the capital share parameter a in the Cobb-Douglas production function, require a value for the corporate tax rate. Since my primary concern is the federal revenue effect of changes in business taxes which are deductible at the statutory corporate tax rate, I simply assume that κ is the statutory rate in 1983 ($\kappa = 0.46$); this implies a nonresidential capital share of $a = 0.18$.

No attempt is made to account for other sources of state and local revenue, including user charges, selective excise taxes, gift and estate taxes, and severance taxes, as well as the land portion of business property taxes. The revenues that are included in state and local sales and capital taxes in the model represent roughly 60 percent of all state and local revenues.

The median voter was simply assumed to be the median income taxpayer for each sector. The utility function of the median voter is assumed to be a constant elasticity of substitution (CES) function, with an elasticity of substitution equal to 0.5. This implies an uncompensated price elasticity of demand of 0.5—toward the middle or upper portion of the range of published estimates (see Inman 1979, Ladd 1984, and Netzer 1985). The CES specification simplifies the analysis at the cost of assuming a unitary income elasticity, which is higher than that suggested by the literature; accordingly, the changes in government service demands are overstated in sector two (which gains income) but understated in sector one (which loses income).

Information on federal grants is obtained from *Advisory Commission on Intergovernmental Relations* (1985b), where revenue sharing is treated as lump-sum grants (S_j), and the remaining grants are treated as matching grants. To obtain realistic matching rates, the grants amount is reduced by the proportion of tax revenues which are not included in the above determinations of sales taxes and capital taxes. Total federal tax revenue is calculated using an expression analogous to equation (17) except that equation (4) is used to calculate explicitly federal personal income taxes paid for each bracket in the two sectors; the fraction of itemizers in each bracket is determined from the Feenberg-Rosen data, and is assumed to be constant throughout the simulations.

In the initial equilibrium, $\phi = \theta = 1$. The calculated initial values of the tax rates and other variables and parameters are substituted into equation (11) for $j = 1, 2$ to solve for the values of the distributive share parameters in the CES utility functions (which differ across the two sectors), and into equations (14–15) to solve for the values of the two "net shifting" perception parameters μ_{Nj}.[14] (Equations (16–17) are satisfied by construction in the initial equilibrium.) These values are then used to calculate new equilibria in response to exogenous reductions in the extent of state and local tax deductibility (ϕ).

Three sets of results are presented. The first set corresponds to an equilibrium situation where the government institutes the reduction in θ predicted by the static revenue described above and runs a deficit if revenues are insufficient. Matching grants are assumed to be constant for this calculation. These results are presented in tables 6.1a–c, where the three cases described above ($N^* = 29, 19, 39$) are considered. The values for $N^* = 29$ provide the best estimates, while the values for $N^* = 19$ and $N^* = 39$ provide reasonable bounds for the various quantities listed.

Several features of the results are common to all three cases. In terms of tax rates, the sector one revenue mix changes drastically as k_1 increases by 43 percent (41, 47) for $N^* = 29$ (19, 39) and t_1 falls by 30 percent (29, 32). The revenue mix in sector two changes less dramatically in the opposite direction, as k_2 falls by 11% (10, 14) and t_2 increases by 5% (5, 9). The effects on revenues are of course quite different in the three cases. When $N^* = 29$, the changes in total state and local capital and sales tax revenues due to changes in the sector one tax rates are offset by roughly 10–12 percent because of changes in the opposite direction in sector two. For example, R_{K1} increases by

Table 6.1a   **Equilibrium Effects of Eliminating Deductibility**
N* = 29, "Static" θ, Grants Constant

Variable	φ = 0:	j = 1	j = 2	φ = 1:	j = 1	j = 2
Capital tax rates		0.211	0.157		0.302	0.139
Sales tax rates		0.132	0.095		0.092	0.100
Gross wages		0.944	0.958		0.931	0.975
Capital fractions		0.577	0.423		0.534	0.466
Net return to capital		0.040	0.040		0.038	0.038
Tax rate variable θ		1.000	1.000		0.898	0.898

Variable	Change for j = 1	Change for j = 2	Net Change
Income			
Labor income	− 13.2	11.5	− 1.7
Capital income	—	—	− 8.8
State/Local Tax Revenue			
Sales tax revenue	− 32.9	3.3	− 29.6
Capital tax revenue	18.1	− 2.2	15.9
Total tax revenue	− 14.8	1.1	− 13.7
Federal Tax Revenue			
Personal tax revenue	− 1.4	− 1.9	− 3.3
Corporate tax revenue	− 9.6	2.1	− 7.5
Total tax revenue	− 11.0	0.2	− 10.8

Notes: All revenue figures in tables are in billions of 1983 dollars; details may not add due to rounding. Predicted revenue gain is $28.6 billion.

Table 6.1b   **Equilibrium Effects of Eliminating Deductibility N* = 19,**
"Static" θ, Grants Constant

Variable	φ = 0:	j = 1	j = 2	φ = 1:	j = 1	j = 2
Capital tax rates		0.219	0.164		0.308	0.147
Sales tax rates		0.142	0.097		0.101	0.102
Gross wages		0.942	0.956		0.925	0.968
Capital fractions		0.431	0.569		0.390	0.610
Net return to capital		0.040	0.040		0.039	0.039
Tax rate variable θ		1.000	1.000		0.898	0.898

Variable	Change for j = 1	Change for j = 2	Net Change
Income			
Labor income	− 13.0	11.3	− 1.7
Capital income	—	—	− 5.7
State/Local Tax Revenue			
Sales tax revenue	− 25.5	4.2	− 21.4
Capital tax revenue	13.2	− 2.9	10.2
Total tax revenue	− 12.3	1.2	− 11.1
Federal Tax Revenue			
Personal tax revenue	0.3	− 2.5	− 2.2
Corporate tax revenue	− 7.3	2.5	− 4.9
Total tax revenue	− 7.0	0.0	− 7.1

Notes: All revenue figures in tables are in billions of 1983 dollars; details may not add due to rounding. Predicted revenue gain is $28.7 billion.

Table 6.1c   **Equilibrium Effects of Eliminating Deductibility**
$N^* = 39$, "Static" θ, Grants Constant

Variable	$\phi = 0$:	$j = 1$	$j = 2$	$\phi = 1$:	$j = 1$	$j = 2$
Capital tax rates		0.200	0.138		0.294	0.118
Sales tax rates		0.125	0.079		0.085	0.086
Gross wages		0.947	0.963		0.941	0.987
Capital fractions		0.803	0.197		0.774	0.226
Net return to capital		0.040	0.040		0.036	0.036
Tax rate variable θ		1.000	1.000		0.898	0.898

Variable	Change for $j = 1$	Change for $j = 2$	Net Change
Income			
Labor income	−8.9	7.6	−1.2
Capital income	—	—	−13.7
State/Local Tax Revenue			
Sales tax revenue	−44.3	1.6	−42.6
Capital tax revenue	26.2	−1.1	25.1
Total tax revenue	−18.0	0.6	−17.5
Federal Tax Revenue			
Personal tax revenue	−3.6	−1.1	−4.7
Corporate tax revenue	−12.9	1.3	−11.7
Total tax revenue	−16.5	0.2	−16.4

Notes: All revenue figures in tables are in billions of 1983 dollars; details may not add due to rounding. Predicted revenue gain is $28.5 billion.

$18.1 billion while R_{K2} decreases by $2.2 billion, and R_{C1} decreases by $32.9 billion while R_{C2} increases by $3.3 billion; total revenues fall by $14.8 billion in sector one while increasing in sector two by $1.1 billion for a net reduction in revenues of $13.7 billion. This corresponds to a reduction of 6.0 percent of the portion of own-revenues analyzed in the model. In contrast when $N^* = 39$, the sector one effects are more dominant, with much more dramatic effects on revenues; total capital tax revenues rise by $25.1 billion and total sales tax revenues fall by $42.6 billion for a net reduction of $17.5 billion or 7.6 percent of own-revenues. More modest revenue effects occur when $N^* = 19$, with a total net reduction of $11.1 billion or 4.9 percent of own-revenues. Note that the reduction in own-revenues is relatively large when virtually all states are modeled as itemizer states, since the increase in the tax price of government services is large for itemizers but zero for non-itemizers. Nevertheless, since the fraction of own revenues analyzed is only 60 percent, the net effect on total government expenditures is modest, and broadly similar to the types of responses suggested by Ladd (1984).

In both cases, the federal revenue gain predicted from the static estimate (as defined above) is approximately $28.6 billion; this implies that θ could be reduced from 1.0 to 0.898 without losing revenues from personal income taxation. Taking into account general equilibrium effects, personal tax revenues are lower in both jurisdictions because of the reduction in the net return to capital implied by the overall increase in taxation of capital (the effects of the increase in k_1 dominate those of the decrease in k_2), and lower in sector one because of lower wages with the opposite effect occurring in sector two. The net effect is a reduction in personal income tax revenues of \$3.3 (2.2, 4.7) billion when $N^* = 29$ (19, 39). (Note that personal tax revenues increase in sector one when $N^* = 19$ because this sector has a disproportionately large share of itemizers.) This revenue loss is increased because corporate revenues from sector one fall because business capital taxes are deducted at a higher k_1, and reduced because of the opposite effect in sector two. The net effect is negative in all three cases, as corporate revenues fall by \$7.5 (4.9, 11.7) billion when $N^* = 29$ (19, 39) as a loss of \$9.6 billion from sector one is partially offset by a gain of \$2.1 billion from sector two. The net effect on federal revenue when $N^* = 29$ (19, 39) is a \$10.8 (7.1, 16.4) billion shortfall or 38 percent (25, 58) of the predicted revenue gain from eliminating deductibility. Note that the revenue losses which occur as a result of general equilibrium effects on the net return to capital and wages are quite important, amounting to roughly 30 percent of the total revenue loss.

These results suggest that the revenue losses due to revenue mix and general equilibrium effects in response to an elimination of deductibility may be quite important. The second set of results pursues this issue further by presenting equilibrium values of the various endogenous variables when θ adjusts endogenously to balance the federal government budget. These results also assume that matching grants do not change in response to changes in own-financed levels of government service provision.

Tables 6.2a–c present equilibrium values for various variables for the same three cases analyzed in tables 6.1a–c ($N^* = 29$, 19, 39). When $N^* = 29$, the reduction in θ financed by the elimination of deductibility is reduced by roughly 43 percent once revenue mix and general equilibrium adjustments are taken into account ($\theta = 0.942$ rather than 0.898). When $N^* = 39$, the result is even more dramatic, as 65 percent of the reduction in marginal tax rates is eliminated, while when $N^* = 19$ only 29 percent of the reduction is eliminated. The increases in k_1 and the reductions in t_1 are larger than in the "deficit" case analyzed in tables 6.1a–c because, with a smaller than expected reduction in θ, the after-tax cost of reducing wages by driving out capital is reduced; for the same reason, the reductions in k_2 and the increases in t_2 are reduced.

The net effect of this greater reliance on capital taxation (relative to the deficit case) is a slightly larger reduction in the net return to capital. In all three cases, K_{T1} falls by roughly 4 percent, which implies an increase in K_{T2} of also roughly 4 percent. The corresponding reductions in sector one wages and increases in sector two wages are fairly modest.

Table 6.2a   **Equilibrium Effects of Eliminating Deductibility
$N^* = 29$, θ Endogenous, Grants Constant**

Variable	$\phi = 0$:	$j = 1$	$j = 2$	$\phi = 1$:	$j = 1$	$j = 2$
Capital tax rates		0.211	0.157		0.306	0.147
Sales tax rates		0.132	0.095		0.090	0.098
Gross wages		0.944	0.958		0.932	0.974
Capital fractions		0.577	0.423		0.534	0.466
Net return to capital		0.040	0.040		0.037	0.037
Tax rate variable θ		1.000	1.000		0.942	0.942

Variable	Change for $j = 1$	Change for $j = 2$	Net Change
Income			
Labor income	−13.0	11.3	−1.7
Capital income	—	—	−9.9
State/Local Tax Revenue			
Sales tax revenue	−44.3	1.6	−42.6
Capital tax revenue	26.2	−1.1	25.1
Total tax revenue	−18.0	0.6	−17.5
Federal Tax Revenue			
Personal tax revenue	6.0	2.5	8.5
Corporate tax revenue	−10.0	1.6	−8.5
Total tax revenue	−4.0	4.1	0.1

Notes: All revenue figures in tables are in billions of 1983 dollars; details may not add due to rounding. Predicted revenue gain is $28.6 billion.

Table 6.2b   **Equilibrium Effects of Eliminating Deductibility
$N^* = 19$, θ Endogenous, Grants Constant**

Variable	$\phi = 0$:	$j = 1$	$j = 2$	$\phi = 1$:	$j = 1$	$j = 2$
Capital tax rates		0.219	0.164		0.311	0.152
Sales tax rates		0.142	0.097		0.100	0.100
Gross wages		0.942	0.956		0.925	0.968
Capital fractions		0.431	0.569		0.390	0.610
Net return to capital		0.040	0.040		0.038	0.038
Tax rate variable θ		1.000	1.000		0.927	0.927

Variable	Change for $j = 1$	Change for $j = 2$	Net Change
Income			
Labor income	−12.9	11.2	−1.7
Capital income	—	—	−6.5
State/Local Tax Revenue			
Sales tax revenue	−26.4	2.8	−23.6
Capital tax revenue	13.6	−2.0	11.7
Total tax revenue	−12.8	0.8	−12.0
Federal Tax Revenue			
Personal tax revenue	4.1	1.6	5.6
Corporate tax revenue	−7.6	2.0	−5.5
Total tax revenue	−3.5	3.5	0.0

Notes: All revenue figures in tables are in billions of 1983 dollars; details may not add due to rounding. Predicted revenue gain is $28.7 billion.

Table 6.2c   **Equilibrium Effects of Eliminating Deductibility**
                      $N^* = 39$, θ Endogenous, Grants Constant

Variable	$\phi = 0$:	$j = 1$	$j = 2$	$\phi = 1$:	$j = 1$	$j = 2$
Capital tax rates		0.200	0.138		0.301	0.131
Sales tax rates		0.125	0.079		0.083	0.081
Gross wages		0.947	0.963		0.941	0.986
Capital fractions		0.803	0.197		0.775	0.225
Net return to capital		0.040	0.040		0.036	0.036
Tax rate variable θ		1.000	1.000		0.964	0.964

Variable	Change for $j = 1$	Change for $j = 2$	Net Change
Income			
Labor income	−8.6	7.4	−1.2
Capital income	—	—	−15.3
State/Local Tax Revenue			
Sales tax revenue	−47.9	0.6	−47.3
Capital tax revenue	28.3	−0.2	28.0
Total tax revenue	−19.7	0.3	−19.3
Federal Tax Revenue			
Personal tax revenue	11.5	1.4	12.9
Corporate tax revenue	−13.9	0.9	−13.0
Total tax revenue	−2.4	2.3	−0.1

Notes: All revenue figures in tables are in billions of 1983 dollars; details may not add due to rounding. Predicted revenue gain is $28.5 billion.

Moreover, the losses in sector one wages are roughly offset by increases in sector two wages. Thus, the primary effect on federal revenues from general equilibrium changes in income is due to changes in capital income, which falls by $9.9 (6.5, 15.3) billion when $N^* = 29$ (19, 39).

The general pattern of revenue changes is similar to that previously discussed. When $N^* = 29$, the increase in R_{K1} of $19.1 billion is offset roughly 6 percent by a reduction in R_{K2} of $1.1 billion for a net increase of $18.0 billion, while the reduction in R_{C1} of $34.7 billion is offset roughly 5 percent by an increase in R_{C2} of $1.8 billion for a net reduction of $32.9 billion. Thus total state and local revenues fall by $14.9 billion. The relatively small equilibrium reduction in marginal tax rates (to $\theta = 0.942$ rather than 0.898) implies an increase in federal personal tax revenues, with a corresponding reduction in federal corporate tax revenues, of $8.5 billion. Results which bound these are obtained for $N^* = 19$ and 39. For example, the increase in federal personal tax revenues and the corresponding decrease in federal corporate tax revenues are $5.5 (12.9) billion for $N^* = 19$ (39).

Finally, table 6.3 presents the same information (for $N^* = 29$) for the case where federal government matching rates are assumed to be held constant, but the dollar value of matching grants is reduced in response to the reduction in own-revenues raised by state and local

Table 6.3   **Equilibrium Effects of Eliminating Deductibility**
                    $N^* = 29$, θ **and Grants Endogenous**

Variable	$\phi = 0$:	$j = 1$	$j = 2$	$\phi = 1$:	$j = 1$	$j = 2$
Capital tax rates		0.211	0.157		0.305	0.145
Sales tax rates		0.132	0.095		0.091	0.098
Gross wages		0.944	0.958		0.932	0.974
Capital fractions		0.431	0.569		0.534	0.466
Net return to capital		0.040	0.040		0.038	0.038
Tax rate variable θ		1.000	1.000		0.930	0.930

Variable	Change for $j = 1$	Change for $j = 2$	Net Change
Income			
Labor income	− 13.0	11.4	− 1.7
Capital income	—	—	− 9.6
State/Local Tax Revenue			
Sales tax revenue	− 34.2	2.2	− 32.0
Capital tax revenue	18.8	− 1.4	17.4
Total tax revenue	− 15.4	0.8	− 14.6
Federal Tax Revenue			
Personal tax revenue	4.0	1.3	5.3
Corporate tax revenue	− 10.0	1.7	− 8.2
Total tax revenue	− 5.9	3.1	− 2.9

Notes: The change in total federal revenue of − $2.9 billion is equal to the reduction in matching grants. All revenue figures in tables are in billions of 1983 dollars; details may not add due to rounding. Predicted revenue gain is $28.6 billion.

governments. Since the reduction in own-revenues is relatively large for median voter itemizers who experience a large change in the effective price of government services, the reduction in federal revenues needed to balance the budget is potentially important. When $N^* = 29$, the percentage of the predicted reduction in marginal tax rates which is eliminated is reduced to 32 percent from 43 percent (θ can be reduced to 0.930 rather than 0.942).

6.5 Conclusion

To the extent the model analyzed in this paper is suggestive of the actual response of state and local governments to the elimination of federal tax deductibility, the results indicate that the increase in federal revenue—or the permitted reduction in marginal tax rates—is likely to be less than that predicted by "static" revenue-estimating techniques. The revenue shortfall predicted ranges from 25–58 percent of the predicted static revenue gain from eliminating state and local tax deductibility; the results presented by Lindsey (in this volume) suggest that a 38 percent revenue shortfall is the best estimate. These results suggest a revenue shortfall larger than the revenue loss of 15–20 percent predicted by the Treasury in generating its revenue estimates (see Nester, 1987) and more in line with the magnitudes suggested by Feldstein and Metcalf (1987). Moreover, the model analyzed here considers only substitution by state and local governments into corporate taxes and nonresidential property taxes on capital; to the extent substitution would occur into revenue sources which are deductible by businesses, such as the land portion of nonresidential property taxes, severance taxes, business user fees, etc., further federal revenue shortfalls would be expected. The results also indicate that changes in federal grants policies are a significant factor. If matching rates stay constant and programs are not added or increased, reduced own-expenditures by state and local governments will reduce federal expenditures, thus attenuating revenue problems due to changes in the state and local revenue mix. However, one could easily argue that eliminating deductibility is likely to increase pressures for more "targeted" federal aid programs, and that increases in such programs will further exacerbate federal revenue shortfalls.

In any case, it is clear that the results of the fairly primitive model analyzed here should be viewed as suggestive. A variety of extensions would enhance the model; these can be divided into three groups. First, the model could be elaborated in a number of ways. Housing and property taxes could be treated explicitly, as could other sources of state and local revenue; this would require modeling of the state and local choice between the taxes analyzed here and other revenue sources such as user charges, selective sales taxes, severance taxes, the land portion of nonresidential property taxes, debt, etc. The determination of the amount of capital income as well as its allocation could be more exact, and a specification of saving behavior could be included so that sales taxes paid would not be overstated for savers. The progressive nature of state and local income taxes could be modeled explicitly, in the same way the progressive structure of the federal tax system is modeled above. A method of allowing for the reduction in the number of itemizers that would occur as the deduction for state and local taxes were eliminated could also be incorporated in the model.

Second, the assumptions regarding the determination of state and local tax and expenditure policy could be altered. For example, modeling a situation where the state and local governments act to maximize a welfare function which weights the utilities of various jurisdictional coalitions—along the lines of the "average voter" model—would seem to be a useful extension; in particular, it would be interesting to construct an average voter model where information regarding the existing mix of state and local taxes would be used to infer the weights in the governmental welfare function. Although the current model may have characteristics similar to an average voter model where itemizers are

relatively important in the political process in one sector and nonitemizers are relatively important in the other sector, a formal analysis is
required before any statements can be made with confidence.

Finally, it would be possible to analyze the model in much more
disaggregated form, applying the general equilibrium modeling techniques popularized by Ballard, Fullerton, Shoven, and Whalley (1985).
In addition (perhaps) to a larger number of production goods, such a
treatment would allow a relatively large number of sectors composed
of broadly similar states. Such a disaggregation would provide a much
clearer picture of the effects of eliminating deductibility across specific
states. This brief discussion suggests that, even if analysis is limited
to the basic model structure utilized in this paper, there are quite a few
directions for future research.

Notes

1. It should be noted that the extent to which Treasury revenue estimates
are "static" is frequently overstated; see Nester (1986).

2. The assumption of a fixed N^* greatly simplifies the analysis. However,
note that N^* ideally should be endogenous, since the number of itemizers in
any jurisdiction will be affected by the elimination of the deduction for state
and local taxes.

3. The value of $N^* = 29$ differs from Lindsey's value of 28 only because the
District of Columbia is included in my sample. See Lindsey (in this volume)
for the explanation of how this figure was derived.

4. See Diewert (1978) for a discussion of the properties of the restricted
profit function.

5. Note that the absence of an explicit treatment of housing also implies that
any effects of eliminating deductibility on the choice between owner-occupied
and rental housing is ignored.

6. No attempt is made to account for either (i) any limitation on the extent
to which sales taxes are only partially deductible because the tables of estimated
sales taxes paid provided to taxpayers by the Internal Revenue Service understate actual sales taxes paid, or (ii) the fraction of sales taxes which are
actually paid by businesses rather than individuals.

7. This formulation assumes federal taxes paid are not deductible against
state and local taxes.

8. This assumption greatly simplifies the governmental optimization problem
because the (relatively small) feedback effects of changes in the government's
capital tax rate on the capital income of the median voter can be ignored.

9. The 1982 *Statistics of Income, Individual Income Tax Returns* issued by
the Internal Revenue Service indicate that less than 9 percent of adjusted gross
income in the $15,000–$20,000 income class is derived from interest, dividends,
and net capital gains.

10. This approach assumes for simplicity that matching grants apply to lump-
sum grant funds; since such funds are held constant throughout the analysis,
the only effect of the assumption is that the matching rate is estimated con-

servatively. Also, note that no attempt is made to model the "flypaper effect" of lump-sum grants; that is, there is no tendency for higher expenditures out of lump-sum grants than out of own revenues.

11. Since the value of β changes 1 percent or less in all the simulations, this seems to be a reasonable assumption.

12. Note however that the results presented here are not directly analogous to those obtained by Lindsey since no attempt is made to weight taxpayers by their probability of voting in determining either the division of states into the itemizer and nonitemizer sectors or the median voter in each sector. Unfortunately, publication time constraints required that a full integration of the Lindsey results with those presented in this paper be left to future research.

13. This corresponds to the allocation of interest, dividends, and net capital gains across these two income classes reported in the 1982 *Statistics of Income, Individual Income Tax Returns* issued by the Internal Revenue Service.

14. For the various simulations reported below, the values of the CES distributive share parameters are around 0.95, the values of μ_{N1} are around -0.4, and the values of μ_{N2} are close to zero or slightly positive. The positive values of μ_{N2} suggest an expectation of greater than full shifting or, more likely, the fact that even jurisdictions where the median voter is a nonitemizer will take into account the fact that some residents are itemizers and use a higher t_2 and lower k_2 than implied in the analysis (a lower k_2 yields a lower implied value of μ_{N2} in the initial equilibrium). Another explanation, suggested by Lindsey (in this volume), is that the relatively low income states which constitute sector two maintain relatively low capital tax rates in the hope of attracting new firms from the relatively high income states that make up sector one.

References

Advisory Commission on Intergovernmental Relations. 1985a. *Intergovernmental perspective: To deduct or not to deduct.* Washington, D.C.: U.S. Government Printing Office.

———. 1985b. *Significant features of fiscal federal.* 1984 ed. Washington, D.C.: U.S. Government Printing Office.

———. 1986. *Measuring state fiscal capacity: Alternative methods and their uses.* Washington, D.C.: U.S. Government Printing Office.

Ballard, C. L., D. Fullerton, J. B. Shoven, and J. Whalley. 1985. *A general equilibrium model for tax policy evaluation.* Chicago: University of Chicago Press.

Board of Governors of the Federal Reserve System. 1986. *Balance sheets for the U.S. economy.* Washington, D.C.: U.S. Government Printing Office.

Chernick, H. and A. Reschovsky. 1987. The deductibility of state and local taxes. *National Tax Journal* 40: 95–102.

Craig, Steven G., and Robert P. Inman, 1985. Education, welfare and the "new" federalism: State budgeting in a federalist public economy. Working Paper no. 1562. Cambridge, Mass.: National Bureau of Economic Research.

Diewert, W. E. 1978. Optimal tax perturbations. *Journal of Public Economics* 10: 139–77.

Feenberg, Daniel R., and Harvey S. Rosen. 1986. State personal income and sales taxes, 1977–1983. In *Studies in State and Local Public Finance,* ed. Harvey S. Rosen. Chicago: University of Chicago Press.

Feldstein, M., L. Dicks-Mireaux, and J. Poterba. 1983. The effective tax rate and the pretax rate of return. *Journal of Public Economics* 21: 129–58.

Feldstein, M., and G. Metcalf. 1987. The effect of federal tax deductibility on state and local taxes and spending. *Journal of Political Economy* 95: 710–36.

Gade, M. N. 1986. Optimal state tax design. Ph.D. diss. Michigan State University.

Gramlich, E. M. 1985. The deductibility of state and local taxes. *National Tax Journal* 38: 447–65.

Hamilton, B. W. 1983. A review: Is the property tax a benefit tax? In *Local provision of public services: The Tiebout model after twenty-five years,* ed. G. R. Zodrow. New York: Academic Press.

Herzog, H. W., Jr., and A. M. Schlottmann. 1986. State and local tax deductibility and metropolitan migration. *National Tax Journal* 39: 189–200.

Hettich, W., and S. Winer. 1984. A positive model of tax structure. *Journal of Public Economics* 24: 67–87.

Inman, R. P. 1978. Testing political economy's "as if" proposition: Is the median income voter really decisive? *Public Choice* 33: 45–65.

———. 1979. The fiscal performance of local governments: An interpretative review. In *Current issues in urban economics,* ed. P. Mieszkowski and M. Straszheim. Baltimore: John Hopkins University Press.

———. 1986. Does deductibility influence local taxation? *Federal-state-local fiscal relations: Technical papers, vol. 1,* 497–531. U.S. Department of the Treasury. Washington, D.C.: U.S. Government Printing Office.

Kenyon, D. A. 1985. Federal deductibility of state and local taxes: Unresolved issues. Mimeo.

———. 1986. Federal income tax deductibility of state and local taxes. In *Federal-state-local fiscal relations: Technical papers, vol. 1,* 417–96. U.S. Department of the Treasury.

———. 1987. Implicit aid to state and local governments through federal tax deductibility. In *Intergovernmental fiscal relations in an era of new federalism,* ed. M. E. Bell. New York: JAI Press.

Ladd, H. F. 1984. Federal aid to state and local governments. In *Federal budget policy in the 1980s,* ed. G. B. Mills and J. L. Palmer. Washington, D.C.: Urban Institute.

Nester, H. W. 1987. Revenue estimates: Macrostatic, microdynamic. *1986 Proceedings of the seventy-ninth annual conference on taxation of the National Tax Association–Tax Institute of America.* Columbus, OH: National Tax Association–Tax Institute of America.

Netzer, D. 1985. Economic consequences of tax simplification: The effect of tax simplification on state and local governments. *Economic consequences of tax simplification.* Boston: Federal Reserve Bank of Boston.

Noto, N. A., and D. Zimmerman. 1983. Limiting state-local tax deductibility in exchange for increased general revenue sharing: An analysis of the economic effects. Committee on Governmental Affairs. 98th Cong., 1st sess. Committee Print 98-77.

Oakland, W. H. 1985. Consequences of the repeal of state and local tax deductibility under the U.S. personal income tax. *Federal-state-local fiscal relations: Technical papers, vol. 1.* U.S. Department of the Treasury. Washington, D.C.: U.S. Government Printing Office.

Office of the President. 1985. *The President's tax proposals to the Congress for fairness, growth, and simplicity.* Washington, D.C.: U.S. Government Printing Office.

Romer, T., and H. Rosenthal. 1983. Voting and spending: Some empirical relationships in the political economy of local public finance. In *Local pro-*

vision of public services: The Tiebout model after twenty-five years, ed. G. R. Zodrow. New York: Academic Press.

Rubinfeld, D. L. 1986. The economics of the local public sector. In *Handbook of public economics,* vol. 2, ed. A. Auerbach and M. Feldstein. Amsterdam: North Holland Press.

U.S. Department of the Treasury. 1984. *Tax reform for fairness, simplicity, and economic growth.* Washington, D.C.: U.S. Government Printing Office.

Zimmerman, D. 1983. Resource misallocation from interstate tax exportation: Estimates of excess spending and welfare loss in a median voter framework. *National Tax Journal* 36: 183–201.

Zodrow, G. R. and P. Mieszkowski. 1983. The incidence of the property tax: The benefit view vs. the new view. In *Local provision of public services: The Tiebout model after twenty-five years,* ed. G. R. Zodrow. New York: Academic Press.

———. 1986. The new view of the property tax: A reformulation. *Regional Science and Urban Economics* 16: 309–27.

Comment   Don Fullerton

For years, the Office of Tax Analysis (OTA) and the Joint Committee on Taxation (JCT) have had responsibility for estimating revenue and other economic effects of alternative tax policies. Academic economists have estimated efficiency and distributional effects of taxes, but they tend to regard tax revenue as a relatively uninteresting by-product or intermediate step in the maximization of social welfare. They have criticized government revenue-estimating models as ad hoc, with institutional detail rather than theoretical foundation, but they have provided few of their own as alternatives. Despite the interest of economists in overall welfare, the recent tax reform experience makes clear that important policy decisions are often based primarily on considerations of revenue. Thus academic economists are beginning to provide more research on the methodology of revenue estimation.

This paper, by George R. Zodrow, is a welcome addition to this relatively new line of research. It is also a unique addition. On the one hand, the revenue-estimating models of OTA and JCT use data with considerable disaggregation and computer programs with considerable coverage of tax law provisions. They incorporate behavioral adjustments, but elasticity parameters are prespecified. Analyses are typically based on partial equilibrium models. On the other hand, academic economists have provided econometric models, using past behavioral reactions to infer how agents would respond to proposed tax law changes.

Don Fullerton is an associate professor of economics at the University of Virginia and a research associate of the National Bureau of Economic Research.
I thank George Zodrow and Harvey Rosen for clarifications.

They use the latest statistical techniques, but typically the parameters are estimated from reduced form equations that are consistent with a number of alternative theories or structural models. The estimated elasticity parameters are essential for producing better revenue estimates, but often the data are not sufficiently robust to distinguish among these structural models. As a consequence, it is difficult to isolate exactly how and why behaviors adjust. These models also are typically partial equilibrium models.

In contrast, Professor Zodrow's paper provides neither elasticity estimates nor institutional detail, yet it nicely complements the other lines of research. It is a general equilibrium model. It uses exogenous behavioral parameters, specific functional forms for utility and production, and market-clearing equilibrium conditions, and it sorts out the net effects of tax changes in the pure world of the computer simulation model. It employs the minimum detail necessary to demonstrate exactly how and why various behaviors might adjust in response to tax policy.

The topic in this case is the repeal of deductibility at the federal level for state and local taxes paid by individuals. Despite Congress's rejection of the proposals by the Treasury and the president to repeal deductibility of all such taxes, the topic is still alive. Deductibility was repealed for selective excise taxes in 1964, for gasoline excise taxes in 1978, and for general sales taxes in 1986. The recent proposals have effectively put the deductibility of all state and local taxes on the table for the discussion with respect to future revenue needs.

The analysis in this paper is complicated by the fact that it deals with more than just individual behavioral adjustments that can be based on utility maximization. It also deals with the decisions of institutions for which there is no such solid theory of behavior. State and local governments are induced to switch from sales or personal taxes that have lost deductibility to business taxes that are still deductible. The model must therefore specify how different state and local governments react to voters that are affected in different ways, and how the economy reacts to the change in the tax mix. Hence a median voter model with two sectors (one controlled by itemizers, the other by nonitemizers), two tax instruments (one on individuals that loses deductibility, the other on businesses), and two factors (capital that is mobile, and labor that is immobile).

The paper does not answer all possible questions, however, and the author nicely recognizes its limitations. The paper points out how results are sensitive to certain parameter assumptions, how some state and local taxes are omitted, and how the current model might be changed to incorporate average voter behavior, more disaggregation, changes in the supply of labor and saving, progressive state and local taxes, explicit treatment of housing, and endogenous decisions to itemize. The remaining discussion will simply clarify and expand on potential limitations.

First, in the choice between a median voter model and an average voter model, the results often do not differ very much. Indeed, for many distributions, the mean and the median themselves do not differ very much. In this case, however, the models would be very different. In this median voter model, one sector is completely controlled by itemizers who want their government to switch from personal taxes to deductible business taxes, even though capital leaves the jurisdiction. The other sector is completely controlled by nonitemizers who are able to take advantage of the lower price for capital that enters the jurisdiction. In an average voter model, however, neither sector would be so extreme. Depending on the weights for itemizers and nonitemizers in each sector, all state and local governments might shift partially into deductible business taxes, instead of one sector shifting a lot. However, capital would not be able to avoid the tax by moving elsewhere, so factor prices and other results might be quite different. In fact, if both sectors were a mixture of itemizers and nonitemizers, it is not clear that there would be any point in having two sectors.

Second, as in all Harberger models of this type, it is difficult to interpret the length of the time period under consideration. Short-run aspects are mixed with long-run aspects. In particular, the time frame in this model allows all state and local governments to put the issue to the voters, to adjust their tax mix in response to that vote, to shift expenditures, and to change the size of the local public sector. It allows capital to flee from one sector to the other, and it allows labor to move within each sector to equalize the wage. However, this amount of time is not enough for labor to cross sectors, for technology to change, or for capital to grow. The odd result, to somewhat overstate the point, is that labor can move from New York to California if both are controlled by itemizers, but not from New York to Connecticut if the latter is controlled by nonitemizers.

Third, the model usefully concentrates on one kind of adjustment, but it therefore ignores others. In response to repeal of deductibility, state and local governments change their tax mix. Also, however, we might expect individuals to shift toward purchase of commodities for which prices implicitly or explicitly include taxes that are still deductible. Some at the margin might be induced to rent homes, so that landlords could deduct property taxes, rather than to own homes themselves. Others might change itemization status. It is the combination of many such effects that is incorporated in conventional econometric estimates, even though the exact source of the net effect is not always clear from these models.

Fourth, Professor Zodrow chooses to assume that all capital income is received by taxpayers in the top two tax brackets. As a consequence, the median voter never receives any capital income. The data generally show, however, that the ratio of capital income to labor income is quite high in low-income brackets that include many retired individuals. This ratio falls in middle-income brackets with predominately wage-earners, and it then rises again in high-income brackets. This U-shaped pattern could create serious difficulties for a median voter model. In general, for such a model, the voters must be ranked by a single criterion so that the voter with the median value can determine the outcome. Often we assume that income is the important criterion. If this reform affects relative factor returns, however, then the capital-labor ratio of income might be important. The ranking by income is not the same as the ranking by capital-labor ratio.

Fifth, despite my earlier comments that academics have overemphasized welfare effects while ignoring revenue-estimating techniques, this paper does the reverse. It provides revenue estimates that are based on a solid theoretical foundation of utility-maximizing individuals and profit-maximizing firms in competitive equilibrium. Given this foundation, it would be relatively straightforward to calculate equivalent or compensating variations for each group and thus show distributional and efficiency effects. In particular, the current deductibility of personal taxes only in the itemizer sector implies a differential subsidy to that sector. In the absence of offsetting externalities or other distortions, this differential subsidy would create a welfare loss. Its removal would increase efficiency in the sense that the gains to the nonitemizing sector would exceed the losses to the itemizing sector. Such calculations would not establish the absence of any spillover benefit of local public expenditure that could justify a differential subsidy, but they could quantify the implications of such an assumption. This is exactly the type of calculation provided in other general equilibrium models of taxation, so the results would be of further interest for comparison purposes.

Finally, this paper shows the degree of error associated with making static revenue estimates, but the definition of "static" is necessarily arbitrary. In fact, the term has become quite value-laden since government revenue estimates have been criticized as static for ignoring any number of possible behavioral adjustments despite the inclusion of many important ones. This paper compares results from the general equilibrium model to results assuming no behavioral adjustment. It implicitly criticizes an easy target, however, because nobody ever assumes such fixed behavior. In this case, government revenue estimates showed that 15–20 percent of revenue would be offset by certain behavioral adjustments. Other standards might be more useful for comparison. In particular, it is straightforward to incorporate behavioral adjustments in a partial equilibrium model, so the contribution here is the general equilibrium modeling rather than the behavioral adjustments per se. It might be interesting then to compare these general equilibrium results to analogous partial equilibrium results that assume the same type of behavioral adjustment.

I suspect that a set of good partial equilibrium models would provide many of the same qualitative results that are obtained here. Results would still be sensitive to the number of states dominated by itemizers, the elasticities of substitution, and the choice of mobility assumptions. The value of a general equilibrium model is to calculate plausible changes in relative prices.

These comments represent further discussion of the paper rather than criticisms of it. The question arises whether relative price results of the current model could be incorporated usefully into government revenue estimates. In this case, I think not. The relative price effects from this model capture a very interesting but very particular effect, not the overall impact on relative prices of complicated proposals for comprehensive tax reform. Since no general equilibrium model can be large enough or robust enough to calculate equilibrium wages and rates of return after tax reform, or even to establish unambiguously the direction of change, government revenue estimates might already incorporate the best available procedures by fixing those relative prices.

7 Income Originating in the State and Local Sector

Charles R. Hulten and Robert M. Schwab

7.1 Introduction

Viewed as an industry, state and local governments constitute one of the largest sectors of the U.S. economy. In 1985, state and local governments accounted for 8 percent of GNP and 13 percent of total employment, according to data from the U.S. National Income and Product Accounts (NIPA). Only two two-digit SIC industries, real estate and retail trade, contributed more to GNP, and only retail trade accounted for more employment.

State and local government is, however, not generally regarded as an industrial sector of the economy. Whereas analysis of industry data proceeds within the framework of production theory, analysis of the state and local sector is typically based on the theory of demand. The theoretical literature stresses problems of demand revelation for public goods (e.g., the literature inspired by Tiebout), and the empirical literature is oriented toward explaining the demand for public expenditures with a heavy emphasis on the median voter model.

This difference in perspective is doubtless the result of institutional differences between the public and private sectors. Private goods are exchanged in voluntary transactions between consumers and producers, and it is natural to separate supply and demand decisions. Public sector goods, on the other hand, are generally distributed directly to consumers and paid for indirectly through taxation. Since supply decisions are made by governments controlled by consumer-voters, it is

Charles R. Hulten is a professor of economics at the University of Maryland and a research associate of the National Bureau of Economic Research. Robert M. Schwab is an associate professor of economics at the University of Maryland.

We thank Joan Soulsby for her very fine work as a research assistant on this project and Helen Ladd and John Haltiwanger for their comments and suggestions.

easy to ignore the distinction between production and consumption and to focus only on the demand for public sector goods.

This demand-side focus obscures some important supply-side aspects of the state and local sector. In particular, the demand-side approach fails to account for the income flows originating in the sector, and this failure has a number of important implications. First, conventional measures of income originating in the general component of the state and local sector only include wages and salaries. Capital income is implicitly assumed to be zero, despite the fact that (as we show below) this sector is one of the most capital intensive in the U.S. economy. Consequently, NIPA dramatically understates the relative size of the sector.

Second, the failure to account for capital income obscures the true nature of federal government subsidies. In the recent debate over federal tax reform, termination of the tax-exempt status of municipal bond interest and the elimination of the deduction for state and local taxes were two options considered. It was not generally recognized that the subsidy to the sector arises from the nonrecognition of the "equity" income accruing to state and local capital. State and local capital is treated like owner-occupied housing under the federal tax code; the noninterest portion of income accruing to capital is excluded from the tax base.

Third, the demand-side approach to the state and local sector cannot readily deal with the distinction between general subsidies, such as the deductibility of state and local taxes and general revenue sharing, and subsidies for capital formation, such as the exemption of municipal bond interest and matching capital grant programs. This distinction is important, because capital subsidies encourage the use of capital through output and factor substitution effects while general subsidies only involve output effects. The inability to distinguish between the two types of subsidies is analogous to the inability to distinguish between excise taxes and an investment tax credit in the private sector.

Fortunately, there is no inherent reason to exclude supply-side considerations from the analysis of the state and local sector. As shown in Hulten (1984), the production of public sector goods is analogous to the production of household goods (including owner-occupied housing); capital, labor, and intermediate inputs are purchased and transformed into output, which is distributed directly within the household. There is no explicit measure of output in either case, but in both cases a shadow value of output is implicit in the maximization of utility subject to the relevant expenditure constraint.

This shadow valuation of output gives rise to an implicit system of income and product accounts for the state and local sector. The purpose of this paper is to develop this accounting framework. The remainder of the paper has the following organization. In section 7.2, we develop a theoretical model of a simple economy in order to clarify the role of capital income in the state and local sector. Section 7.3 implements the accounting framework developed in 7.2. We present aggregate estimates of the gross output of state and local governments for the 1959–85 period and then compare them to the estimates in NIPA. Section 7.4 offers a brief summary and conclusions.

7.2 Theoretical Considerations

Nearly all local public goods and services are provided directly to consumers without charge and then financed indirectly through taxes. Since these goods are not bought and sold in markets, no direct measure of the value of the goods and services produced in this sector is available. It is therefore impossible to develop independent measures of both sides of the conventional accounting equation which relates the value of output to the value of inputs.

This observation does not, however, imply that it is impossible to construct an appropriate income and product account for the state and local sector. In this section of the paper we show that such a system of accounts is implicit in standard optimization models of state and local governments. In order to make our argument clear, we first develop a very general model of a simple economy. We then add important institutional details to our model which allow us to focus on the provision of local public goods.

7.2.1 A Static One-Sector Model

We begin with a one-good model in which output Q is produced with capital K and labor L via a production function $Q = F(K,L)$. Under constant returns to scale, Euler's equation yields $Q = F_K K + F_L L$, where F_K and F_L are the marginal products of capital and labor. This expression implies a rudimentary accounting framework which allocates the value of output to the inputs since F_K and F_L can be interpreted as the shadow prices of capital and labor.

Profit maximization adds additional structure to this simple accounting framework. If product and factor markets are perfectly competitive, then the necessary conditions for profit maximization require firms to hire each input up to the point that the value of the marginal product of that input equals its factor price. Thus $F_K = P^K/P^Q$ and $F_L = P^L/P^Q$, where P^K, P^L, and P^Q are the prices of capital, labor, and output. Euler's equation then implies that

$$(1) \qquad P^Q Q = P^K K + P^L L$$

for each firm. Aggregating over firms yields the fundamental equation of income and product accounting. It states that the value of output (revenue) observed from market transactions equals the payment for capital services (dividends, interest, rents, retained earnings, etc.) and the wage bill. This equation therefore generates a simple T-account and corresponds to Section A, Table 1, of the U.S. National Income and Product Accounts.

Households play two roles in such a model. First, they supply capital and labor to firms. Second, these households purchase a quantity of Q which satisfies the constraint that their expenditures equal the sum of their capital and labor income. The aggregation of this budget constraint requires that $P^Q Q$ equals the sum of $P^K K$ and $P^L L$ and therefore generates a set of personal income and outlay accounts which are analogous to Table 2 of Section A of NIPA. Factor and goods prices are determined through the interaction of supply and demand. We can characterize this economy with a familiar "circular flow" diagram shown in figure 7.1.

This simple accounting model could be generated without the assumption of optimizing behavior by tracking commodity and money flows between agents in the economy. It is important to stress, however, that such a set of accounts also arises from optimizing models where markets are not present. In an optimally planned economy without money or markets, the clockwise flow of commodities would be gen-

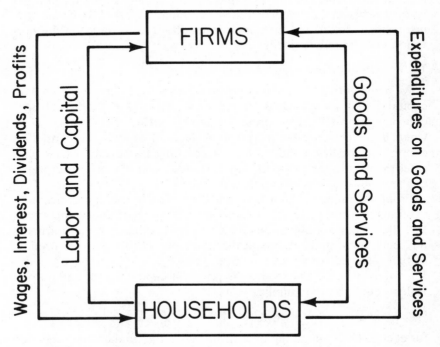

Fig. 7.1   A circular flow model.

erated by the planners, but an implicit counterclockwise flow of values exists via shadow prices implied by optimization. We draw on this result when we turn to the accounting for public goods for which there are no explicit markets.

7.2.2 Intertemporal Aspects of the Simple Model

The model presented in the preceding section is essentially static in that the capital stock is fixed and the technology is constant. We can introduce dynamic aspects into the model by allowing consumers to make intertemporal decisions, either because they live for more than one period or because they wish to leave a bequest to their heirs.

In such a model, consumers can trade consumption in one period for consumption in another by setting aside some of one period's output to increase the stock of capital. Society faces two constraints. First, the aggregate production function constraint in this model requires that $Q_t + I_t = F(K_t, L_t, t)$, where Q_t is consumption at time t and I_t is the amount of the homogeneous good set aside for investment. Second, society is constrained by the identity that the stock of capital at the end of year $t + 1$ is equal to the existing stock after depreciation plus any investment made during the year. We assume that capital depreciates at a constant rate δ, and therefore the perpetual inventory equation can be written[1]

$$(2) \qquad K_{t+1} = I_t + (1 - \delta)K_t.$$

The dynamic version of our simple model requires us to draw a distinction between the asset price of capital and the user cost of capital. A consumer who purchases a unit of capital for his portfolio pays the asset price P_t^I, which in our one good model must equal the price of the consumption good P_t^Q. The replacement value of the capital stock held by the household sector, which owns all factors of production, is therefore $P_t^Q K_t$.

The price of capital from the standpoint of the producer is the cost of using (or, renting) one unit of the consumers' capital for one period. It is this price, P_t^K, which is equated to the value of the marginal product of capital under profit maximization. P_t^K is also the amount which is received by households (in the form of dividends, interest, rents, etc.). Therefore, the value of owning one unit of capital W_t is the present value of the P_t^K generated over the life of the asset. Since capital depreciates at the rate δ, this must be given by[2]

$$(3) \qquad W_t = \sum_{\tau=0}^{\infty} \frac{(1 - \delta)^\tau P_{t+\tau}^K}{(1 + r)^{\tau+1}}.$$

The discount rate r in equation (3) is derived from the intertemporal utility maximization problem and represents the tradeoff between consumption in successive years. That is, the marginal rate of substitution between consumption in year t and year $t + 1$ is $1/(1 + r)$. For simplicity, we assume that r is constant.

The capital values P_t^Q and W_t are not necessarily equal. Tobin's marginal "q" ratio is, indeed, defined as the ratio of the two values:

$$(4) \qquad q_t = \frac{W_t}{P_t^Q}.$$

However, the optimal investment program implied by the optimization of the intertemporal utility function has the property that, in the absence of adjustment costs in changing the stock of capital, $q_t = 1$. That is, the value of the income generated by the stock of capital is equal to the reproduction cost of the stock.

If the economy is in equilibrium and therefore prices are constant, equation (3) yields the well known Hall and Jorgenson (1967) expression for the user cost of capital.[3]

$$(5) \qquad P^K = P^Q(r + \delta).$$

As we argue in subsequent sections of this paper, the public sector analogue to (5) is extremely useful in attributing capital income in the state and local sectors, since communities typically own the capital they use and annual payments to capital are not observed.

A balance sheet for our simple economy is embedded in the framework underlying equation (4). The asset side of the ledger contains the reproduction value of the capital stock, $P_t^Q K_t$; this is the amount that could be obtained if the physical capital were sold. The liability side of the ledger contains claims on the income flow generated by the capital, W_t; this is the amount that could be obtained if the rights to the income were sold. This distinction is somewhat artificial in our simple model, but takes on significance when we allow consumers to transfer physical capital to firms in exchange for financial claims against the capital (e.g., stocks and bonds).

Intertemporal considerations also influence the structure of the income and product accounts. The flow of capital payments from firms to households must now include a depreciation component. Net national income in this economy will then equal gross income, measured either as the sum of factor payments or as the value of output, less depreciation. An investment and saving account must be constructed to balance the production of investment goods with consumer saving.

7.2.3   A Three-Consumer-Good Model with a Public Sector

The jump from a one-sector accounting model to an N-sector model is, in principle, straightforward. Each sector is characterized by its own technology and its own income and product account, each developed along the lines set out above. The separate sectoral flows can then be aggregated to form an economy-wide set of accounts. The main complication arises when some sectors use the output of other sectors. In this case, intermediate inputs must be netted out in the aggregation across sectors.[4] We ignore this complication in this discussion.

With this in mind, we turn to the problem of accounting for public sector output. For reasons which will become apparent below, we begin with a simple model in which three goods are produced; a private sector good Z, housing H, and a local public good X. As above, Z and H are produced by profit-maximizing firms operating in perfectly competitive markets.

Initially we assume that communities rent capital and that they charge a user fee equal to marginal cost, P^X. If a community is to attract households it must produce local public goods at minimum cost. The necessary conditions for cost minimization imply that marginal cost equals the price of each input divided by that factor's marginal product, and therefore P^X equals P^K/F_K and P^L/F_L. Under constant returns, marginal cost is independent of the scale of output and the value of the output equals the value of the inputs used to produce that output:

$$(6) \qquad P^X X = P^K K^X + P^L L^X.$$

It is therefore clear that the fact that one of the goods is produced by state and local governments does not in any fundamental way change the set of accounts we would construct to characterize this economy.

Suppose, now, that instead of renting capital, the community buys the stock of capital it needs for the production of local public goods. By analogy to the private sector, the change in the form of ownership will have no impact on the nature of our accounting framework. Private firms typically own the capital they use. The implicit income from this capital equals the explicit rent that would be charged in competitive markets; in a simple world without taxes, the appropriate per unit rental would be the Hall and Jorgenson user cost in equation (5).

This may seem a trivial observation, but it contains a fundamental insight that is lost in most analyses of the public sector; the allocation of capital to the public sector production implies a return to capital. This return is equal to $P^K K^X$, and reflects the fact that consumers allocate their capital so that at the margin the net return from all uses is equal, i.e., the income from allocating capital in one use equals the opportunity cost of using capital in other uses.

This is a rather unconventional view of the public sector, in that it suggests that income should be attributed to the residents of a community because they "own" streets, schools, etc. Clearly, communities never send their citizens a check which represents a payment for the use of capital; how, then, can it be claimed that capital "income" from schools and streets should be attributed to the local citizenry?

In order to address this issue, it is helpful to again consider the private sector for the moment. A share of stock represents a claim to a portion of the future income of a corporation and, equivalently, a claim to a portion of the corporation's physical stock of capital. These shares can be bought and sold and their value is determined in a stock market.

Is there a public sector analogue to the stock market? When a consumer purchases a home in a community, that consumer simultaneously purchases a share in a corporation which produces goods, i.e., the consumer purchases a share of the community's capital stock. These shares may be bought and sold, though the market does not function quite like a stock market since the shares in these public corporations can only be transferred when a home is transferred. These public corporations also differ from private corporations in that the goods they produce are only consumed by the owners of the enterprise. These differences aside, the value of a house must equal the value of housing capital and the value of a share, i.e., the value of a community's public capital stock (net of outstanding debt) is capitalized into the value of homes in that community.

This capitalization argument allows us to characterize the user cost for a community which owns the stock of public capital. Suppose a community purchases a unit of capital at the beginning of a year with P^I tax dollars. The community uses the increment to its capital stock to produce local public goods and, in the process, the unit of capital depreciates to $(1 - \delta)$; housing values are thus higher by $(1 - \delta)P^I$ at the end of the year as a result of the unit investment. The community incurs an opportunity cost of rP^I since the P^I dollars required to purchase the capital could have been invested at the rate r. Therefore the cost of using this unit of capital for one year is $P^I + rP^I - (1 - \delta) P^I$, or $(r + \delta) P^I$. But clearly this is equivalent to the user cost P^K in equation (5); given capitalization, the cost of capital facing communities who own capital is the same as the imputed user cost. P^K can then be interpreted as the additional end-of-year rent that the community would charge for the rental of its housing, in view of the additional public capital owned by the community.

Now consider the form of this payment. We could think of local governments setting a tax on its citizens as consumers equal to the cost of producing local public goods $P^K K + P^L L$ and then using a part of those tax proceeds to pay a "dividend" to its citizens as shareholders equal to $P^K K$. Of course, communities do not do this; they simply net out the dividend and set a tax of $P^L L$. Therefore the returns on public capital take the form of lower taxes. It then becomes necessary to impute the income generated by the public capital stock, just as the income from owner occupied housing must be imputed.

Finally, as we noted above, state and local governments rarely rely on user fees. But a local government acting solely in the interest of its citizens will act as if decisions were made by a utility-maximizing representative voter. In a median voter model, this representative voter is the one who prefers the median level of local public goods; in a Tiebout model, communities are homogeneous and therefore any voter can be considered as the representative voter. The relevant cost of local public goods in this maximization problem is its shadow price P^X. Therefore local taxes in these models are equivalent to user fees and all of the points that we made above in a world where governments set user charges equal to the unit cost of production continue to hold.

7.2.4 Bond Financed Public Capital

It is not difficult to show that in the context of our simple model the method of financing the acquisition of public sector capital has no impact on the cost of using that capital. Suppose the community we have considered had issued P^I dollars of bonds when it bought a unit of capital. The interest on those bonds would be rP^I dollars. The value of housing in this community would rise by $P^I(1 - \delta)$ dollars as a result of the larger capital stock and fall by P^I dollars because of the debt which must be repaid. These three terms together represent the cost of using capital for one period; they equal $P^I(r + \delta)$, as in the all-equity case.

7.2.5 The Federal Government

The federal government influences the cost of local public goods in at least two important ways. First, local taxes are deductible. Therefore, if the federal tax rate is t, then the marginal cost of local public goods from the perspective of the community is $(1 - t)P^K/F_K$ and $(1 - t)P^L/F_L$. From society's perspective, marginal cost is unchanged and therefore federal taxation introduces a wedge between the social cost of producing local public goods and their benefits.

We might then ask, how should we treat this implicit subsidy in our system of accounts if we wish to put the state and local sector and the private sector on the same footing? From the perspective of an income and product account, the inputs used in the state and local sector must be valued at their market prices. This follows directly from the fact that these accounts are derived from Euler's equation. The value of output received by a producer equals the cost of inputs purchased by that producer. Thus if a firm receives $100 in revenue, which is then paid to the owners of the labor and capital used to produce the firm's output, the set of accounts should value that output at $100, even if a subsidy to the buyer reduces the net cost to $50.[5]

The federal government also influences cost by offering grants to state and local governments which offset part of the cost of acquiring public sector capital. These grants typically take one of three forms.

As Bradford and Oates (1971) argue, nonmatching grants are equivalent to an increase in income for the citizens of a community. An open-ended matching grant under which the federal government pays θ percent of the cost of all units of capital effectively reduces the cost of acquiring capital to $(1 - \theta)P^I$. Therefore a more general expression for the cost of public sector capital is

(7) $$P^K = P^I(1 - \theta)(r + \delta).$$

Matching grants thus play the same role in the cost of capital in the public sector as do investment tax credits in the private sector.

The effects of closed-ended matching capital grants depend on the level of capital chosen by the community. If a community purchases less capital than the maximum level the federal government will subsidize, then the program is functionally equivalent to an open-ended matching grant; in this case the price of public sector capital is $P^I(1 - \theta)(r + \delta)$. If a community purchases more capital than the federal government will subsidize, then the program is functionally equivalent to a nonmatching grant; the relevant price of capital is $P^I(r + \delta)$ and the community receives additional income equal to the subsidy on capital. Finally, if the community chooses exactly the quantity the federal government will subsidize, we can show that it behaves as if it faces a shadow price of capital $\gamma P^I(r + \delta)$, where γ lies between $(1 - \theta)$ and 1.

7.3   The Production of State and Local Public Goods

An important implication of the preceding analysis is that an income and product account can be constructed for the state and local government sector even though there is no independent measure of sectoral output. In this section of the paper we develop estimates of state and local output and input for the period 1959 to 1985. We then compare our results to those obtained directly from NIPA.

We begin by examining the technology used in the production of local public goods. The relationship between purchased inputs and output can change for two reasons. First, technical and managerial innovation may occur. Thus, for example, computers may allow communities to better regulate the flow of traffic, police to respond more quickly to emergencies, and teachers to improve their students' understanding of algebra.

Second, the production of local public goods depends on purchased inputs as well as the characteristics of the citizens. Bradford, Malt, and Oates (1969) drew the important distinction between what they termed D-output and C-output. D-output is the direct output of a local public agency, such as the number of city blocks patrolled, the average time to respond to a reported fire, and the number of hours of mathematics instruction in the public schools. The amount of D-output produced depends only on purchased inputs. C-output is the public service output that enters citizens' utility functions, and would include the level of public safety and the level of education achievement. The level of C-output depends on the amount of D-output and the characteristics of the population. For example, with identical expenditures for education, children in white-collar or upper-income communities may show greater educational achievement than children in blue-collar or low-income communities.

Both effects may alter the quantity of output obtained from a given amount of input. To allow for this possibility, we define A as an index of total factor productivity and assume that A enters the production function as a Hicks neutral change parameter. We also extend our previous specification of technology by including services S and non-durable intermediate goods G as well as labor L and capital K as inputs. The technology can then be written as

$$(8) \qquad X = AF(K, L, S, G).$$

We continue to assume that the production function exhibits constant returns to scale and that communities hire each factor of production up to the point that the value of the marginal product of that factor equals its price, and that output is priced at marginal cost, P^X. As noted above, this implies that the value of output must equal the value of the inputs required to produce that output:

$$(9) \qquad P^X X = P^K K + P^L L + P^S S + P^G G.$$

In the construction of private sector accounts, an independent estimate of $P^X X$ is available. Data on the current account inputs $P^L L$, $P^S S$, and $P^G G$ are also available and capital stock K can be estimated using the perpetual inventory method, equation (2), given estimates of investment spending. The user cost can therefore be estimated as the residual that causes equation (9) to hold.

The situation is obviously different for the public sector. Independent estimates of $P^X X$ are not available, but $P^X X$ can be imputed given estimates of the values on the right-hand side of (9). The values $P^L L$, $P^S S$, and $P^G G$ are available from NIPA, and K can be estimated using a perpetual inventory method. This implies that $P^X X$ can be imputed given an exogenous value for the unobserved user cost P^K. This procedure is thus the converse of the procedure for constructing the private sector account, and the "value" of output constructed in this way is a cost-based measure.

Equation (9) defines the value of the goods and services produced by state and local governments in a manner which is consistent with theory and the underlying technology. It differs from the total purchases of state and local governments E which is the measure of output in many studies, and which is defined as

(10) $$E = P^I I + P^L L + P^S S + P^G G.$$

The difference between these two concepts is $(P^I I - P^K K)$; purchases are not an adequate measure of output becaue they include the acquisition of capital and exclude the cost of using the services from the existing stock.

The estimation of real output X also requires indirect methods. Total differentiation of the technology in equation (8) implies

(11) $$d\ln X = d\ln A + s^K d\ln K^X + s^L d\ln L^X + s^G d\ln G + s^S d\ln S$$

where s^K, s^L, s^G, and s^S represent output elasticities. The marginal productivity conditions imply that these output elasticities equal each factor's share of the community's cost of producing local public goods, e.g., $s^K = (P^K K^X) / (P^X X)$.

If X were a private good, then we would have independent estimates of the growth rates of X, K, L, S, and G. In that case we could infer productivity growth (the growth rate of A) as a residual. But X cannot be observed directly; we can estimate $P^X X$ but we cannot separate price and quantity without additional information.

We are therefore forced to construct our accounts in a somewhat different way. We impose an estimate of productivity growth (zero in the estimates presented below), and then infer the growth rate of output as the share-weighted growth rates of inputs.[6] While this is clearly an arbitrary assumption, it is consistent with the estimates in Hulten (1984) and elsewhere. We choose 1982 as our benchmark and then use these growth rates to estimate constant dollar aggregate output for the state and local sector for the 1959 to 1985 period.

The estimation of X via (11) permits $P^X X$ to be separated into price and quantity components. P^X has the ready interpretation as the marginal cost of producing X. We therefore rely on the assumption that communities are cost minimizers in our estimation of the real output of the state and local sector.

The assumptions underlying our estimates are clearly arguable. It may not be appropriate to characterize the various functions of state and local governments by a single production function. Furthermore, public decision makers may have objectives other than the efficient production of goods and services. The assumption of a zero rate of productivity growth is at best a compromise between competing points of view.

The framework of this paper is not, however, without merit. As Solow (1957) argues, the production theoretic framework should not be viewed as true per se, but rather as a systematic and explicit framework for organizing data. In this context, it should be noted that this framework, however imperfect, has the virtue of defining the theoretically correct measure of public sector output. It is clearly superior to a framework which implicitly assumes that there is no public sector capital (or that it has no value); police officers ride in squad cars, children sit in classrooms, and water flows through pipes. While our estimates of P^K and K^X may be problematic, they must represent an improvement over current practice.

Moreover, the total purchases approach to output measurement will almost never yield a valid measure. While total purchases may be the right concept for the analysis of cash flow and budget constraint problems, it is hard to justify its use in problems relating to the demand for and production of goods and services, except in the extreme circumstance of steady state growth.

In a more positive vein, our approach—embedded in the identity in (9)—has the sensible property that it defines the value of gross output as the value of resources withdrawn from the production of other goods and services. While this value is not necessarily equal to the value to the consumer of the goods produced, it does focus on the cost of producing those goods.

7.3.1 Data

The basic data source for our estimates is Part 3 of the U.S. National Income and Product Accounts. NIPA provides data on various aspects of state and local economic activity, including the purchases of goods and services, transfer payments, and the activities of government enterprises. Since the focus of the paper is the production of goods and services, we omit transfer payments from the analysis and include government enterprises with general government.

Table 7.1 sets forth state and local current dollar expenditures on structures and equipment, employee compensation, and purchases of intermediate goods and services; table 7.2 presents the corresponding data in constant 1982 dollars. It is clear from table 7.2 that real gross investment fell sharply after 1968, and this decline has sparked a deep concern over the condition of the public infrastructure.[7] Real labor compensation continued to rise through the 1970s and then remained roughly constant until 1985.

Table 7.3 expresses the expenditure data as shares. It shows that relative expenditures on services and nondurables rose very rapidly over the period. In 1959, these two categories together represented 18.7 percent of total state and local expenditures; by 1984 this figure had risen to 28.8 percent. Labor's share remained roughly constant during this time. In sharp contrast, the share of state and local expen-

Table 7.1   **Total Purchases State and Local Government Sector (billions of current dollars)**

Years	Total Purchases	Compensation of Employees	Nondurable Goods	Services	Expenditure on Capital Goods	Expenditure on Structures	Expenditure on Equipment
1959	47.4	24.4	3.7	5.2	14.2	12.8	1.4
1960	50.8	27.0	3.9	5.6	14.3	12.7	1.6
1961	55.2	29.3	4.2	6.1	15.5	13.8	1.7
1962	58.6	31.8	4.2	6.2	16.3	14.5	1.8
1963	63.8	34.6	4.4	6.7	18.0	16.0	2.0
1964	69.1	37.8	4.5	7.2	19.5	17.2	2.3
1965	76.3	41.4	5.0	8.5	21.4	18.9	2.5
1966	85.0	46.4	5.3	9.6	23.8	21.0	2.8
1967	94.5	51.9	5.7	10.8	26.1	23.1	3.0
1968	105.7	58.5	6.3	12.4	28.4	25.2	3.2
1969	116.3	65.6	7.3	14.2	29.2	25.6	3.6
1970	129.4	74.5	8.5	16.7	29.7	25.8	3.9
1971	143.6	83.1	9.9	19.4	31.2	27.0	4.2
1972	156.5	92.0	10.8	21.8	31.9	27.1	4.8
1973	174.1	102.9	12.4	24.2	34.7	29.1	5.6
1974	199.2	113.3	15.8	28.6	41.6	34.7	6.9
1975	224.9	127.6	19.8	33.2	44.3	36.5	7.8
1976	242.2	140.1	23.0	35.7	43.4	35.0	8.4
1977	260.9	152.9	26.7	39.0	42.3	33.3	9.0
1978	291.8	167.6	29.4	44.6	50.2	40.2	10.0
1979	322.7	183.4	34.3	49.5	55.4	44.1	11.3
1980	360.8	203.3	40.1	54.9	62.5	49.9	12.6
1981	390.5	221.8	45.1	62.7	60.8	47.3	13.5
1982	418.4	240.3	47.3	71.3	59.5	44.8	14.7
1983	444.9	256.1	48.7	79.2	60.9	44.3	16.6
1984	479.1	274.1	51.2	86.8	66.9	48.2	18.7
1985	521.8	318.1	46.3	81.6	75.8	55.0	20.8

Table 7.2   Total Purchases State and Local Government Sector (billions of constant 1982 dollars)

Year	Total Purchases	Compensation of Employees	Nondurable Goods	Services	Expenditure on Capital Goods	Expenditure on Structures	Expenditure on Equipment
1959	192.7	108.6	12.4	19.0	52.8	48.6	4.2
1960	200.7	114.3	13.1	20.1	53.3	48.6	4.7
1961	212.2	119.8	13.8	21.3	57.4	52.6	4.8
1962	218.8	123.7	13.9	21.7	59.5	54.4	5.1
1963	232.2	129.5	14.7	23.5	64.5	58.8	5.7
1964	246.8	137.8	15.0	25.0	69.0	62.7	6.3
1965	264.9	146.1	16.4	28.6	73.8	67.0	6.8
1966	281.7	154.7	16.8	31.5	78.7	71.3	7.4
1967	295.6	160.2	17.5	34.4	83.5	75.8	7.7
1968	312.9	168.3	19.3	37.9	87.3	79.3	8.0
1969	321.4	175.4	21.8	40.7	83.5	75.0	8.5
1970	331.5	183.2	25.2	44.7	78.3	69.4	8.9
1971	344.4	191.1	28.6	48.4	76.3	67.1	9.2
1972	354.9	198.5	30.7	51.9	73.8	63.6	10.2
1973	366.9	205.9	31.9	54.4	74.6	63.1	11.5
1974	379.7	213.0	32.7	58.2	75.8	63.1	12.7
1975	389.0	218.1	36.7	61.6	72.6	59.9	12.7
1976	393.2	220.8	41.0	62.1	69.3	56.4	12.9
1977	396.6	225.2	44.7	62.9	63.9	50.8	13.1
1978	412.2	231.1	46.4	66.4	68.3	54.8	13.5
1979	416.9	236.4	46.3	67.9	66.3	52.2	14.1
1980	418.9	239.9	44.8	67.3	66.9	52.5	14.4
1981	417.6	241.7	45.2	68.8	61.9	47.7	14.2
1982	418.4	240.3	47.3	71.3	59.5	44.8	14.7
1983	425.1	240.7	49.7	74.5	60.2	43.9	16.3
1984	435.7	242.6	51.7	77.2	64.1	46.2	17.9
1985	449.0	264.0	46.7	69.4	69.0	49.5	19.5

Table 7.3   Expenditure Shares

Year	Compensation of Employees	Nondurables	Services	Capital Expenditure
1959	0.514	0.077	0.110	0.300
1960	0.531	0.077	0.111	0.281
1961	0.532	0.077	0.110	0.281
1962	0.543	0.072	0.106	0.279
1963	0.543	0.070	0.105	0.282
1964	0.548	0.065	0.105	0.282
1965	0.543	0.065	0.111	0.281
1966	0.545	0.063	0.113	0.279
1967	0.549	0.061	0.114	0.276
1968	0.554	0.060	0.117	0.269
1969	0.564	0.063	0.122	0.251
1970	0.575	0.066	0.129	0.230
1971	0.579	0.069	0.135	0.217
1972	0.588	0.069	0.139	0.204
1973	0.591	0.071	0.139	0.199
1974	0.568	0.079	0.143	0.209
1975	0.567	0.088	0.147	0.197
1976	0.578	0.095	0.147	0.179
1977	0.586	0.102	0.149	0.162
1978	0.575	0.101	0.153	0.172
1979	0.568	0.106	0.154	0.172
1980	0.563	0.111	0.152	0.173
1981	0.568	0.115	0.161	0.156
1982	0.574	0.113	0.170	0.142
1983	0.576	0.109	0.178	0.137
1984	0.572	0.107	0.181	0.140
1985	0.610	0.089	0.156	0.145

ditures devoted to capital expenditures fell from 30.0 percent in 1959 to 14.5 percent in 1985, a decline of more than one-half.

As we argued above, the basic difference between the total purchases concept of expenditure summarized in tables 7.1 through 7.3 and the value of gross output lies in the treatment of capital. In particular, the theoretically correct measure of output requires us to replace investment expenditures (column 6 in tables 7.1 and 7.2) with an estimate of the value of the current flow of capital services.

The valuation of capital services requires two steps: (1) the calculation of constant dollar stocks of each of three types of capital assets, and (2) estimation of the per unit service price for each asset. The stocks of depreciable assets, structures and equipment, can be estimated through the perpetual inventory method in equation (2); the capital stock in the current year equals the capital stock in the previous year less depreciation plus investment during the previous year. The real investment series in equation (2), I_t, for structures and equipment are based on columns 6 and 7 of table 7.2 for the 1959–85 period and unpublished data from the Bureau of Economic Analysis (BEA) for the earlier period. Sufficiently long time series are available so that the initial stocks can be ignored in the recursive application of (2).[8]

The estimation of the rate of depreciation, δ, is another matter, however. No systematic data are available and therefore indirect methods are required. The study by Boskin, Robinson, and Huber (1986), based on the depreciation study of Hulten and Wykoff (1981), estimates depreciation rates of approximately 13.1 percent for equipment and 1.9 percent for structures, and we have used those estimates in our work. These rates of depreciation are somewhat lower than the rates implied by the BEA assumptions on asset life and retirement distribution.

BEA provides unpublished estimates of current dollar land purchases. We use a 1958 benchmark from Goldsmith (1962) and a price deflator for land based on the Bureau of the Census index for land in the nonagricultural sector and Department of Agriculture estimates of the value of rural land.

Table 7.4 presents estimates of the stocks of structures, equipment, and land in current and constant dollars. The deflators for structures and equipment are obtained from NIPA, and refer to the replacement cost of these assets.[9]

If all assets were rented in competitive markets, then the observed rental prices would serve as the appropriate rental prices in the calculation of the value of local public goods as specified in equation (10) and the growth of output as specified in equation (11). Unfortunately, this is not the case and we must therefore impute these rental prices.

Equation (7) provides the basis for this imputation. The user cost of capital, as shown in (7), equals $P^I(1 - \theta)(r + \delta)$, where θ is the federal matching rate, r is the discount rate, δ is the rate of economic depreciation, and P^I is the asset price of capital. The estimates of the rate of depreciation and the asset price embedded in our user cost calculations are the same as those we discussed above. Estimates of the subsidy parameter are based on Schneiderman (1975) and U.S. General Accounting Office (1983).[10]

As noted above, the user cost of capital is determined endogenously in growth analyses of the private sector. Specifically, the private rate of return in (5) is allowed to adjust so as to equate the right- and left-hand sides of (9). This procedure yields an ex post estimate of the rate of return which can be shown to provide an adjustment for capacity utilization (Berndt and Fuss 1986; Hulten 1986b). This approach is not available in the public sector and we require an exogenous value of r in order to impute P^K on the right side of (9).

The choice of an appropriate discount rate is not clear. In equilibrium, arbitrage should insure that the rate of return on all capital in the same risk class is the same. But, recent work by Gordon and Slemrod (1983,

Table 7.4 Price and Quantity of the Capital Stock (value in billions of current dollars)

Year	Structures Price	Structures Quantity	Structures Value	Equipment Price	Equipment Quantity	Equipment Value	Land Price	Land Quantity	Land Value
1959	0.264	653.8	172.4	0.333	24.0	8.0	0.260	107.7	28.0
1960	0.261	689.4	180.1	0.340	25.0	8.5	0.261	111.0	29.0
1961	0.263	724.4	190.5	0.354	26.4	9.4	0.261	114.6	29.9
1962	0.267	762.6	203.8	0.353	27.7	9.8	0.261	118.7	31.0
1963	0.272	802.0	218.1	0.351	29.2	10.2	0.262	122.9	32.2
1964	0.274	844.9	231.7	0.365	31.0	11.3	0.265	127.8	33.8
1965	0.282	890.9	251.4	0.368	33.2	12.2	0.272	132.9	36.2
1966	0.294	940.4	276.5	0.378	35.6	13.5	0.282	138.0	38.9
1967	0.304	993.0	302.2	0.390	38.3	14.9	0.291	142.9	41.6
1968	0.318	1049.2	333.6	0.400	41.0	16.4	0.306	147.5	45.1
1969	0.341	1107.8	377.7	0.424	43.6	18.5	0.329	152.0	50.0
1970	0.372	1160.9	431.5	0.438	46.3	20.3	0.348	156.2	54.3
1971	0.402	1207.3	485.1	0.457	49.1	22.4	0.373	160.6	59.9
1972	0.426	1250.6	532.2	0.471	51.8	24.4	0.400	164.6	65.8
1973	0.461	1289.5	594.1	0.487	55.2	26.9	0.433	168.6	73.0
1974	0.550	1327.1	730.4	0.543	59.4	32.3	0.490	172.3	84.5
1975	0.610	1364.0	831.6	0.614	64.3	39.5	0.547	175.9	96.3
1976	0.621	1396.9	867.6	0.651	68.5	44.6	0.588	179.3	105.4
1977	0.655	1425.7	933.9	0.687	72.3	49.7	0.641	182.1	116.7
1978	0.734	1448.3	1063.3	0.741	75.9	56.2	0.707	184.6	130.5
1979	0.846	1474.4	1246.7	0.801	79.4	63.6	0.784	186.8	146.4
1980	0.950	1497.5	1422.3	0.875	83.0	72.6	0.868	189.1	164.1
1981	0.992	1520.4	1508.1	0.951	86.5	82.2	0.952	191.4	182.1
1982	1.000	1538.0	1538.0	1.000	89.2	89.2	1.000	193.6	193.6
1983	1.010	1552.4	1568.6	1.018	92.2	93.9	1.005	195.8	196.7
1984	1.044	1565.6	1634.3	1.045	96.3	100.6	1.031	198.0	204.1
1985	1.111	1580.8	1756.2	1.067	101.5	108.3	1.046	200.4	209.6

1984) and Hulten (1986a) suggests that the arbitrage assumption may not be a good guide to the selection of an appropriate discount rate. Lacking a better alternative (or, at least, one that commands widespread acceptance), we select the long-term nominal interest rate on municipal bonds, less long-term expected inflation, as our rate of discount for public sector capital income. This assumption is attractive in that the municipal bond market is the major source of funds for the acquisition of public sector capital.

We thus require a measure of long-term expected inflation. There has been a great deal of research on the formation of short-term expectations, and a number of alternative approaches have been developed, including distributed lag models, rational expectations models, and the use of survey data.[11] Long-term expected inflation, however, has received less attention. We have used the following procedure. Joseph Livingston, a Philadelphia journalist, began in 1946 to survey roughly 50 economists for their forecasts of inflation (as measured by the Consumer Price Index) for the coming 6 and 12 months. We base our long-term estimate of inflation on these short-term forecasts, using the following method. We denote the 12-month Livingston forecasts made in period t by π^e_{t+1}.[12] We assume that the Livingston respondents form their expectations by looking at past actual inflation, π_{t-s}, according to the process

$$(12) \qquad \pi^e_{t+1} = \alpha_0 + \Sigma \, \alpha \, {}_s\pi_{t-s}.$$

We estimate the parameters of (12) and then generate forecasts for future periods π^e_{t+2}, π^e_{t+3}, etc. by replacing past actual inflation in (13) with forecasts for earlier years. Long-term expected inflation is the average forecast rate for the coming five years.

Our estimates of long-term expected inflation are shown in the second column of table 7.5. Standard and Poor's nominal interest rates on high-grade municipal bonds are shown in the third column. The last column represents our estimates of the real interest rate in the state and local sector. These estimates are consistent with the patterns noted by Blanchard and Summers (1984) and others; real interest rates remained roughly constant through the 1960s, fell during the 1970s, and then rose sharply in the first half of the 1980s.

Inasmuch as the choice of appropriate discount rate is problematic, we present alternative estimates (which parallel the calculations presented in the text) in an appendix. These alternative calculations assume that the appropriate discount rate is the real ex post return in the private sector.[13] The estimates of gross product in the appendix can then be interpreted as the marginal opportunity cost of resources employed to produce local public goods.

Table 7.5   **Real and Nominal Interest Rates**

Year	Expected Inflation	Nominal Interest Rate	Real Interest Rate
1958	0.21	3.56	3.35
1959	0.93	3.95	3.02
1960	0.96	3.75	2.77
1961	0.92	3.46	2.54
1962	1.01	3.18	2.17
1963	0.73	3.23	2.50
1964	0.84	3.22	2.38
1965	0.74	3.27	2.53
1966	1.16	3.82	2.66
1967	1.34	3.98	2.64
1968	2.09	4.51	2.42
1969	2.11	5.81	3.70
1970	2.64	6.51	3.87
1971	3.11	5.70	2.59
1972	3.24	5.27	2.03
1973	3.25	5.18	1.93
1974	4.37	6.09	1.72
1975	3.93	6.89	2.96
1976	4.91	6.49	1.58
1977	5.27	5.56	0.29
1978	5.10	5.90	0.80
1979	5.88	6.39	0.51
1980	6.82	8.51	1.69
1981	6.74	11.23	4.49
1982	5.89	11.57	5.68
1983	5.28	9.47	4.19
1984	5.00	10.15	5.15
1985	3.48	9.18	5.70

7.3.2 Current Dollar Accounts

The gross output account for the state and local sector is shown in table 7.6 and represents our implementation of equation (9). The last column is the sum of the implicit rentals on three types of capital: structures, equipment, and land. The third, fourth, and fifth columns show employee compensation, expenditures on nondurable goods, and services. The second column is the sum of the last four, i.e., the value of output equals the sum of the factor payments given Euler's theorem (under constant returns to scale). Table 7.7 presents the corresponding factor shares.

Tables 7.6 and 7.7, which focus on gross output, present a rather different picture of the state and local sector than do tables 7.1 and 7.3, which focus on expenditure. As shown in table 7.3, capital's share of expenditures fell by nearly 16 percentage points from 1959 to 1985; in contrast, capital's share of gross output was unchanged.

Table 7.6   **Gross Output Account for the State and Local Sector**
                   (billions of current dollars)

Year	Output	Labor Compensation	Nondurables	Services	Capital
1959	41.4	24.4	3.7	5.2	8.2
1960	45.0	27.0	3.9	5.6	8.5
1961	48.3	29.3	4.2	6.1	8.7
1962	50.7	31.8	4.2	6.2	8.4
1963	55.2	34.6	4.4	6.7	9.5
1964	59.2	37.8	4.5	7.2	9.6
1965	65.9	41.4	5.0	8.5	11.1
1966	73.8	46.4	5.3	9.6	12.5
1967	82.4	51.9	5.7	10.8	13.9
1968	91.9	58.5	6.3	12.4	14.6
1969	108.2	65.6	7.3	14.2	21.1
1970	123.2	74.5	8.5	16.7	23.5
1971	132.8	83.1	9.9	19.4	20.3
1972	144.1	92.0	10.8	21.8	19.4
1973	160.0	102.9	12.4	24.2	20.6
1974	181.0	113.3	15.8	28.6	23.4
1975	215.6	127.6	19.8	33.2	35.1
1976	223.8	140.1	23.0	35.7	25.0
1977	235.0	152.9	26.7	39.0	16.4
1978	264.8	167.6	29.4	44.6	23.3
1979	292.0	183.4	34.3	49.5	24.8
1980	338.9	203.3	40.1	54.9	40.6
1981	403.1	221.8	45.1	62.7	73.4
1982	450.6	240.3	47.3	71.3	91.7
1983	462.3	256.1	48.7	79.2	78.3
1984	506.1	274.1	51.2	86.8	93.9
1985	556.2	318.1	46.3	81.6	110.2

This pattern reflects the rapid accumulation of capital in the state and local sector during the 1950s and 1960s. This was a period when the baby boom generation began to reach school age and therefore the needs for additional educational facilities rose sharply. Further, the ambitious interstate highway program was begun during this period, while rapid suburbanization led to additional infrastructure requirements. These factors led to an investment boom. After the boom ended, the consequent larger capital stock continued to generate the capital income imputed in this paper. Therefore capital's share of output remained roughly constant while its share of expenditures fell sharply. High real rates in the 1980s also played an important role.

These considerations have some important implications for measuring the growth of output over time. As shown in tables 7.1 and 7.6, current dollar gross output in 1959 was about 15 percent lower than expenditure; in 1985 it was 6 percent higher. Our estimates therefore

Table 7.7   Income Shares of Gross Output

Year	Labor	Nondurables	Services	Capital	Structures	Equipment	Land
1959	0.589	0.088	0.126	0.198	0.158	0.024	0.016
1960	0.598	0.087	0.125	0.190	0.151	0.024	0.014
1961	0.607	0.088	0.125	0.180	0.143	0.024	0.013
1962	0.628	0.083	0.122	0.166	0.132	0.024	0.010
1963	0.627	0.080	0.122	0.171	0.138	0.023	0.011
1964	0.639	0.076	0.122	0.162	0.129	0.023	0.010
1965	0.628	0.076	0.128	0.168	0.134	0.023	0.011
1966	0.628	0.072	0.130	0.170	0.136	0.023	0.011
1967	0.630	0.070	0.131	0.169	0.136	0.023	0.011
1968	0.637	0.069	0.135	0.159	0.127	0.022	0.009
1969	0.606	0.068	0.131	0.195	0.159	0.023	0.013
1970	0.604	0.069	0.136	0.191	0.157	0.021	0.013
1971	0.626	0.075	0.146	0.153	0.125	0.020	0.009
1972	0.639	0.075	0.151	0.135	0.109	0.019	0.007
1973	0.643	0.078	0.151	0.129	0.104	0.018	0.006
1974	0.626	0.087	0.158	0.129	0.105	0.019	0.006
1975	0.592	0.092	0.154	0.163	0.133	0.021	0.009
1976	0.626	0.103	0.159	0.112	0.088	0.019	0.005
1977	0.651	0.114	0.166	0.070	0.052	0.017	0.001
1978	0.633	0.111	0.168	0.088	0.068	0.018	0.002
1979	0.628	0.117	0.170	0.085	0.065	0.018	0.002
1980	0.600	0.118	0.162	0.120	0.095	0.020	0.005
1981	0.550	0.112	0.156	0.182	0.148	0.022	0.012
1982	0.533	0.105	0.158	0.203	0.165	0.024	0.015
1983	0.554	0.105	0.171	0.169	0.135	0.023	0.011
1984	0.542	0.101	0.172	0.186	0.149	0.024	0.013
1985	0.572	0.083	0.147	0.198	0.160	0.024	0.014

imply that the production of local public goods grew faster than the total purchases approach suggests. This result has important implications for econometric work on state and local governments; those studies which rely on expenditures as a measure of the output in this sector have systematically mismeasured their dependent variable.

This pattern is more dramatic if we focus on value added rather than gross output. Value added in the private sector is the sum of compensation of employees and the value of capital services, i.e., the private sector analogues to the sum of the third and sixth columns in table 7.6. NIPA defines value added for the state and local sector as the sum of compensation of employees and the adjusted current surplus of government enterprises.

Table 7.8 compares these two measures. Our 1985 estimate of value added for the state and local sector is 122 billion dollars greater than the corresponding NIPA value. Figure 7.2 presents our estimates of value added as a percentage of the NIPA numbers of the 1959–1985

Table 7.8

Year	NIPA Value Added	Hulten-Schwab Value Added
1959	26.8	32.6
1960	29.5	35.5
1961	32.1	38.0
1962	34.7	40.3
1963	37.8	44.1
1964	41.1	47.4
1965	44.8	52.5
1966	49.9	58.9
1967	55.6	65.9
1968	62.4	73.1
1969	69.6	86.7
1970	78.7	98.0
1971	87.5	103.4
1972	96.6	111.4
1973	107.8	123.5
1974	118.1	136.7
1975	132.6	162.6
1976	145.0	165.1
1977	157.7	169.3
1978	172.7	190.9
1979	188.0	208.2
1980	207.4	243.9
1981	225.4	295.3
1982	244.7	332.0
1983	262.2	334.4
1984	282.4	368.1
1985	306.3	428.3

period. It shows that in 1985 NIPA understated the output of this sector by nearly 40 percent.

7.3.3   Constant Dollar Accounts

The preceding sections developed a set of current dollar gross output accounts for the state and local sector. We now turn to a corresponding set of constant dollar accounts. The key issue here is the separation of value into prices and quantities.

We outlined our approach to estimating the growth rate of output earlier; assuming productivity growth is zero, it equals the share-weighted growth rates of the inputs.[14] The growth rates of labor, intermediate goods, and intermediate services are based on the factor payments in table 7.5 and price indices from NIPA; the required share estimates are reported in table 7.7.

For capital, we use 1982 as our benchmark and expand our benchmark to other years with a Divisia index of capital growth. This index

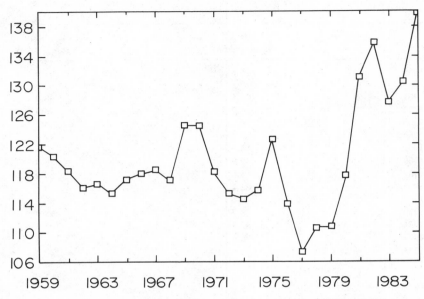

Fig. 7.2   Alternative measures of value added, Hulten-Schwab/NIPA.

is defined as the growth rates of structures, equipment, and land from table 4 weighted by each asset's share of payments to capital. Thus in continuous time, the growth rate of capital would be given by

$$(13) \qquad d\ln K = \Sigma \, v_i d\ln K_i$$

where i refers to structures, land, and equipment and v_i equals the ith factor's share of total rentals $P_i^K K_i / \Sigma P_i^K K_i$. Output is also benchmarked to 1982.

The prices and quantities of output and inputs are shown in table 7.9. That table suggests that we divide 1959–85 into two subperiods. As shown in table 7.10, from 1959 to 1975, the real gross output of state and local governments grew at an average rate of 5.3 percent per year. In sharp contrast, output grew only 2.3 percent per year from 1975 to 1985. This reflects the slower growth of real input used in this sector, which in turn is linked to the slowdown in the growth of government in the 1970s (and possibly to the slowdown in growth throughout the economy during this period).

7.4 Summary and Conclusions

We have developed in this paper an accounting framework for state and local governments which is consistent with representative voter models of this sector. We have shown that this framework is in principle

Table 7.9   Constant Dollar Gross Output Account (quantities in billions of constant 1982 dollars)

Year	Output		Capital		Labor		Services		Nondurables	
	Price	Quantity	Price	Quantity	Price	Quantity	Price	Quantity	Price	Quantity
1959	0.247	167.5	0.011	746.6	0.224	108.6	0.274	19.0	0.295	12.4
1960	0.255	176.5	0.011	784.0	0.236	114.3	0.280	20.1	0.301	13.1
1961	0.261	185.4	0.011	822.1	0.245	119.8	0.285	21.3	0.306	13.8
1962	0.265	191.3	0.010	862.9	0.257	123.7	0.286	21.7	0.303	13.9
1963	0.274	201.5	0.010	905.5	0.267	129.5	0.287	23.5	0.301	14.7
1964	0.277	213.4	0.010	952.8	0.275	137.8	0.290	25.0	0.300	15.0
1965	0.288	228.8	0.011	1004.4	0.283	146.1	0.296	28.6	0.305	16.4
1966	0.304	243.1	0.012	1059.7	0.300	154.2	0.304	31.5	0.317	16.8
1967	0.323	255.0	0.012	1118.8	0.324	160.2	0.313	34.4	0.328	17.5
1968	0.339	271.0	0.012	1180.7	0.348	168.3	0.327	37.9	0.329	19.3
1969	0.377	287.3	0.017	1244.0	0.374	175.4	0.350	40.7	0.335	21.8
1970	0.404	305.1	0.018	1302.7	0.406	183.2	0.374	44.7	0.337	25.2
1971	0.413	321.8	0.015	1355.7	0.435	191.1	0.402	48.4	0.347	28.6
1972	0.428	336.9	0.014	1406.1	0.464	198.5	0.420	51.9	0.353	30.7
1973	0.456	350.8	0.014	1455.1	0.499	205.9	0.444	54.4	0.389	31.9
1974	0.495	365.6	0.016	1505.8	0.532	213.0	0.491	58.2	0.482	32.7
1975	0.563	383.2	0.023	1556.9	0.585	218.1	0.538	61.6	0.540	36.7
1976	0.570	392.6	0.016	1602.9	0.635	220.8	0.574	62.1	0.562	41.0
1977	0.582	403.5	0.010	1646.6	0.679	225.2	0.620	62.9	0.598	44.7
1978	0.634	418.0	0.014	1684.2	0.726	231.1	0.671	66.4	0.632	46.4
1979	0.683	427.6	0.014	1723.7	0.776	236.4	0.730	67.9	0.741	46.3
1980	0.781	434.0	0.023	1759.7	0.847	239.9	0.816	67.3	0.895	44.8
1981	0.908	443.9	0.041	1792.4	0.918	241.7	0.912	68.8	0.997	45.2
1982	1.000	450.6	0.050	1817.4	1.000	240.3	1.000	71.3	1.000	47.3
1983	1.010	457.8	0.043	1839.8	1.064	240.7	1.063	74.5	0.980	49.7
1984	1.084	466.8	0.050	1864.2	1.130	242.6	1.125	77.2	0.989	51.7
1985	1.161	479.0	0.058	1892.5	1.205	264.0	1.176	69.4	0.992	46.7

	Output	Capital	Labor	Services	Nondurables
1959–1975	0.053	0.047	0.044	0.074	0.068
1975–1985	0.023	0.020	0.019	0.012	0.024
1959–1985	0.041	0.037	0.034	0.050	0.051

the same as the accounting framework for other sectors of the economy. We have also shown that the capital income in this sector appears as a reduction in taxes, to the extent that capital is not financed by debt. In addition, we have found that the nondebt value of the public capital stock should be capitalized in housing values, and that the analysis of housing values can yield the implicit rent on public capital.[15]

We have not implemented a complete accounting framework; this would involve the construction of income, expenditure, and wealth accounts for the state and local sector, and substantial revisions in other sectoral accounts (particularly housing). This is beyond the scope of this paper and we have, instead, limited our empirical work to constructing an income and product account for the state and local sector. This has involved the measurement of capital stocks and the imputation of capital income to the sector.

Our empirical results indicate that current national income accounting procedures substantially underestimate the amount of income originating in the state and local sector. In recent years, the size of this understatement is on the order of $100 billion. This can hardly be considered a negligible amount. There is, correspondingly, an overstatement of income in the housing sector, but we have not estimated the size of this effect.

This missing income has important policy implications. The debate over tax reform focused on the various ways that the federal government subsidizes the production of local public goods. The federal tax treatment of part of the income accruing to state and local capital was discussed (the income reflected in municipal bond interest) but, since less than half of state and local capital formation is financed by debt, a large portion of the capital income originating in the sector was ignored.

Our results also present a rather different picture of the sector than might be obtained, for example, from the well-known study by Baumol (1967) or from NIPA. We find that labor productivity (output per unit of labor input) grew at an average annual rate of 0.6 percent, even under our assumption that there was zero total factor productivity growth; by contrast, NIPA procedures imply that labor productivity growth was virtually zero.

Moreoever, we find that the state and local sector is in fact relatively capital intensive. According to data from the Bureau of Labor Statistics, the capital-output ratio in private business was approximately 3.1 in 1982. For the state and local sector, we find that the ratio of capital to gross output was 4.1 in that year; the ratio of capital to value added was 5.6. If productivity growth in this sector has in fact been slow, it cannot be attributed to the fact that the production of local public goods is labor intensive.

The assumptions underlying some of our methods and some of our conclusions are clearly arguable. But our point is not that NIPA misstates the size of the state and local sector by $75 billion, $100 billion, or $150 billion. Rather, our point is that capital income in the state and local sector is not zero, and that our estimates suggest that the magnitude of the measurement error for this sector is large.

Appendix

This appendix presents an alternative set of accounts based on the assumption that the appropriate discount rate for the state and local sector is the real ex post return in the private sector. The numbering of these tables parallels the text. Thus, for example, table 7.A.6 in this appendix (which presents estimates of current dollar gross output based on the alternative real rate) is the analogue to table 7.6 in the text.

As can be seen, the estimates in the appendix and the estimates in the text of the paper are very similar. For example, as shown in table 7.A.8, 1985 value added in the state and local sector under our ex post real rate series is $415.7 billion; under our ex ante real rate series, value added is $428.3 billion.

Table 7.A.6   **Gross Output Account for the State and Local Sector (billions of current dollars)**

Year	Output	Labor Compensation	Nondurables	Services	Capital
1959	41.8	24.4	3.7	5.2	8.6
1960	45.2	27.0	3.9	5.6	8.7
1961	48.8	29.3	4.2	6.1	9.1
1962	53.8	31.8	4.2	6.2	11.6
1963	58.9	34.6	4.4	6.7	13.2
1964	64.8	37.8	4.5	7.2	15.2
1965	74.2	41.4	5.0	8.5	19.4
1966	82.8	46.4	5.3	9.6	21.6
1967	90.4	51.9	5.7	10.8	21.9
1968	99.0	58.5	6.3	12.4	21.7
1969	108.7	65.6	7.3	14.2	21.6
1970	119.9	74.5	8.5	16.7	20.3
1971	136.7	83.1	9.9	19.4	24.2
1972	152.7	92.0	10.8	21.8	28.1
1973	167.9	102.9	12.4	24.2	28.4
1974	182.8	113.3	15.8	28.6	25.2
1975	217.3	127.6	19.8	33.2	36.8
1976	235.6	140.1	23.0	35.7	36.8
1977	258.0	152.9	26.7	39.0	39.4
1978	287.9	167.6	29.4	44.6	46.4
1979	317.7	183.4	34.3	49.5	50.5
1980	350.8	203.3	40.1	54.9	52.5
1981	389.8	221.8	45.1	62.7	60.1
1982	422.9	240.3	47.3	71.3	64.0
1983	456.0	256.1	48.7	79.2	72.0
1984	502.0	274.1	51.2	86.8	89.9
1985	543.6	318.1	46.3	81.6	97.6

Note: The figures in this table are based upon an alternative real rate of interest.

Table 7.A.7   **Income Shares of Gross Output**

Year	Labor	Nondurables	Services	Capital	Structures	Equipment	Land
1959	0.583	0.087	0.124	0.206	0.165	0.024	0.017
1960	0.596	0.087	0.124	0.193	0.154	0.024	0.015
1961	0.602	0.087	0.124	0.187	0.149	0.025	0.014
1962	0.591	0.078	0.115	0.215	0.174	0.024	0.017
1963	0.587	0.075	0.114	0.224	0.182	0.024	0.018
1964	0.584	0.070	0.112	0.235	0.191	0.024	0.020
1965	0.558	0.067	0.114	0.261	0.213	0.025	0.023
1966	0.560	0.064	0.116	0.260	0.213	0.025	0.022
1967	0.575	0.063	0.119	0.243	0.198	0.025	0.020
1968	0.591	0.064	0.125	0.219	0.179	0.024	0.017
1969	0.603	0.067	0.131	0.199	0.162	0.023	0.014
1970	0.621	0.071	0.140	0.169	0.138	0.021	0.010
1971	0.608	0.073	0.142	0.177	0.145	0.020	0.011
1972	0.603	0.071	0.143	0.184	0.151	0.020	0.012
1973	0.613	0.074	0.144	0.169	0.139	0.019	0.011
1974	0.620	0.086	0.156	0.138	0.112	0.019	0.006
1975	0.587	0.091	0.153	0.169	0.139	0.021	0.010
1976	0.595	0.098	0.151	0.156	0.127	0.020	0.010
1977	0.593	0.103	0.151	0.153	0.124	0.019	0.010
1978	0.582	0.102	0.155	0.161	0.130	0.020	0.010
1979	0.577	0.108	0.156	0.159	0.129	0.020	0.009
1980	0.580	0.114	0.156	0.150	0.121	0.021	0.008
1981	0.569	0.116	0.161	0.154	0.124	0.021	0.009
1982	0.568	0.112	0.169	0.151	0.120	0.022	0.009
1983	0.562	0.107	0.174	0.158	0.125	0.022	0.010
1984	0.546	0.102	0.173	0.179	0.143	0.023	0.012
1985	0.585	0.085	0.150	0.180	0.144	0.024	0.012

Note: The figures in this table are based upon an alternative real rate of interest.

Table 7.A.8

Year	NIPA Value Added	Hulten-Schwab Value Added
1959	26.8	33.0
1960	29.5	35.7
1961	32.1	38.5
1962	34.7	43.4
1963	37.8	47.8
1964	41.1	53.1
1965	44.8	60.8
1966	49.9	67.9
1967	55.6	73.9
1968	62.4	80.3
1969	69.6	87.2
1970	78.7	94.7
1971	87.5	107.3
1972	96.6	120.1
1973	107.8	131.3
1974	118.1	138.4
1975	132.6	164.4
1976	145.0	176.9
1977	157.7	192.3
1978	172.7	214.0
1979	188.0	233.9
1980	207.4	255.8
1981	225.4	281.9
1982	244.7	304.3
1983	262.2	328.1
1984	282.4	364.0
1985	306.3	415.7

Note: The figures in this table are based upon an alternative real rate of interest.

Table 7.A.9   Constant Dollar Gross Output Account (quantities in billions of constant 1982 dollars)

Year	Output		Capital		Labor		Services		Nondurables	
	Price	Quantity	Price	Quantity	Price	Quantity	Price	Quantity	Price	Quantity
1959	0.260	160.7	0.011	760.4	0.224	108.6	0.274	19.0	0.295	12.4
1960	0.267	169.2	0.011	798.4	0.236	114.3	0.280	20.1	0.301	13.1
1961	0.274	177.9	0.011	837.3	0.245	119.8	0.285	21.3	0.306	13.8
1962	0.293	183.9	0.013	878.7	0.257	123.7	0.286	21.7	0.303	13.9
1963	0.304	193.7	0.014	921.8	0.267	129.5	0.287	23.5	0.301	14.7
1964	0.316	205.1	0.016	969.3	0.275	137.8	0.290	25.0	0.300	15.0
1965	0.337	219.9	0.019	1020.9	0.283	146.1	0.296	28.6	0.305	16.4
1966	0.355	233.5	0.020	1076.1	0.300	154.7	0.304	31.5	0.317	16.8
1967	0.369	244.7	0.019	1135.0	0.324	160.2	0.313	34.4	0.328	17.5
1968	0.381	259.8	0.018	1196.8	0.348	168.3	0.327	37.9	0.329	19.3
1969	0.397	274.0	0.017	1260.5	0.374	175.4	0.350	40.7	0.335	21.8
1970	0.413	290.6	0.015	1320.1	0.406	183.2	0.374	44.7	0.337	25.2
1971	0.445	307.2	0.018	1373.8	0.435	191.1	0.402	48.4	0.347	28.6
1972	0.474	321.9	0.020	1424.2	0.464	198.5	0.420	51.9	0.353	30.7
1973	0.501	334.9	0.019	1472.2	0.499	205.9	0.444	54.4	0.389	31.9
1974	0.525	348.2	0.017	1522.2	0.532	213.0	0.491	58.2	0.482	32.7
1975	0.596	364.8	0.023	1573.4	0.585	218.1	0.538	61.6	0.540	36.7
1976	0.630	374.1	0.023	1618.4	0.635	220.8	0.574	62.1	0.562	41.0
1977	0.671	384.7	0.024	1658.1	0.679	225.2	0.620	62.9	0.598	44.7
1978	0.724	397.8	0.027	1690.8	0.726	231.1	0.671	66.4	0.632	46.4
1979	0.781	406.9	0.029	1726.1	0.776	236.4	0.730	67.9	0.741	46.3
1980	0.853	411.2	0.030	1759.1	0.847	239.9	0.816	67.3	0.895	44.8
1981	0.933	417.7	0.034	1791.6	0.918	241.7	0.912	68.8	0.997	45.2
1982	1.000	422.9	0.035	1817.4	1.000	240.3	1.000	71.3	1.000	47.3
1983	1.059	430.4	0.039	1840.6	1.064	240.7	1.063	74.5	0.980	49.7
1984	1.143	439.1	0.048	1865.3	1.130	242.6	1.125	77.2	0.989	51.7
1985	1.207	450.3	0.052	1894.1	1.205	264.0	1.176	69.4	0.992	46.7

Note: The figures in this table are based upon an alternative real rate of interest.

Notes

1. In a discrete time model, it is important to specify the timing of all transactions. We have adopted the following convention. At the beginning of period t, firms "inherit" a stock of capital K_t and contract with labor L_t. Production takes place during the period. At the end of the period, output is sold, workers are paid, and an investment I_t is made. The perpetual inventory equation in (2) and the cost of capital discussed below are consistent with this convention.

2. The $P_{t+\tau}^K$ in (3) refers to the user cost of a *new* asset τ years in the future. The expression $(1 - \delta)^\tau P_{t+\tau}^K$ is thus equal to the user cost of a τ-year-old asset which has "shrunk" to $(1 - \delta)^\tau$ of its original "size".

3. We assume that there is no inflation so that the distinction between nominal and real rates of return can be ignored, and that there are no taxes or subsidies. Our assumption about inflation implies that the investment good price does not change, and therefore that there is no capital gain term in (5). The implicit rental payment is assumed to occur at the end of the year.

4. There are actually two types of T-accounts that can be constructed at the sectoral level; (i) gross output accounts that include the value of intermediate inputs, and (ii) value-added accounts which net out intermediate inputs and which therefore measure the sector's contribution to total GNP. The latter measures the income which originates in the sector (i.e., capital and labor income); the former measures the output which is produced and the allocation of the value of this output to the factors of production. Except under certain restrictive assumptions, gross output is the appropriate concept in the econometric estimation of production functions.

5. To see this point in another context, consider other federal programs which subsidize consumption directly (such as food stamps) or indirectly (such as the deduction for medical expenses). The national accounts would measure the output of the food and medical sectors as the sum of the payments to factors of production.

6. As we argued above, $d\ln A$ captures productivity growth as we normally think of it in the private sector as well as the effects of changes in community characteristics, so a zero rate does not necessarily imply a static technology. For example, a change in society which increases criminal activity could offset technical improvements in law enforcement, leaving output (public safety) unchanged.

7. See for example, National Council on Public Works Improvement (1986) and Hulten and Peterson (1984).

8. The investment series extends back to 1850 for structures and back to 1902 for equipment. Since the capital stock estimates in this paper begin in 1958, the influence of the initial benchmark is very small. At a 1.9 percent rate of depreciation, only 12.4 percent of the 1850 structures benchmark survives in 1959.

9. It should be noted that the estimates in table 7.4 refer to stocks rather than to a flow of services. In the absence of data or procedures (e.g., Berndt and Fuss 1986) to correct for variations in the rate of utilization, we are forced to assume that the utilization rate remains constant. This may be a highly dubious assumption for public sector capital, since much of this capital is in networks (e.g., roads, sewers, water distribution) and it is frequently cost effective to build capacity in advance of need. Conversely, it is hard to expand existing capacity as demand increases (roads in crowded urban areas), or to

reduce the capital stock as demand decreases. Returns to scale in the construction of infrastructure, and regional and demographic shifts, almost certainly lead to variations in the utilization of the measured stock of capital.

10. By law, virtually all capital grants are matching grants. It might be reasonable, however, to argue that in fact these grants have many of the characteristics of lump-sum grants. Under this view, the federal government establishes an aggregate level of funding and invites communities to compete for these funds. Our formulation of the user cost implicitly assumes that the grants are in fact matching grants.

11. See Huizinga and Mishkin (1986) for a review of the literature in this field.

12. See Carlson (1977) for a discussion of the Livingston survey.

13. We thank Barbara Fraumeni for providing this series to us.

14. Our calculations are based on the discrete approximation to equation (9) in which differences in logarithms weighted by the average share in two successive periods replace the share-weighted logarithmic differentials. Diewert (1976) shows that this approximation is exact if the underlying technology is translog.

15. We believe that this last result points to a promising area for future research; hedonic studies of housing values may ultimately lead to direct estimates of user cost of capital and thus obviate the need for the imputation methods developed in this paper. But, even if this proves to be impossible, future research should examine the imputation of rental income to the housing sector. Part of the income and wealth attributed to the housing sector properly belongs in the government sector, and this may suggest a revision of current national income accounting procedures.

References

Baumol, W. J. 1967. Macroeconomics of unbalanced growth: The anatomy of urban crisis. *American Economic Review* 57: 415–26.

Berndt, E., and M. Fuss. 1986. Productivity measurement with adjustments for variations in capacity utilization and other forms of temporary equilibrium. *Journal of Econometrics* 33: 7–29.

Blanchard, O. J., and L. H. Summers. 1984. Perspectives on high real world interest rates. *Brookings Papers on Economic Activity* 2: 273–324.

Boskin, M., M. Robinson, and A. Huber. 1986. New estimates of state and local government tangible capital and net investment. Research Paper, National Bureau of Economic Research, Conference on State and Local Government Finance, December 1986.

Bradford, D., and W. Oates. 1971. The analysis of revenue sharing in a new approach to collective fiscal decisions. *Quarterly Journal of Economics* 85: 416–39.

Bradford, D., R. Malt, and W. Oates. 1969. The rising cost of local public services: Some evidence and reflections. *National Tax Journal* 22, no. 2: 185–202.

Carlson, J. A. 1977. A study of price forecasts. *Annals of Economic and Social Measurement*, 6: 27–56.

Diewert, W. E. 1976. Exact and superlative index numbers. *Journal of Econometrics* 4: 115–46.

Goldsmith, R. W. 1962. *The national wealth of the United States in the postwar period*. Princeton: Princeton University Press.
Gordon, R. H., and J. Slemrod. 1983. A general equilibrium simulation study of subsidies to municipal expenditures. *Journal of Finance* 38: 585–94.
———. 1984. An empirical examination of municipal financial policy. Research Paper, National Bureau of Economic Research.
Hall, R. E., and D. W. Jorgenson. 1967. Tax policy and investment behavior. *American Economic Review* 57: 391–414.
Huizinga, J., and F. S. Mishkin. 1986. Monetary policy regime shifts and the unusual behavior of real interest rates. *Carnegie-Rochester Conference Series on Public Policy,* 231–74. Amsterdam: North-Holland Press.
Hulten, C. R., 1984. Productivity change in state and local governments. *Review of Economics and Statistics* 66, no. 2: 256–65.
———. 1986a. The impact of federal tax reform on state and local governments. In *Federal-State-Local Fiscal Relations, Technical Papers, vol. 1*. U.S. Treasury Department. Washington, D.C.: U.S. Government Printing Office.
———. 1986b. Productivity change, capacity utilization, and the sources of efficiency growth. *Journal of Econometrics* 33: 31–50.
Hulten, C. R., and G. E. Peterson. 1984. "The public capital stock: Needs, trends, performance." *American Economic Review,* 74: 166–73.
Hulten, C. R., and F. C. Wykoff. 1981. The measurement of economic depreciation. In *Depreciation, inflation and the taxation of income from capital,* ed. Charles Hulten. Washington, D.C.: The Urban Institute.
National Council on Public Works Improvement. 1986. The nation's public works: Defining the issues. Washington, D.C.
Schneiderman, P. 1975. State and local government gross fixed capital formation, 1958–1973. *Survey of Current Business* 55, no. 10: 17–26.
Solow, R. 1957. Technical change and the aggregate production function. *Review of Economics and Statistics* 39: 312–20.
U.S. Department of Commerce, Bureau of Economic Analysis. 1982. *Fixed reproducible tangible wealth in the United States, 1925–79*. Washington, D.C.: U.S. Government Printing Office.
U.S. Department of Commerce, Bureau of Economic Analysis. 1986. *The national income and product accounts of the United States, 1929–1982, Statistical Tables*. Washington, D.C.: U.S. Government Printing Office.
U.S. General Accounting Office. 1983. Trends and changes in the municipal bond market as they relate to financing state and local public infrastructure. Washington D.C.: U.S. Government Printing Office.

Comment   Helen F. Ladd

By analogy to the production of household goods, Hulten and Schwab argue carefully and persuasively that capital used in the state and local public sector yields an implicit rate of return to local citizens and that the annual value of capital services is a more appropriate measure of capital's contribution to output than is expenditure on capital goods.

Helen F. Ladd is a professor of public policy studies at Duke University.

Why this paper is included in a volume of fiscal federalism is not clear. The authors make only limited reference to the relationships among levels of government or to intergovernmental aid issues. Nonetheless, the paper is a high-quality piece of work that makes an important contribution to our understanding of the role of capital in the state-local public sector.

The National Income and Product Accounts (NIPA) measure the size of the state-local sector in terms of expenditures on inputs. This means capital's contribution to the sector is measured by purchases of capital goods. Hulten and Schwab's goal, in contrast, is to measure size in terms of gross output. Hence, the appropriate way to account for capital is in terms of the annual value of services it generates. Starting with the equivalence between the value of output and payments to inputs, the annual value of services is equivalent to the amount of capital in the state and local sector multiplied by the implicit return to capital, as measured by the user cost of capital.

The strength of this approach is that it makes accounting for the state-local public sector consistent with that for the private sector and allows analysts to consider supply-side aspects of the sector. The approach requires strong assumptions, however, including constant returns to scale, homogeneous capital, cost-minimizing behavior of state and local governments, and no adjustment costs. Although the assumptions may be strong and not fully realistic, the Hulten-Schwab approach represents a useful contribution to national income accounting and a clear step in the right direction for measuring capital income originating in the state and local sector.

Five conclusions emerge from the paper. The first is that in recent years capital income in the state and local sector has substantially exceeded annual expenditure on capital goods, as reported in the National Income and Product Accounts. Large capital investments in the late 1960s continue to produce services and to yield implicit returns despite the recent dramatic decline in investment by state and local governments. For example, the authors estimate that the value of capital services exceeded expenditures on capital goods by 45 percent in 1985. This, in turn, means that the NIPA expenditure approach underestimates the size of the state and local public sector by about 7 percent. The conclusion is reversed for earlier years when capital outlays were high relative to the services from existing capital; capital outlays in 1959, for example, exceeded the value of capital services by over 70 percent and total state and local expenditures exceeded gross output by 14 percent.

Second, capital's contribution to state and local output has not declined as much as indicated by the standard accounting framework. The authors' preferred estimates show that as a percentage of gross output the value of capital services was about the same in the early 1980s as in the early 1960s. This contrasts dramatically with the NIPA expenditure approach which shows that capital outlays declined as a percentage of total state and local spending from a peak of 28.2 percent in the early 1960s to a low of 13.7 percent in 1983.

Third, contrary to accepted wisdom, the state and local sector is relatively capital intensive. According to the authors' estimates, the capital-output ratio in the state-local sector is about 4 to 1 while that in the private sector is about 3 to 1. This means that below-average productivity growth in the state-local sector should not be attributed to the sector's labor intensity alone.

Fourth, real output in the state local sector grew at about 5.3 percent per year in the 1959–75 period and about 2.3 percent per year in the 1975–85 period. Based on the assumption of no change in overall factor productivity, these estimates simply reflect changes in the quantity of inputs. A subsidiary conclusion is that labor productivity—output per unit of labor input—grew at an average annual rate of 0.6 percent per year, a substantial increase over the zero growth of labor productivity implicit in the NIPA approach.

A final, more theoretical, implication of the authors' analysis relates to the ownership of the capital used in the state and local sector. A natural question is who earns the implicit rate of return to state and local capital. The authors argue that one can view state and local officials as reducing taxes rather than paying dividends and that these reduced taxes get capitalized into higher housing prices. This implies that part of the income and wealth attributed to the housing sector in the national income accounts really belongs in the government sector.

Central to the approach are the authors' assumptions that state and local governments minimize costs and that the marginal cost of public sector production equals its value to consumers. These assumptions of efficient production are less reasonable for the public sector where goods and services are provided through the budgetary mechanism than they are for the private sector with its discipline of private markets. The Tiebout mechanism provides one possible source of discipline on public sector production: public officials must minimize costs and produce services in line with consumer preferences to keep taxpayer voters from moving to other jurisdictions. At best, however, such a model applies to relatively homogeneous suburban jurisdictions within a metropolitan area. Its general applicability to other local governments and to state governments is questionable.

The voting mechanism provides an alternative source of discipline. Unless elected officials provide services in line with consumer preferences and minimize production costs they are subject to being turned out of office. But the voting mechanism is an indirect and imprecise method for translating taxpayer preferences into public services.

These observations about decision making in the public sector imply that total payments to factors of production may not translate into the value to citizens of the output produced. The authors recognize this, but counter with the argument that a theoretically consistent framework is preferable to an inconsistent one. Only in the special case of steady-state growth would purchases of capital goods be justified as a measure of capital income or services produced. Moreover, the authors argue that even if their output measure does not represent value to citizens, their approach makes sense as a cost-based measure of output. That is, it represents the value of resources withdrawn from the production of other goods and services.

Of more concern are the assumptions of homogeneous capital, constant returns to scale, and no adjustment costs. Hulten and Schwab calculate the annual value of services from capital as the product of the capital stock and the marginal productivity of capital as measured by the user cost of capital services. Key components of the user cost of capital are the discount rate and the matching rate for federal aid. Their assumptions imply that a fall in the discount rate or an increase in the matching rate (both of which decrease the user cost of capital) decreases the marginal productivity of all units of capital. The intuition here, given their assumptions, is that the fall in the user cost of capital induces more investment and that this additional investment lowers the productivity of all of the homogeneous units of capital.

But state and local capital is not homogeneous, in large part because of its spatial dimension. If the state of North Carolina responds to a lower user cost by investing in more roads, for example, there is little reason to believe that the value of the marginal product of roads in California would fall. This is because roads in California are not the same good as roads in Maryland. This criticism can be mitigated by assuming that all cities and states face the same user cost of capital and that there are no costs of adjusting capital stocks. In this case, not only North Carolina, but also California and every other state would invest in more roads in response to a fall in the user cost of capital. Provided production is characterized by constant returns to scale and that capital is homogeneous within each state, this then would lead to a lower value of product on each and every unit of capital (roads) throughout the country.

Adjustment costs should also be considered. The long-lived characteristic of capital goods makes it difficult to reduce capital stocks over a short period of time and the lumpiness of many capital investments makes it hard to invest in small increments. This implies that even if all states face the same reduction in the user cost of capital, some may respond by increasing investment in the current period and others may not. Hence, the current user charge of capital will not be a good measure of the marginal productivity of capital in those states that do not respond in the current period. This means that multiplying the existing aggregate capital stock by the current user cost of capital gives a misleading picture of the value of capital services. Note that adjustment lags create a problem for the accounting of private sector activities as well. What makes them so relevant here is their interaction with the spatial dimension of state and local infrastructure.

Consider what this implies for the authors' estimates of the value of capital services. If the federal government decreases its share of the cost of waste treatment plants from 80 percent to 60 percent, the user cost of capital faced by local governments would increase by 100 percent (from 20 percent of the original costs to 40 percent). While it is reasonable to believe that local officials would refrain from investing in new plants unless the returns are substantially higher than before the change in federal aid, high adjustment costs make it implausible that the higher return applies to all existing plants in the current period as is implicit in the authors' calculations.

The same argument holds for changes in the discount rate. If the discount rate did not change much over time, the assumption of costless adjustment would be less of a concern. But the authors' preferred method for estimating the discount rate implies large changes over time in the discount rate and consequently large changes in the value of capital services. Hulten and Schwab correctly point out that economic theory yields no clear choice of a discount rate. Their preferred discount rate is the long-term nominal interest rate on municipal bonds minus carefully estimated measures of long-term expected inflation. The resulting series of real interest rates varies substantially over time. The rate was about 2.5 percent in the early 1960s, jumped up to over 3.5 percent in 1969 and 1970, fell to under 0.3 percent in 1977, and rose to 5.7 percent in 1985 (based on their table 7.5).

The effect of this variation over time in the discount rate is substantial. In an earlier version of the appendix to their paper, Hulten and Schwab reported estimates of capital income based on a constant discount rate of 2.83 percent (the average over the period) that could be compared to the tables in the text based on the varying discount rate. The comparison is striking. Based on the authors' preferred estimates, the value of capital services as a share of gross output was exactly the same in 1985 as in 1959 (although it fell substantially in the late 1970s when real interest rates were low). This suggests that concerns about declining capital in the state and local sector may be misplaced. In contrast, estimates based on a constant discount rate indicate that the share decreased steadily over time from about 21 percent in 1959 to 14 percent in 1985, which is more in line with the picture that emerges based on the more common measure, capital outlays.

My purpose here is not to criticize the authors' choice of a discount rate. Their preferred rate is sensible. Moreover, appendix tables show that an alternative rate, the real return in the private sector, yields estimates of capital income reasonably similar to those in the text. Instead, my purpose is to highlight the importance of costless adjustment in a world with nonhomogeneous capital. In such a world, the standard approach is to argue that a rise in the interest rate affects existing capital by lowering its value. The productivity of that existing capital does not change, but the rate of return rises on all capital through the downward revaluation of the capital stock. This change in valuation is not part of Hulton and Schwab's analysis. Their estimate of the stock of capital in the state and local public sector depends only on annual investment and the rate of economic depreciation. A rise in the interest rate affects the return on new investment. Only if all capital is homogeneous and can be adjusted costlessly would the rise in the interest rate affect the value of services produced by existing capital. Because adjustment lags are ignored in this paper, the authors overstate the value of capital services when real interest rates are rising and understate them when real interest rates are falling.

Finally, I turn to the authors' assumptions about the rate of economic depreciation. The depreciation rate enters the calculations in two ways. First it is a key determinant of the size of the capital stock which the authors estimate based on the perpetual inventory method. The lower is the rate of depreciation, the larger is the capital stock at any point in time for any pattern of investment, and consequently the larger is the value of capital services, all else constant. Working in the other direction is its impact on the user cost of capital. A lower rate of depreciation lowers the user cost of capital and consequently lowers the estimated value of capital services.

Hulten and Schwab use a rate of 13.1 percent for equipment and 1.9 percent for structures, both of which are lower than depreciation rates used by the Bureau of Economic Analysis. These rates, based on previous work, represent careful estimates derived from observed behavior in the private sector. Weaker incentives to maintain property in the public sector than in the private sector, however, may mean these depreciation rates are too low. State and local officials have a number of incentives to undermaintain capital projects. First, federal aid programs for capital projects may bias officials toward new construction and away from maintaining the existing stock. Second, the short-run perspective of many elected public officials combined with the relative invisibility of capital deterioration in the short run may also lead to undermaintenance. Clearly not all components of the public capital stock are equally undermaintained. Evidence suggests that those financed by an earmarked revenue source or user charges tend to be better maintained than those whose financing is subject to the political process. But this observation only reinforces the possibility that much of the capital in the state and local sector may be less well maintained than capital used in the private sector.

If the depreciation rates used by Hulten and Schwab are too low, their estimates of the capital stock are too high, but their estimates of the user cost of capital are too low. How these net out is not clear, but deserves further investigation.

In sum, Hulten and Schwab have provided a systematic and theoretically consistent accounting framework for the state and local public sector. The framework requires some strong and questionable assumptions, but the basic approach is solid and worthy of further research and refinement.

Contributors

Alan J. Auerbach
Department of Economics
University of Pennsylvania
3718 Locust Walk
Philadelphia, PA 19104

Daniel Feenberg
National Bureau of Economic
  Research
1050 Massachusetts Avenue
Cambridge, MA 02138

Ronald Fisher
Department of Economics
Michigan State University
East Lansing, MI 48824

Don Fullerton
Department of Economics
University of Virginia
Charlottesville, VA 22901

James R. Hines, Jr.
Woodrow Wilson School
Princeton University
Princeton, NJ 08544

Douglas Holtz-Eakin
Department of Economics
Columbia University
International Affairs Building
New York, NY 10027

Charles R. Hulten
Department of Economics
University of Maryland
College Park, MD 20742

Robert Inman
Department of Finance
Wharton School of Management
University of Pennsylvania
Philadelphia, PA 19104

Helen F. Ladd
Institute of Policy Sciences
  and Public Affairs
Duke University
Durham, NC 27706

Lawrence Lindsey
Department of Economics
Harvard University
Littauer Center 231
Cambridge, MA 02138

Wallace E. Oates
Department of Economics
University of Maryland
College Park, MD 20742

Thomas Romer
Graduate School of Industrial
  Administration
Carnegie-Mellon University
Pittsburgh, PA 15213

Harvey S. Rosen
Department of Economics
Princeton University
Princeton, NJ 08544

Robert M. Schwab
Department of Economics
University of Maryland
College Park, MD 20742

John Joseph Wallis
Department of Economics
University of Maryland
College Park, MD 20742

Jeffrey S. Zax
National Bureau of Economic
    Research
269 Mercer Street, 8th Floor
New York, NY 10003

George R. Zodrow
Department of Economics
Rice University
Houston, TX 77251

Index